LITTLE
BIG
MINDS

LITTLE
BIG
MINDS

Sharing Philosophy with Kids

MARIETTA
McCARTY

JEREMY P. TARCHER/PENGUIN

a member of Penguin Group (USA) Inc.

New York

JEREMY P. TARCHER/PENGUIN
Published by the Penguin Group
Penguin Group (USA) Inc., 375 Hudson Street, New York, New York 10014, USA •
Penguin Group (Canada), 90 Eglinton Avenue East, Suite 700, Toronto, Ontario M4P2Y3,
Canada (a division of Pearson Penguin Canada Inc.) • Penguin Books Ltd, 80 Strand,
London WC2R 0RL, England • Penguin Ireland, 25 St Stephen's Green, Dublin 2,
Ireland (a division of Penguin Books Ltd) • Penguin Group (Australia), 250 Camberwell
Road, Camberwell, Victoria 3124, Australia (a division of Pearson Australia Group Pty
Ltd) • Penguin Books India Pvt Ltd, 11 Community Centre, Panchsheel Park, New
Delhi–110 017, India • Penguin Group (NZ), Cnr Airborne and Rosedale Roads, Albany,
Auckland 1310, New Zealand (a division of Pearson New Zealand Ltd) • Penguin Books
(South Africa) (Pty) Ltd, 24 Sturdee Avenue, Rosebank, Johannesburg 2196, South Africa

Penguin Books Ltd, Registered Offices: 80 Strand, London WC2R 0RL, England

Most Tarcher/Penguin books are available at special quantity discounts for bulk purchase
for sales promotions, premiums, fund-raising, and educational needs. Special books or book
excerpts also can be created to fit specific needs. For details, write Penguin Group (USA)
Inc. Special Markets, 375 Hudson Street, New York, NY 10014.

Library of Congress Cataloging-in-Publication Data

McCarty, Marietta, date.
Little big minds : sharing philosophy with kids / Marietta McCarty.
p.   cm.
ISBN-13: 978-1-58542-515-0
ISBN-10: 1-58542-515-X
1. Children and philosophy.   2. Philosophy—Study and teaching (Elementary).   I. Title.
B105.C45M39   2006   2006029099
108.3—dc22

Printed in the United States of America
1   3   5   7   9   10   8   6   4   2

Book design by Meighan Cavanaugh

While the author has made every effort to provide accurate telephone numbers and Internet
addresses at the time of publication, neither the publisher nor the author assumes any responsibility for errors, or for changes that occur after publication. Further, the publisher does
not have any control over and does not assume any responsibility for author or third-party
websites or their content.

For June 'n' Mac,
who gave me my childhood

CONTENTS

INTRODUCTION

Welcome to the world of ideas.

Little Big Minds is an invitation to discover philosophy (or rediscover it, if you have studied it previously) and to consider how we as adults can most effectively share this subject with children. Having spent the last fifteen years happily philosophizing in circles of hand-raising, foot-tapping children, I can tell you that kids are natural philosophers. They approach philosophical topics with great big minds that are uncluttered by the baggage that can accumulate as one gets older.

Kids are unrelenting in their inquiries; they see no topic as off-limits for discussion. Tackling concepts like courage, death, and prejudice without blinking, they seldom back off from a mental challenge. They seem to have an easier time than many of us do in recognizing when to push full force through a difficult subject and when to allow life's mysteries to remain invitingly unknown. A child can ask, "Do you think nothing is something?" and an hour's uninterrupted entertainment ensues. A child will wonder, "When they made time, what time was it?" and laughter and conversation abound. My appreciation for childlike candor and intuition has grown tremendously over the years!

Little big minds show grown-ups that a degree in philosophy is not necessary for one to engage in exciting philosophical conversations. Children feed our hunger for a reinvigorated mental life. Many times I have watched adults as they hang about in doorways or kneel in corners captivated as a group of kids philosophize. As I can see from their expressions, the fringe benefits are plentiful for adults who join in a circle and share ideas with children. For me, spending time with young philosophers discussing some of life's most important questions has made the world feel wide open once again.

I teach philosophy at Piedmont Virginia Community College in Charlottesville, Virginia. Why in the world did I first decide to pull up a small chair to a short table of third-graders? Don't I know that philosophy is a serious discipline restricted to professional academics? I might once have been skeptical about the possibility of children "doing" philosophy, but here's what happened to convince me otherwise.

For fourteen summers when I was director of a tennis camp, the young athletes gave me back my childhood. They were curious about *everything*, more than willing to change their tennis game and their sense of fair play, and so appreciative of life's simple pleasures. Gender, age, ability, background, and nationality became unimportant in our ten-day sessions together. The campers were eager to share their awe with me, as the Blue Ridge Mountains gradually turned blue at sunset or when their serves went over the net for the first time.

Putting tennis racquet aside to work with inner-city children in Charlottesville for the following four summers, I learned in an intimate way that life for many children is neither easy nor fair.

While they taught me firsthand that our social problems are many and serious, I also saw a bold display of endurance and the noble strength of the human spirit. Like the tennis campers, these children, too, were imaginative philosophers. Each morning as we contemplated social problems, I was buoyed by many kids' determination to improve their lives and their stubborn refusal to accept the inevitability of hardship. Their pure pleasure in coming upon a pond or holding their faces up to a sudden, soft rain reminded me to take nothing for granted. These children looked unflinchingly at a reality that was tough yet promising.

Early in my teaching as a community college professor, no longer working in any organized way with children, I began to think about ways I could use philosophy, or the art of clear thinking, to serve the larger community as well as my college students. Immediately I knew to follow the yellow school bus. Doubters questioned whether a child could comprehend philosophy, but I had seen for myself that kids naturally philosophize—thinking, wondering, imagining, and exploring the unknown.

I have taken my children's philosophy program throughout Virginia and headed west with it to Chicago, Phoenix, and Redlands, California. At first I focused my teaching on third-graders. Most kids at this age are both uninhibited and articulate, their lives a blend of experience and innocence, and this combination makes them excellent philosophers. While third-graders will always be my first loves, equally sharp thinkers are waiting to be found in kindergarten classrooms and middle-school hallways. Children of all ages are willing to work with a grown-up who has faith in their abilities and trusts them. With *Little Big Minds,* I hope to inspire you to reach out and give as many children as possible the opportunity to make philosophy a permanent part of their lives. This book is your do-it-yourself teaching kit. Whether you're a plumber, a nurse, a musician, or a grandma, let your life experience and your personality shape the way you share philosophy with children. This "manual" can help you get started by pointing you in *your* direction.

Philosophy travels well. I've shared philosophy with groups of children and adults in a fish store, in libraries, gardens, living rooms, parks, at recreation centers, and on playgrounds. As a teacher, you can include philosophy in your curriculum or start an after-school philosophy club. As a parent, you can put the basketball down and go one-on-one in the philosophical arena. Great-aunts can use it to entertain an extended family of cousins. Grown-up neighbors can team-teach a group of children in their community. Philosophy can become an activity at *any* camp. And Boys and Girls Clubs and Big Brother/Big Sister volunteers may have a new game to play with their young friends.

What can you expect to accomplish through teaching children an array of philosophical theories, encouraging them to ask questions, engaging them in hearty dialogue, showing respect for their ideas, and joining them in philosophizing? From something so simple, the rewards are remarkable. Both teachers and parents confirm that critical thinking skills gleaned from philosophy make the entire process of learning more fun and productive for child philosophers. Many teachers tell me that studying philosophy deepened the connection among classmates by giving the group a common language to use to suit any need or challenge, and that many of their students applied philosophical topics easily to their other subjects. With the freedom to open their minds and to think for themselves, the young philosophers can welcome a big world with confidence rather than fear. You can empower children by giving them the tools for character development and the chance to craft their own childhood. Far from diminishing youthful innocence and hope, philosophical investigation grounds young spirits and gives them a place to rest. Also, witnessing some of the child philosophers grow up provides compelling evidence of the enduring benefits of early philosophizing. I see in many now mostly grown-up child philosophers the capacity for happiness, appreciation of simplicity, tolerance of difference, and natural humility borne of their continuing sense of amazement. These young adult philosophers strike me as comfortable in their bodies, and they are both good listeners and at ease in expressing themselves.

In ancient Athens, Plato (PLAY-toh) looked forward to the time when philosophers would govern the state. He insisted that peace is possible only if thinkers who embrace the world of ideas make the decisions that affect everyone. Grasping the ideas of compassion and justice, of love and responsibility, such leaders would make wise choices and create social harmony. Plato believed that flexible, open minds engaged in public service could make good living possible. In American society, we expect children to possess good computer skills at an early age. Encouragement abounds for a child to learn to play a sport or a musical instrument. Adults not only approve of these pursuits but quite often become involved themselves, coaching the soccer team and playing a piano duet. Applause rings out for a smooth slide both on the guitar and into second base. What if we make it a priority that children also learn to practice philosophy? What if we recognize the ability to philosophize as part of the foundation of the process of becoming an educated person? Philosophy enriches a mind in ways that neither age nor difficulty can dull. At any point in their lives, once-young philosophers will be willing to change their minds and find a clearer path. Quite possibly, Plato's ideal society is a world of grown-up child philosophers.

Philosophy isn't contained only in dusty books. Every day presents an opportunity to consider important questions about how we choose to live our lives, about the basic beliefs and assumptions that underlie our actions. Through philosophy, kids learn to think about how they can improve not only their lives but the larger society as well. The influence of a child whose open mind and heart breed tolerance is unlimited, and this child, mercifully, may grow up to better the world. I feel a growing conviction that a renewed interest in philosophy can lead in only one direction: peace. As you plant the seeds, trust, as Plato and I do, that a rich harvest awaits all of us.

HOW TO USE THIS BOOK

Little Big Minds is a guide to sharing philosophy with kids. In this book, you'll find plenty of specific advice on the how, what, and why of presenting philosophical topics to children. However, I've also tried to provide a framework that allows you to be spontaneous and open to the amazing situations that arise when you sit down and talk with a group of young philosophers. In my experience, anything can happen, and it's usually the kids themselves who lead us to the most stunning insights. I've designed this book so that you don't have to use the exact resources or discussion questions I've recommended—you can turn to old favorites that you love and want to share, or draw from your own personal experience to create discussion ideas that will inspire your group. In other words, feel free to take the spirit of what I've offered and have fun discovering your own way of doing it.

BOOK LAYOUT

This book examines fifteen topics that I have found children respond to most passionately. These are the topics that, in my experience, matter most to kids. Each chapter is devoted to a theme and presents two philosphers whose work illuminates the subject at hand. Each chapter provides two angles of discussion, or subtopics, that you might want to introduce to your group in order to enrich your discussion and draw attention to the subject's relevance to the kids' daily lives. Also included in each chapter are suggested discussion questions, teaching tips, exercises, and a list of resources, which I hope you will find particularly helpful as you enter the world of Little Big Minds.

DESIGNING PHILOSOPHY SESSIONS
APPROPRIATE FOR YOUR AGE GROUP

One of the first questions I'm asked by adults who are interested in teaching philosophy to children is: "How will I know what material is age-appropriate for the kids I'm working with?" Interestingly, I've found there is no guarantee that one approach or presentation will work for a particular age group, and that it's best to trust your intuition about whether or how to approach a topic with your class or child. I have met second-graders who discussed death with ease, and seventh-graders who were uncomfortable talking about friendship. It's important not to assume immediately that a topic is appropriate or inappropriate on the basis of a child's age. Children's maturity levels, interests, backgrounds, and verbal abilities vary. I believe that any topic can be discussed once you determine the general maturity level of your group and shift gears as needed. If a suggested exercise or discussion question in *Little Big Minds* feels too advanced for the kids you're working with, you can either adapt it or substitute another question, song, or story.

TEACHING TECHNIQUES

THE TWO RULES

1. Never speak when someone else is talking, no matter who it is.

2. Never make fun of what someone says. Laugh at a remark
   only when you are sure the speaker intends it to be funny.
   (Usually it's a good indication if the speaker is laughing too.)

With these two simple requests, I have enjoyed more than fifteen
years of productive philosophizing with kids. I think these two
rules are so effective because they are simple and easy to remember.

SIT IN A CIRCLE

Sitting in a circle is essential for good conversation and instills a
sense of belonging. You become part of the circle, and kids love
to feel that the teacher is learning along with them. They can *see*
you listening and paying attention to their ideas. I make sure that
the children learn to speak to one another in the give-and-take of
philosophical dialogue, and I stress the importance of making eye
contact. Rather than looking at me when they respond to a classmate's remark, the children learn to turn toward the speaker and
to have a go at the back-and-forth conversation that is essential to
genuine philosophizing. With gentle and consistent reinforce-
ment, comfort with eye contact and ease in personal interactions
can carry over naturally into each child's daily interactions.

START WITH QUIET TIME

I begin each session with a few minutes of quiet time. Children
gradually experience the benefits of becoming still, realizing
that being calm makes clear thinking possible. Simply sitting in
silence reduces mental clutter in any life, and kids find it curi-
ously powerful to settle themselves.

INCLUDE A BRIEF STORY IN EACH LESSON

Children warm to you and to the study of philosophy when you
share a quick story with them. Everyone likes a good story, and

when the story comes from your personal experience, your honesty is an invitation to the children to open up. *Everyone* has a story to tell, and the phrase "tell me your story" will become a frequent part of your philosophical dialogue. Since philosophizing brings out difficult personal issues, you want to create a sense of community quickly. Bringing my dog, Mel, breaks barriers more readily than I alone could. You can bring photographs, your child, or a friend. . . .

PAY ATTENTION TO THE CHILDREN'S COMFORT LEVEL

Keep in mind anything about a child's life or the group's chemistry that may be an issue. Has a child suffered the loss of a family member, or is there excessive competition between two students? Be aware of any nonparticipants. Are they engaged in the conversation and simply quiet, or restless and perhaps uncomfortable? Did tension creep into the discussion at a particular point? Are they not quite ready for the philosopher or special topic that you had planned for them? Take frequent mental steps back to see how the child philosophers are responding. Your sensitivity is important in creating a comfortable atmosphere for everyone. Save time for individual children after class and let them know that you're available to talk.

BE PREPARED WITH DEFINITIONS OF THE PHILOSOPHICAL CONCEPT

Encourage your child philosophers to look for a brief, crisp, direct definition of the philosophical concept under investigation, and be prepared with your own definition. Here are a few of mine: *Responsibility* is an invitation to give what you can because you can. *Compassion* is the art of pure feeling. *Friendship* is meeting yourself in another form and holding on. *Justice* is the opportunity to live to your full potential. Reducing the definition to one sentence is a terrific mental exercise. Limiting the words is like focusing the lens of a camera. What is unnecessary is filtered out so that the photographer gets a clear picture or, as in our case, the philosopher understands a clear idea. Frequent use of this technique sharpens the mind. Limiting a description to a certain number of words—I often choose five words—moves the child past trite and obvious expressions. I find that frequently used words, such as *friendship* and *love,* require a fresh investigation rather than mindless repetition of customary phrases. Whenever I ask young philosophers what it was like to have so few words to use, the word I hear most often is *relaxing.* This technique teaches them to think . . . and then raise their hands. The confusion that comes when they speak before they are ready, correcting themselves while growing less sure, detracts from the enjoyment and the incentive to speak their minds in the future.

CLARIFY MEANINGS OF ALL WORDS USED

Whenever you use a new, unfamiliar word in teaching philosophy or giving an assignment to the children, be sure to clarify its meaning and give an example or two of its use. Be on the lookout for language that is too complicated; their philosophical talents may make you forget their age. Simplify and clarify at the least doubt, because often the children are too shy to ask what a word means, especially if everyone else seems to understand. You may understand *simplify* and *clarify,* but "Give a simple description" and "Make your meaning clear" are better choices for children. Listen for what the children call "vocab words," words that require an explanation. Your ear will become attuned quickly. For example, *attuned?*

AVOID GENERALIZATIONS AND PROJECTIONS

Anyone can fall easily into the trap of making sweeping statements, such as "all celebrities" or "all doctors." I watch for such generalizations in my own language and in my interactions with the child philosophers. I stop the children early on when they make a generalization. I explain that such restrictive statements rule out individuality and can lead to prejudice. We work together on becoming aware of generalizations, as well as the human tendency to project our own views of the world on others. "That's the way *those people* are. They don't want to change." "They are all afraid because of the way they live." "People who believe that are just plain mean."

DISCUSS REASONS FOR ASSIGNMENTS
Always ask, "Why do you think I am giving you this assignment?" This is a good question because the children appreciate being included, and it makes them ponder the thinking that produced the assignment. The more intriguing variety in your assignments, the more engaged in philosophizing the children become. Innovative work that has not been part of their educational experience up to this point keeps them on their toes and actually makes them eager to find out what's coming next. Enjoy trying something for the first time.

PARTICIPATE WITHOUT DOING THE ASSIGNMENT FOR THEM
Children really like having adults discuss philosophy with them. I try as best I can to participate in a way that shows my involvement without allowing them to copy or paraphrase my ideas. Sometimes I wait for them to finish and take my turn last. At other times I speak first and quickly downplay the importance of my response. I wait to join them in artwork until they are well under way. Making it possible for children to stretch for their own ideas, rather than giving your views, is the heart of the philosophical experience. The job of the philosopher is to teach in a way that invites

questions and gives momentum to dialogue. The goal is to provide the opportunity for a child to expand his or her *own* mind.

GIVE A SENSE OF COMPLETION

Give the kids a sense of satisfaction in their look at each topic. Making a clear connection between a particular concept through future assignments and projects is essential. Having them keep a philosophy journal between meetings gives the children their first philosophy book and a strong sense of continuity. I know children who still treasure their journals ten years later. It is helpful to refer to previously studied philosophers who are relevant to the current topic under investigation.

USE OTHER MEDIUMS FOR INVESTIGATION

Art: Often I use art as a tool for the children to express ideas that are difficult to verbalize. Most kids relish any chance to draw. My usual restrictions are that they can't draw human beings or use any words. These limitations awaken their imaginations and allow the young artists to think more deeply. Relying on words or representing humans makes it easy for children to copy the drawing they saw on a greeting card or to repeat a familiar phrase to signify love. They miss the opportunity to explore the concept in an original way. Their artwork is uniquely their own and belongs to them. It has its own merit and is neither right nor wrong. Any materials will work: pencil, watercolor, pastel, charcoal. Black on white interests them because they are so accustomed to color. You may want to take them outside and let them select what nature provides. A collection of fallen leaves, twigs, pebbles, and dirt can become materials for a piece of sculpture in small hands.

Music: Music is our first language. Listening to music lightens and elevates the children's mood. I expose them to many different kinds of music as a way to learn about other cultures, back-grounds, and time periods. Philosophical themes are everywhere, especially in the spaces between the notes. Instrumental music breathes life into young imaginations as they wonder what the instruments are saying to one another. What did the composer have in mind? What is it like to compose music? What is it about music that everyone enjoys? Opera can showcase philosophical themes, and bluegrass makes for quick entry to Appalachia. Is there an idea that they would like to explore through playing their flutes or drums for the class?

Poetry: As with art, children enjoy expressing their understanding of ideas through the freedom of writing poetry. Listening to poetry encourages children to write their own. Read to them and have them recite poetry, as well. If a poem comes from the heart, it can never be *wrong*. Many kids learn to enjoy writing by composing poetry and find their voices reciting it aloud.

Literature: With practice the children learn to find philosophical themes in their reading. Fiction or nonfiction, a short story or a novel, a passage will trigger the memory of a theory or discussion. Philosophy becomes more natural, more everyday, as the children can see that it is woven throughout so many disciplines. Suggest a good book to read over the weekend or during a holiday. Remind the children that some philosophers, Camus and Anzaldúa, for example, write fiction as well because novels are a good way to set forth philosophical ideas.

CONNECT PHILOSOPHY TO THEIR LIVES

This is a big one. The best way to give philosophy staying power in the minds and hearts of students is to be sure that they can directly apply the philosopher's theories to their everyday lives. I frequently remind little big minds that the point of studying philosophy is to use it as a means to improve the quality of their lives. With clear thinking, young philosophers can discover how to become an important part of the world. Everyone has talents to share and many ways to give. On most occasions, through dialogue and encouragement, children discover excellent ideas for putting philosophy to use. Be sure to have some possibilities for individual action or a group project, in case the children don't come up with any suggestions at first. Make sure that their plan for a group activity is realistic. I encourage projects that require time rather than money. You want to be sensitive to economic reality so that the children are not disappointed in the execution of their positive efforts.

PHILOSOPHY

While I have life and strength, I shall never
cease from practicing and teaching philosophy.

—SOCRATES, IN PLATO'S *Apology*

THE TOPIC

When did we humans first begin to think about our place in
the universe and what it all means? What moved us from thinking only about such basic life-sustaining actions as building
a fire to musing about what is real, what is true? Or is it just
human nature to wonder about a world that contains so many
secrets?

The word *philosophy* means "love of wisdom." Inspired by a
sense of wonder and countless questions, philosophers investigate
life. Ordinary things usually taken for granted acquire new meaning when we look deeper and ask ourselves, "What's going on?"
The more often such a seemingly simple question is asked, the
bigger the world appears and the more curious the questioner
becomes about that world. Regardless of age, *anyone* who sets out

to explore the unexplained, to ponder the mysterious, is by definition a philosopher.

I like to tell my as-yet-unrealized philosophers at the start of our journey together that everyone has a philosopher inside and that kids always impress me with their seemingly endless ability to wonder. How high does the sky go? Why are there so many different languages? Does the world look the same to a frog as it does to me? Why do people hurt one another? Does my dog know how much I love him? Who or what is an alien? What's more important, numbers or letters? Is there a reason I'm on the earth? How was the world invented? What's going to happen in the future? I tell them that all these questions they've been pondering and perhaps asking their parents since they were very small are philosophical questions.

"Do any of you know what the word *philosophy* means?" is my first question on opening day. When I asked this long-rehearsed question to my *very first* group of child philosophers, I was surprised to see one hand shoot up immediately. Children already know what philosophy is? Here's what eight-year-old Rebekah had to say: "I think I know what philosophers do, but first I have a question that I've *always* wanted to ask. *Why is life?*"

It's clear to me that children have such questions in mind from a very early age, and philosophy is their chance to go exploring. They want to talk about their questions and travel the world of ideas with the assurance that they'll be listened to. The philosopher within comes out and is ready to go!

Beginning with the assertion that the key to good living is clear thinking, Socrates (SAH-kruh-teez) and his star pupil, Plato, are the perfect philosophers to introduce children to the bigness of their minds.

TEACHING TIPS: THE TOPIC

- You, the child philosophers, and any visitors should wear name tags. This encourages everyone to learn one another's names and will lend a personal touch to philosophical conversation. Encourage those speaking back and forth to turn and face each other so they can get to know everyone better.
- Teach kids right away not to use the word that they are defining in their definition. "Being fearful" is not a good definition of *fear* because it uses the word that is being defined.
- Ask the children for a *one*-word definition or example. This helps kids sharpen their thought processes. Finding sharp, focused words makes clear thinking easier.

 DISCUSSION QUESTIONS: THE TOPIC

- How would you explain what philosophy is to someone who has never heard the word?
- How do you define *imagination*? How does it feel to be imaginative?
- How could thinking clearly about certain ideas help you in your life? What ideas are you going to try to understand better?
- How have you benefited so far from learning about philosophy? How would you explain these benefits to someone who can't quite understand why you have become a philosopher?

EXERCISES: THE TOPIC

- Introduce the children to a poet who could be their friend for life, Emily Dickinson. The kids will probably need a little help defining words and putting phrases together, but it is well worth the effort. Three of her poems in particular match the spirit of philosophy. Recite "I Dwell in Possibility," and if you like, hand out copies for them to read along with you. Talk to them about what philosophy makes possible. Ask them to write their own poem titled "Possibility." Next, try Dickinson's "There Is No Frigate Like a Book." Ask the child philosophers how a book can be like a ship "to take us lands away." Where can a book take a reader? Have the kids write in their philosophy journals a brief plot for their very own adventure story. Remind them that their adventure is completely a creation of their imaginations. Discuss with them how philosophy can help them write about places they've never seen and people they've never met. Finally, most kids get a kick out of "I'm Nobody. Who Are You?" Ask the kids why they think Dickinson writes "how dreary to be somebody." Have them write a poem titled "I'm a Philosopher. Are You?"

- Read aloud *The Little Prince* by Antoine de Saint-Exupéry over a period of time that works for your group. As children become immersed in this book and think along with the little prince, they will find themselves actually "practicing philosophy." Ask the kids what thought-provoking ideas occurred to them from the previous week's reading. The book is full of references to philosophical ideas and one profound example is in chapter 21. Here the little prince makes the very Platonic declaration: "And now here is my secret, a very simple secret: It is only with the heart that one can see rightly; what is essential is invisible to the eye." I use this quote to inspire dialogue about how real ideas are even though they are not available to our senses.

THE PHILOSOPHERS

The life which is unexamined is not worth living.

—SOCRATES, IN PLATO'S *Apology*

Often referred to as the founder of Western philosophy, Socrates was born in 470 B.C.E. in Athens, Greece. Socrates turned his inquisitive mind into his own form of art and took what had been previously only a pastime (philosophy) and turned it into a vocation. Young boys with time to spare found great entertainment in Socrates' persistent questioning and subsequent humiliation of authority figures. This led to a trial against him, with corruption of the youth of Athens as the major accusation. The guilty verdict resulted in a death sentence that he accepted as the price to be paid for disturbing Athenian complacency through his insistence on a vigorous mental life for its citizens.

Socrates' philosophy and personality are known mainly through the writings of his pupil Plato. There is no written work that bears Socrates' name. While the dialogues Plato wrote late in his life moved beyond his teacher's theories, the works written in the early and middle stages of Plato's career show the blending of his theories with those of Socrates. The two Platonic works that I favor using with child philosophers, "The Myth of the Cave" and the *Apology,* set forth their shared philosophical theories.

I share Plato's "Myth of the Cave" every time I introduce children to the world of ideas. I explain to the children before telling the story that Plato wants us to understand that each of us is a prisoner if we live without wonder and curiosity, and we must be willing to explore the world of ideas if we want to be free. I ask them to sit staring straight ahead and imagine that they are handcuffed to their desks. Then I begin the story.

"Imagine a very dark cave. There are people inside who have been there all their lives and they have never once been outside. Just like you, they are chained where they sit and cannot move. The only light in the cave comes from a fire behind them, and all they can see are the shadows cast on the wall in front of them by all sorts of objects that have been placed in front of the fire. These objects might be things like bushes, boats, or animals, but all the prisoners can see are the objects' *shadows* on the wall of the cave. Since this is the *only* world the prisoners know and all that they have ever seen, to them the shadows seem to be more than just shadows. To the prisoners, the *shadow* of the boat *is* the boat, and the *shadow* of the bush *is* the bush.

"One of the prisoners, Socrates, manages to escape from his chains and crawl toward the world outside the cave. The path is very steep and long, and it is an extremely hard climb. When he reaches the opening of the cave, the sunlight blinds Socrates at first because it is so bright in comparison to the cave's darkness. When his eyes adjust to the light, however, Socrates looks all around at the *real* world. Here are real bushes, real boats, and real animals! He no longer sees only shadows but sees the true world."

I explain to the kids that Plato tells this story as a way of presenting his main philosophical theory. The prisoners in the cave are exactly like people who ignore the exciting world of ideas in favor of easy, fuzzy thinking. His myth is like an alarm clock going off, screaming at our minds to "wake up!" It is the job of philosophy to help us focus on our ability to understand ideas. For the kids, I compare our minds to lightbulbs covered in heavy dust, and I explain that clear thinking will be the dust cloth that lets the light shine through again. A number of children have found it "kind of funny to think about taking care of my *brain*." It seems quite different from brushing your teeth! I tell them that Plato would say that the best way to begin dusting off their bulbs is to talk about ideas.

I ask the child philosophers for examples of ideas to make sure that they can distinguish concepts from physical things that can be known by the senses. Some examples they have agreed on include loyalty, thankfulness, and honesty. After listening to their examples, I ask the children if they can explain what an idea *is*. I've been told most often that "ideas are what's in our minds." This usually leads to a discussion of our inability to see or touch ideas. Child philosophers find it quite curious that something invisible is also real! I ask them if *all* ideas are real and give them this test as an example: "If you have an idea of a purple horse with wings, is it real?" Kids from kindergarten through eighth grade often make the distinction that "the imaginary horse isn't real, but your *idea* of it *is* real."

I tell children that Plato will be their companion in one important way for every philosophical topic we discuss. Plato insists that we think hard and talk with others to uncover the one true, unchanging meaning of a particular idea. I assure kids that as we become philosophers together, we may not always determine to our satisfaction one definition for an idea that is true for all. But Plato challenges us to make the mental effort that provides better clarity and less confusion about our ideas. This effort is essential because what we think motivates every action we take.

☑ TEACHING TIPS: THE PHILOSOPHERS

- Bringing in photographs of caves assists the kids in picturing Plato's Cave and Socrates making his escape into the sunlight.

After talking about Plato's myth and reading selected passages, let the children choose how to express artistically their picture of the Cave in their imaginations.

* Show the kids photographs of the Parthenon and other buildings and places that recall the Athens of Socrates and Plato.

 DISCUSSION QUESTIONS:
THE PHILOSOPHERS

* Why do you think Socrates' questions bothered people so much? What do you like about asking questions?
* Why do you think you should take good care of your mind, as Plato and Socrates suggest? Why would anyone not appreciate the mind's ability?
* If you had been a student in Plato's school, The Academy, what do you think a school day would be like?

 EXERCISE: THE PHILOSOPHERS

* Listen to Haydn's Symphony No. 22. Haydn did not name this symphony, and kids are most intrigued that an anonymous person named it "The Philosopher." As the children are listening to a recording, have a good time discussing why someone chose that name for this particular symphony. Haydn is a good example of a composer who used his imagination and tried out new ideas. This symphony is an experimental piece; its slow first movement was very unusual for his time period. Haydn lets listeners make of his music what they will. As they listen to the symphony, have the children draw one particular idea that keeps coming to mind. Encourage their creativity by asking them not

to draw human beings or write words. Ask them if they can imagine this music playing at the entrance of Plato's Cave.

THE EXAMINED LIFE

Socrates was devoted to the vocation of philosophy, endeavoring to bring an active mental life to Athenian citizens. It was with dismay that he realized that most people in the Greek city-state that he loved cared only for bodily pleasure and material possessions. This preoccupation cost them dearly, as they neglected the most important thing of all: the quality of their minds. To Socrates, social problems as well as personal difficulties result from dusty minds, and it seemed so very clear to him that a good life and a good character come from clean, crisp thinking. What could he do?

Socrates claimed that he was wise in only one way. He knew how little he knew. This gave him the opportunity to grow in knowledge and to avoid the pitfalls experienced by those who believe they know everything. Describing himself as the "gadfly" of Athens, he resolved to seek out those who assumed this posture of expertise and question them about their knowledge. His legend grew in proportion to the irritation of the experts and those citizens who were comfortable with the world as they knew it. And Socrates continued to ask questions.

I suggest to the children that we get on Socrates' side and admit that there are some things that we don't know. Kids appreciate it when I begin with some of the things on *my* endless list. While something new that I don't know occurs to me every time I work with children on philosophy, some of their favorite examples of things I have told them that I don't know include the following: "What is lightning?" and "I wonder why my brain makes me a conscious person and my kneecap doesn't. . . ." What *they* don't know can range from "why I'm alive" to "how to be happy like I used to be" to "why I don't have two mouths and three eyes." Admitting so many things that remain a mystery paves the way for a good discussion of the benefits of examining your life. "The capacity to learn and the organ with which to do so are present in every person's soul" (Plato, *The Republic*).

I ask the children what Socrates might mean by examining their lives. Many of them have said that it means that they would have to look inside themselves and be honest about it, and that it's up to them what to do with what they find. Together we search for problems that could be addressed through better understanding of ideas. I begin by giving the example of the many environmental problems we face and how a stronger grip on the meaning of responsibility could help all of us care for the earth. Some of the kids' examples include: "I might not disappoint my friend over and over if I understood the idea of trust better." "I guess I don't really understand patience because I get frustrated every time I have to wait around." After all his classmates had contributed their ideas, one quiet eight-year-old boy stated that "the reason for war is that everybody has forgotten what peace means."

Kids quickly recognize that the Socratic challenge to look hard at their lives is not exactly an easy one to accept. Some have told me that "it would be nice to live in *and* out of the Cave." Several times children have acted out having one leg in each world, and it is quite a stretch! I assure the child philosophers that almost everyone experiences the desire to be a thinking person and also to have lazy days. But what if every day were a "lazy day"? Asking children to describe their picture of an *un*examined life helps them to see the benefits of an examined one. Many have imagined it as a life in which they "just go along with everybody else," while others have described it as a life in which you're never "*really* satisfied" or "happy in your heart." Through discussion, kids can see the connection between a "mixed-up mind" and a life that's "much harder than it needs to be."

I've found it valuable to look at the importance of an examined life by asking children how they would try to philosophize with someone who expressed no interest. They love imagining that they are gadflies like Socrates. Some suggestions from the kids: "I'll ask them if they ever wonder what's going on. I mean, something big *is* going on." "I would just quietly ask what they think it means to be alive and be nice and just hang around." "I'd nudge them and ask them if they ever thought our world was just part of someone else's dream." An interesting suggestion from a first-grader: "I will ask them when you think, what do you think about?"

 TEACHING TIP: THE EXAMINED LIFE

- On opening day the child philosophers should receive their first professional "Philosophy Journal." It need not be fancy, as long as it's bound in some way so that their reflections on the world of ideas can be ongoing.

 DISCUSSION QUESTIONS:
THE EXAMINED LIFE

- As a philosopher, how would you describe "the good life"?
- What is the one question that you would most like to have answered? Do you think you will ever know the answer?

 EXERCISE: THE EXAMINED LIFE

- Recite "The Red Wheelbarrow" by William Carlos Williams. This poem teaches children that *anyone* can write poetry about *anything.* You can write this short poem on the board and watch the children laugh as they wait for the surprise of the next line. What's with those white chickens? What in this world depends on a red wheelbarrow? Invite the kids to enter the poet's imagination and wonder with them what Williams was thinking as he created his masterpiece. Join the kids in writing a poem titled "The _____," about absolutely anything that could spark others' curiosity and make them wonder. . . .

GOOD CONVERSATION

As I begin the first philosophy session with any group of children, I chat with them about the importance of good conversation in becoming a philosopher. Most children have participated in conversations that have been all about winning an argument and getting in the last word. I describe this unproductive form of communication to kids as "verbal tag," and explain that while the game of tag can be great fun at recess, keeping everyone *in* the game is the goal of true philosophizing. The philosophical dialogue that is so dear to Socrates is *not* about proving your point or being "right." I tell them we will learn to talk *together.* I compare philosophers to jugglers who, rather than keeping many balls in the air, instead hold many ideas in their minds during philosophical conversation.

Socrates insisted that asking questions and talking, allowing the conversation to follow the questions wherever they may lead, enables philosophers to get closer and closer to the truth. Even on the day he died, he spent all his time in dialogue with his friends and followers, reminding them never to lose faith in the power of discourse to reveal the meaning of ideas. You will see this willingness to continue in hot pursuit of understanding in your child philosophers. As their guide, you encourage their interest every time you ask a question, whenever you indicate that there's something you don't know that's really piqued your curiosity, and any time you praise them for their philosophical abilities.

I ask kids as they are learning the art of good conversation to pretend that they are students in Plato's Academy. I want to show them how the world opens up to us as we discover how little we know, so I ask them a question about something that many people assume they know and perhaps never questioned before. One that has worked very well for me is "What does it mean to be a good person?" Hands go up quickly and come down, and then come quick answers accompanied by looks of dissatisfaction, then shrugs of disbelief that the question is so hard. They welcome the chance to go back to the beginning and talk about what it could mean to be this "good person." You will see that most children find it thrilling that something that seemed obvious can be so remarkably elusive. And what they love is the excitement of conversation with an adult about "important stuff" when "my ideas matter." The chance to join you in *your* quest for knowledge is an enticing incentive for a child to engage in philosophy.

At the end of one of my philosophy sessions, which parents had observed silently on the outskirts of our circle, one new child philosopher invited her mother to join in with this remarkable question: "Mom, now that you've heard about the Cave, what's yours? What's your own Cave?" In their semiprivate conversation afterward, Quanshe explained to her mother that everyone has her own Cave because everyone's different. This six-year-old told her mom that hers was fear because "You know, it's hard for me to stand up to stuff. I was scared to change schools. And I was a little afraid to ask you that question just now." Quanshe concluded their exchange with her acknowledgment that she was going to work on understanding the idea of courage better.

TEACHING TIPS: GOOD CONVERSATION

- Be sure to keep any one child from taking over the dialogue. Calling on different children makes it clear that philosophizing is for everyone. Show your appreciation for enthusiasm too!
- I never insist that any child *must* speak, and I make this known at the beginning of the first class. Shy children can be paralyzed by the fear of being called on and forced to answer before they're ready. Eventually, with several sessions under their belts, all will participate in their own way.

 DISCUSSION QUESTIONS: GOOD CONVERSATION

- Why would some people feel as if they have to be right all the time? What makes someone want to prove a point over and over?
- What are some things that you don't know that you thought you knew? Which of these discoveries surprised you and why?

 EXERCISE: GOOD CONVERSATION

- Do an experiment that shows the variety of ways people interpret physical experiences. One the kids really enjoy involves a taste-testing. I provide crackers or pretzels for them to dip in a jar of mustard and ask for a one-word description of how it tastes. What could be simpler than mustard? In one sitting, I got reports of "hot," "spicy," "bitter," "sweet," "nasty," "sharp,"

"nothing," and "fruity." Philosophy can make the taste of mustard mysterious! Next, work with your child philosophers to compare how people's different ideas about life can be just as wide-ranging as their experiences of mustard. Ask them to tell the group about a time when they were surprised by another person's view on a subject because it was so different from their own.

After you have been philosophizing with kids for a while, it's great fun to ask them what they make of this philosophy business. Horatio told me that he had been having trouble in school until he became a philosopher, but now philosophy is his favorite subject. What makes him so good at it is that "I just say that not every question has an answer or that I don't know and this makes me a good student!" Third-grader Jenny thought for a long time before finding words suitable for a description of philosophy's effect on her: "It makes me fall into my body and think hard, really hard." Brendan, a lively seven-year-old, confessed that every single time we talk about ideas, the question pops into his head, "Do we really want everything we think we want?" Brendan and I had a great conversation about this question, and so can you and your little big minds.

With the kids, I have enjoyed the beauty of keeping philosophy simple. The child philosophers led me from the Cave into the sunlight.

Resources

- *Apology* by Plato.
- *The Republic* by Plato. "The Myth of the Cave" is in Book VII.
- *Meno* by Plato. In this short, early work, the Socratic method of

teaching by asking questions is demonstrated through a Q&A session between Socrates and a boy who has no formal education.

- *Phaedo* by Plato. This dialogue presents major theories shared by Plato and Socrates through Socrates' dialogue with his friends on the day he dies.
- *The Little Prince* by Antoine de Saint-Exupéry.
- Symphony No. 22 in E-Flat by Franz Joseph Haydn. Among the many possible recordings available on CD, *Haydn: Symphonies Nos. 22–25* by The Hanover Band / Roy Goodman is a fine one.
- "The Red Wheelbarrow" by William Carlos Williams. You can find the chickens and the wheelbarrow in his *Collected Poems: 1909–1939*, volume 1.
- "I Dwell in Possibility," "There Is No Frigate Like a Book," and "I'm Nobody. Who Are You?" by Emily Dickinson. These poems are included in a nice presentation of her complete work, *The Poems of Emily Dickinson,* edited by R. W. Franklin.

FRIENDSHIP

Loving friendships provide us with a space
to experience the joy of community in
a relationship where we learn to process
all our issues, to cope with differences
and conflict while staying connected.

—BELL HOOKS, *all about love*

THE TOPIC

For more than twenty-five hundred years friendship has remained a perennial topic for Eastern and Western philosophers alike. In fact, many have described it as one of the main ingredients of human happiness. Friendship is an integral part of a satisfying life. Philosophers know it. Adults know it. Children know it.

Is it possible for the bond of friendship to be pure and selfless, or is it simply human nature to protect our own interests at all costs? Is the affection between friends unconditional, or does it fluctuate like the direction of the wind? What makes friendship possible and how does it work? What *is* friendship?

In discussing this topic with kids, I define *friendship* as meeting yourself in another form and holding on. Among some of the fine definitions I've heard from child philosophers in elementary schools: "holding hands," "tight connection," "two people who can hang out without talking," "being alone when you're together," "like a spiral," and "back and forth."

In their analysis of friendship, philosophers have been confounded by the ways in which we complicate communication and connection unnecessarily, in spite of our deep desire for both. Why do we get in our own way? We know when we are shutting down and pushing someone away from us. We are aware when we are not making an effort, yet we continue to let friendships fade. For many of us, it is a challenge to allow our friendships to find their own rhythm, and instead we manipulate them to suit our needs.

Children understand the value of friendship, and many have already experienced the devastation that comes from losing a friend. In almost every classroom I've visited, conversations about friendship are quick to heat up, with kids eager to share memories of their first friend or the day they met their best friend in kindergarten. Children are also very open about experiences of a friend disappearing or turning on them, and many have told me they believe they'll never get over such heartache. Children fear being without a friend and know that there are real chances of being hurt in the attempt to make and keep one. Think about how joyous and painful the ups and downs of friendship were in your childhood. Do you remember how you felt? It's still the same.

bell hooks and Karl Jaspers (YAH-spurs) have complementary ideas about friendship and communication. Both focus on authenticity, the human need for honest relationships, and all the benefits that come from the bonds that we share. These two philosophers give little big minds a better understanding of the meaning of friendship and provide them with new ideas for strengthening and expanding the friendships in their lives.

✓ TEACHING TIPS: THE TOPIC

• Some children experience friendship for the first time in kinship with a special place in nature or hearing the welcoming bark of a dog. Leave the scope of friendship open for exploration.

• I minimize the importance of my definition of friendship in order to encourage the children to define it for themselves.

• When introducing new philosophical concepts to children, allow blocks of silent time for the ideas to take shape and simmer in their minds. Likewise, when asking questions, ask the children to think about the question for a little while *before* raising their hands.

• Before they begin any assignment, ask the children what they think the purpose of the assignment is. In doing this, I have witnessed puzzled looks turn enthusiastic. Asking this question helps young philosophers to take each assignment seriously.

• Kids love to hear stories about adults befriending children and learning that friendship transcends age. I usually tell them about my friend Marshall, the four-year-old son of a friend of mine. As we held hands walking along the beach, he assured me that when I was his age, he was there to hold my hand. Marshall thinks we were friends before he was born! The child philosophers want to ask him questions *now.*

? DISCUSSION QUESTIONS: THE TOPIC

• Is friendship important to you? Why or why not?

• Can you think of any characteristics that all friendships have in common?

• What are some different kinds of friendships?

EXERCISES: THE TOPIC

- Give the children time to think about five important friendships in their lives. Ask them to describe each friendship in no more than five words, focusing on an important trait of that friend or an important experience they shared with that friend. Some examples: "one who waited, oh that face, laugh that jiggles my heart, those hands, and bends to my level." Divide the children into pairs and have them share their word pictures. Next, with as much explanation as they like, have them elaborate on each description, so that friends come alive for their partners.

- Listen to Kate Wolf's beautiful song "Friend of Mine"—a lovely tribute to her friends. Let the kids know that Kate's friends have helped to keep her northern California folk music alive since she died of leukemia at an early age. Have them compose their own lyrics for their song entitled "Friend of Mine." Ask the young composers if music is a good way to celebrate friendship, and ask them to explain their answer fully in their philosophy journals.

- Read May Swenson's poem "The Centaur." Ride along with a ten-year-old girl on her faithful horse Rob Roy. "My head and my neck were mine, / yet they were shaped like a horse." Ask the children to volunteer a story about their bond with an animal. Talk with them about how friendships form without the use of words. Invite them to make a composite drawing of themselves and their animal friend as Swenson pictures herself with Rob Roy to illustrate the union friendship creates.

- Gather the children to read and share the drawings in *Horton Hatches the Egg*. Lazybird Mayzie flies away and leaves her unhatched egg behind. Horton exemplifies important qualities in a friendship as he remains "faithful one hundred percent" to Mayzie's egg, eventually hatching an "elephant-bird." Horton is trustworthy. Discuss the quality of being "faithful one hundred percent" with the kids by looking at Horton's trustworthy nature. What would the behavior of such a person be like? Do they know anyone who is "faithful one hundred percent"? Is such faithfulness possible or worth the effort? This is a perfect time to share stories of faithful friends. In their philosophy journals, ask the children to explain why being trustworthy is an important ingredient in friendship. Let them write some private suggestions to refer to and make additions to on how they can develop a trustworthy nature.

THE PHILOSOPHERS

If we do not experience love in our extended families of origin (which is the first site for community offered us), the other place where children in particular have the opportunity to build community and know love is in friendship.

—BELL HOOKS, *all about love*

Born Gloria Watkins, bell hooks took her great-grandmother's name to honor the voice that went unheard in her own day. The name is also a tribute to the legacy left to hooks by her mother and grandmother. bell hooks maintains that the use of lowercase letters is intended to downplay her own importance as a writer and to allow her readers to consider her ideas on their own merit. (Ironically, both child and college philosophy students focus immediately on this unusual lack of capitalization!)

bell hooks calls for cultural change in ways that are hard to ignore. She exposes our lack of understanding of love and friendship in *all about love*. In *Teaching to Transgress,* hooks takes a soulful look at our educational system, expressing her belief that the

educational process should be rooted in freedom, and its goal
should be the education of free individuals. She challenges us
to prepare our children to rise above the barriers to friendship
imposed by race, gender, and class.

According to hooks, the principles of love apply to any relationship. "When we are loving we openly and honestly express care,
affection, responsibility, respect, commitment, and trust" (*all about
love*). In a loving friendship we put those ingredients together and
hold fast to our understanding of what constitutes a loving relationship. Throughout her work, hooks emphasizes the importance of
having a clear understanding of love and friendship when young.
The many misguided societal ideas about relationships begin in
childhood. hooks's own hard childhood was her confirmation of
the confusion that can hinder a young mind. "Whether our homes
are happy or troubled, our families functional or dysfunctional, it's
the original school of love" (*all about love*). Talking with your children about the meaning of loving friendship gives them a fresh start.

There should be neither hurt nor neglect in friendship, hooks
says. Friendship forms in the effort to get behind our friends and
help their inner lives flourish. A friend supports who you are, recognizes your hopes and dreams, and the two of you can join together in mutually fulfilled lives. However, the rewards of friendship
come with a price, she warns. You must take care of yourself in a
loving way so that you have much to give. You need to respect
and to trust yourself in order to respect and trust others, hooks
reminds us.

At this point, I ask the children to think of qualities they appreciate in a friend, and to consider how important it is to develop these
qualities in themselves, for themselves *as well as* for others. Children
are drawn to the idea of always being assured of having a friend if
they can establish a good relationship with themselves. Some kids
express surprise that if they are their own good friend, they will not

demand so much from their other friends. Understanding the core being of another is the essence of friendship. Knowing your own heart prepares you for this sensitive entry into another life.

hooks emphasizes that the ability to forgive is another necessary part of the work that friendship requires. Most kids can name a friendship that they lost because of the unwillingness of someone to say "I'm sorry." We talk about the sad feeling that these friendships now seem irretrievable, and this conversation is an excellent lesson in the merits of forgiveness. Forgiveness does not mean that you aren't hurt; nor does it mean that you simply forget the experience. The power of forgiveness is that it releases your friend from guilt as it releases you from anger. "Forgiveness is an act of generosity" (all about love), a sign of respect for your friend and a choice to care for your own well-being. It clears the way for the connection to strengthen.

Friendships are the building blocks that create communities out of isolated individuals. hooks watches the thread of friendship expand as it wraps around this connected group. With effort spent on our friendships, the sense of community blossoms effortlessly. We feel better about ourselves and the world because of a friend's commitment to us. Friendship provides security. Friendships spill up and over, and fear diminishes along with the feeling that an unfamiliar face is the face of a *stranger*. Now we can smile at people we don't know and acknowledge that we are sharing time and space together on the same planet. Speaking and making eye contact come more naturally, and nodding one's head in passing can improve another's day.

It is clear that it has taken a large part of hooks' life to uncover her definitions of love, friendship, and community. "Definitions are vital starting points for the imagination. What we cannot imagine cannot come into being. A good definition marks our starting point and lets us know where we want to end up" (all about love).

Some children have defined community as "any connected group that is tied together." It is interesting that so many offer their families as an example of community. A few of their less obvious examples: 4-H club, choir, the kids I wait for the bus with, the birds that show up every day at the feeder. Thinking about community excites children because almost all child philosophers in some way express a desire to feel that they belong.

> The thesis of my philosophizing is: The individual cannot become human by himself. Self-being is only real in communication with another self-being.
>
> —KARL JASPERS, *Existenzphilosophie*

Karl Jaspers found his home in philosophy after careers in both law and psychiatry. He lived through two world wars in Germany. His wife, Gertrud, was Jewish, and in *The Question of German Guilt* Jaspers took a rigorous look at the collective guilt of the German people for the rise of Hitler's Third Reich. He and Gertrud left Germany after the war so that Jaspers could take a teaching position at the University of Basel in Switzerland.

Existentialist philosophers focus on the human condition in all its complexity. They probe the moods, whims, desires, and mix of reason and emotion that are part of the human puzzle. As an existential philosopher, Jaspers' central concern was an understanding of what it means to be human and how to live a full-bodied life. He feared that the scientific advances, as well as the economic and political realities of the twentieth century, posed a serious threat to authentic living. In his major work *Existenzphilosophie,* Jaspers explores the essence of a human being that is free and open to a world of possibility. This genuine core, which he terms *Existenz,* is our authentic center that makes friendship possible. Intimate communication comes alive in this "meeting of two selves."

Aware of the loneliness that can occur even among a group of so-called friends, Jaspers finds the rewards of merging one *Existenz* with another innumerable. He wonders why we settle for superficial encounters while still desperate for deep friendships. We can feel most alone and hunger most earnestly for true friendship while in a group of seemingly happy acquaintances. As soon as I ask a group if they understand how Jaspers might have felt alone at a big party, they respond variously: "separate," "shy," "afraid," and "worse than if he had stayed home." The kids commiserate with him, talking about feeling lonely "even while jumping rope at recess with ten people" and about feeling miserable while "pretending to have a good time at a big sleepover." The kids and I talk at length about their awareness that being around people or spending a lot of time with others in no way guarantees good conversation. Most kids are willing to admit that we take a risk when we try to make friends. "Small talk is easy but hardly ever gets you a buddy." "We experience limits of communication: something is lacking even when it succeeds" (Jaspers, *Existenzphilosophie*). What makes unlimited communication impossible? How do we plumb communication to the depth of its possibilities?

We must be willing to move below the surface within ourselves to find deeper friendships with others. Only with our hearts wide open and our minds awake is intimate communication possible. For Jaspers, the best way to begin our effort to understand ourselves and the world is with a *genuine* attempt to communicate with someone else who seeks understanding as well. I ask the kids for examples of ways to talk from the heart to another person. They've given me lots of suggestions, for example: "I can ask them why they're sad," "I can find out what kind of music they like," "I can tell them my hardest subject in school and find out what theirs is," and "I can see if they want to try a little philosophy." While friendship requires effort and can be frustratingly difficult, it should be lovingly embraced all the same. Not only does intimate communication reveal a friend's inner nature, but it also provides realizations about oneself that would never be possible in solitude. Strengths and weaknesses become apparent for what they are, and understanding motivations and tendencies becomes easier. Questions appear one after another as we become more involved in our lives and the lives of others. When two authentic individuals put their full effort into honest talk and concentrated listening, they can discover together life's highest truths.

Children understand just as adults do that we can gain clarity and peace talking through things with a friend. The child philosophers I have taught often marvel that they get smarter when they are with their best friends and wonder why a problem becomes smaller when shared. Kids will go to great lengths to make sure that I understand the distinction between a real friend and a fake friend, and they make me pass their test by giving an example or two! "It's important that you understand," I'm told, "because your real friends can teach you a lot." One enthusiastic girl clapped her hands and summed up the importance of such communication by asking me this question: "Why do you think they invented language?" "Knowledge attains its full meaning only through the bond that unites men . . ." (Jaspers, *Existenz philosophie*).

✓ TEACHING TIPS: THE PHILOSOPHERS

- Make sure the children know the meaning of every word. *Community* and *genuine,* for example, may need defining. When in doubt, clarify. I always ask the children for their definition first.
- Break concepts down into simple phrases and be sure to have them prominently on display—either on the blackboard or on a

poster board. Catchy key phrases are more likely to stick in children's memories. For example, in reinforcing bell hooks, you may choose the phrase: better friends = stronger community.

DISCUSSION QUESTIONS: THE PHILOSOPHERS

- Hand out the following passage from The Epistle of Paul to the Hebrews: "Be not forgetful to entertain strangers: for thereby some have entertained angels unawares" (13:2). How does this relate to bell hooks' ideas on friendship?
- What are your qualifications for being a good friend?
- When do people become our friends? When they invite you over to their house? When you do your homework together? What if someone picks you to be on her team in gym? What if your parents are friends?
- Has a friend ever let you down? How so? Can you think of a time when you may have let one of your friends down?
- Do you believe a friendship can last through any kind of change? Separation? Why or why not?
- What are some examples of community? In what ways do neighbors create a community, or your class become a community of students, or the members of the school orchestra learn to think of themselves as a community?

EXERCISES: THE PHILOSOPHERS

- Have two students recite together one of Paul Fleischman's poems from his *Joyful Noise, Poems for Two Voices* collection. These poems become duets as two young voices in harmony fall tenderly on the ears. Reading poetry together can create a sense of community for children on a small scale. "House Crickets" is a favorite, giving two children a chance to chirp "Crick-et, crick-et" in unison. "Book Lice" offers up the repeated refrain "We're book lice, we're book lice." Have the children write and perform their very own poems for two. This work should take some time as they get it just right, and you can offer suggestions as they go along.

- Have the children think of friendships they treasure that might be in trouble. Is the friendship worth saving? What could they do to help mend it? Ask them to think of little things they can do to help heal the friendship. For their private use, in their philosophy journals they can reflect on what they've learned about themselves in this process.

- Have the children draw what friendship means to them *without* depicting people. Young philosophers naturally move their thinking to a deeper level with these boundaries. Artistic representations of friendship by kids have included a very large birthday cake—to signify that age doesn't matter since this eleven-year-old deemed his grandfather to be his best friend. One first-grader cut out a megaphone from construction paper to broadcast to the whole world that his brother was his best friend. Another drew a light bulb since she was able to figure out stuff by talking to her friend. My all-time-favorite masterpiece was created by a fourth-grader. He presented a drawing of what appeared to be a harp, and a figure of some kind, with wings attached, wearing a pair of very, very short pants. "Mine is of an angel unawares," he told the class. I thanked him and gently explained that the warning from Hebrews is to treat strangers well because you could be talking to an angel *unawares,* not in underwear. (Another example of the importance of clarifying vocabulary!)

LISTENING

Communication is impossible without listening. Words simply reverberate off the walls. Intense listening is a prerequisite for Jaspers' goal of intimate communion, *Existenz* to *Existenz*, essence to essence. Yet many children learn at an early age how to pretend not to hear what is being said. In my experience in and outside the classroom, I see preoccupation with one's own concerns and general restlessness as the two main sources of difficulty in concentrating on what someone else is saying. Kids know how to get a request repeated indefinitely and delight in demanding seemingly endless explanations. Get ready for *what* bus? Feed *my* dog? You asked me to pay *attention*? They've already learned the difficulty in having a heart-to-heart conversation, and that a deaf ear is a powerful device for procrastination and often succeeds in wearing out the speaker.

Children *do* realize that there are benefits to being a good listener and that listening is essential to friendship. They ask why in the world you would want to talk about true feelings if the other person was doing something else. They are very sensitive to the times their own voices have gone unheard. How do they know when adults or their peers aren't listening? Among countless proofs of not being heard that kids have reported to me are the following: reading the mail, typing on the computer, looking away during conversation, wearing headphones, or simply talking over the children's voices. "Early in my life and then later again and again I was perplexed by people's rigid inaccessibility and their failure to listen to reasons, their disregard of facts, their indifference which prohibited discussion, their defensive attitude that kept you at a distance and at the decisive moment buried any possibility of a close approach . . ." (Jaspers, *Existenzphilosophie*). I encourage the children to let me know if ever I fail to listen to them carefully. Often the child philosophers tell me that one of their favorite things about our dialogues is that "you listen to a kid." Their delight in being heard is an indication that it should happen more. hooks reminds us that all relationships, including friendships, wither if neglected. Listening conveys the respect and attention that friendship requires.

Children acknowledge how nice it feels to be listened to. Jaspers and hooks extol the comfort and wonderful quiet that can occur in a friendship grounded in listening. Kids express their appreciation for the way a friend who listens absorbs their words, feelings, and facial expressions. Listening only to you, your friend is not diverted in any other direction. Your attentive friends do not redirect your words in such a way so as to hear what they want to hear or expect an echo of what they already think. There is no need for listeners to rehearse their responses while their friends are speaking. Most kids make the leap from their appreciation of being heard to their obligation to try harder to listen to others. Leaving themselves plenty of wiggle room, a number of children have said that *maybe* they *might* listen and even stop interrupting, *most* of the time.

 TEACHING TIPS: LISTENING

- This topic is perfect for reminding the children of the humiliation that results from experiencing a drowned-out voice, and it is the *first* rule in working with a group: Never speak when someone else is talking, *regardless* of who it is. This rule protects the speaker and encourages others to pay attention. If you can't interrupt the speaker, listening is your alternative.
- Be sure to open up an honest dialogue with the class by sharing your own thoughts, stories, and examples. I always exchange my own descriptions of my friends with the child

philosophers' descriptions of theirs. Joining them in assignments emboldens children to be honest and builds an atmosphere of trust.

 DISCUSSION QUESTIONS: LISTENING

• How does one become a good listener? Why is it so hard to listen to someone else with full attention? How does it feel to be listened to?
• Do you know what it means to listen to your own thoughts? Do you listen to yourself?

 EXERCISE: LISTENING

• Listen to or watch a narrated version of *Peter and the Wolf,* which Sergei Proko fiev wrote for his own children. Peter's buddy, a bird on a branch, calls him out to play against his grandfather's warnings of the possibility of a wolf in the woods. With an ingenious plan, Peter and the bird capture the wolf and lead him to the zoo. Each character in the story—the duck, cat, bird, and wolf, as well as Peter—is represented by a musical instrument. Listening to the instruments closely to identify the characters they represent improves listening skills. Can you tell how each character is feeling by the tone and the tempo of the individual instruments? Discuss the kind of friendships Peter has with his grandfather and with the bird. What about the animals' friendship with one another? Have the children write an alternative ending to the story with the bullying wolf somehow becoming a part of the community. This gives the kids a chance to think about friendly ways of pulling a bully into the group.

BULLYING

A discussion of friendship is the perfect context in which to talk about bullying. Bullying is the antithesis of befriending, since it destroys hooks' ideal of community and prevents Jaspers' goal of genuine communication. Whenever I go to a school, it is not long before a teacher or a principal asks me to discuss bullying with the students. This problem is a harsh reality throughout the country in all sorts of schools. Bullying poses a serious threat to the joys of childhood, calling for our immediate attention and determined action to put an end to it. When you listen to children talking about the damage inflicted by bullies, it is impossible to ignore this problem. A bully hunts out the weak and vulnerable and exhibits a special kind of cruelty. Whether or not a child has been hurt physically, the psychological wounds are long-lasting. The victim lives in fear and learns despair much too early. Sometimes a child adopts hostility as the only available response to a bully, and the problem worsens.

In my conversations with children, they often express their understanding that it is the bully who is weak, but knowing this does not solve the problem. When children talk freely about the crisis of bullying in search of its causes and possible solutions, they somehow know to focus on understanding the mind-set of their tormentor. The bully's problems, whatever they are, must be fixed. Despite their own misery as the result of a bullying encounter, kids suspect that bullies "must be very sad" or "feel terrible about themselves."

The value our two philosophers place on friendship makes the position they would take on bullying clear. "Young people are cynical about love. Ultimately, cynicism is the great mask of the disappointed and betrayed heart" (hooks, *all about love*). The cynicism and anger of disappointed youth turns into the quest for

domination. The bully wants to have control over someone, something, anything. Since bullies are not part of a community linked
by friendships, they have no real sense of belonging. Through the
eyes of his wife, Jaspers watched bullying feed on itself. Ultimately it escalated to the unthinkable horror of the Holocaust.

Bullies' parents face tremendous responsibility because bullies
grow up, and the potential for causing harm grows with them. In
the bully's mind, no rules apply to them. Many more parents,
mothers and fathers of the victims, bandage and console their
children and share their relentless heartache. The best-planned family dinner is ruined as a child's tearful recollection of taunts experienced while walking to class impacts the family. A bully on a
swim team can be the unspoken reason for an avid swimmer's decision to quit the "team." Can a bully in the troop be a "sister to
every Girl Scout"? Bullying makes the Scout pledge meaningless
because it destroys any sense of community. Bullying taints every
moment in the life of a child who's filled with fear, and whose
parents endure the constant nightmare of being unsure how to
protect their child.

? DISCUSSION QUESTIONS: BULLYING

• What is a bully? Has anyone ever bullied you? Have you ever
  bullied someone else? Why do bullies bully?

EXERCISE: BULLYING

• Perhaps your class can devise a solution to bullying similar to
  the following one. After learning of bell hooks' emphasis on
  friendships and community, the children at one school devised a

"Bully-Busters" project. They made brochures, posters, and fly-ers describing the dangers of bullying. They set up a website where people could ask questions about bullies and seek advice from expert "Bully-Busters." They arranged a makeshift club-house where kids could go to talk about bullying at recess or when the school day was over. The kid organizers also wore buttons that said "Bully-Buster" so other kids knew who they could go to if they had a bully (or a bullying!) problem.

Children show me the human desire for friendship as well as the fear of being hurt by it. Unfortunately, I see in their faces that suffering is not new to them. I find them refreshingly honest when they admit they will continue to make mistakes while still striving to be careful with their friendships. In private conve rsations with me, the child philosophers explain how they know who their friends are and definitely who their friends are not. They have taught me well that though friendship is sometimes hard to explain, it is a tremendous gift that should not be taken for granted.

Over the years, the child philosophers have become my good friends and taught me to be a better listener. The torment that some children experience as a result of being bullied has encouraged me to be attentive to the bully as well. I hope that acknowledging the child bully "leads eventually to a deep compre-hension of the importance of establishing *communication*" (Jaspers, *Existe n zphilosophie*).

Resources

• *all about love* by bell hooks. Chapter 1, "Clarity: Give Love Words," gives hooks' description of love and discusses societal misconceptions about love. Chapter 8, "Community: Living Communion," takes a look at greed, domination, loss, self-love, and honesty.

- *Existenzphilosophie* by Karl Jaspers.
- *Existentialism from Dostoevsky to Sartre,* edited by Walter Kaufmann. This collection includes excerpts from *Existenzphilosophie.* Under the heading "On My Philosophy," the section titled "Drives to the Basic Questions" is full of ideas on what constitutes true communication and why humans thirst for it. This anthology is a good source for many readings from a number of our philosophers.
- "Friend of Mine" by Kate Wolf. This song is available on several of her CDs, including her live concert album, *An Evening in Austin.*
- *Peter and the Wolf* by Sergei Prokofiev. Royal Ballet School, 1997. About thirty minutes long, this choreographed version holds kids' attention as they watch children performing ballet. Many CDs of the music are readily available also.
- *Correspondence, 1926–1969,* a collection of letters between Karl Jaspers and the philosopher Hannah Arendt. The letters are examples of honest communication between a former student and her teacher. Theirs is a friendship that includes others, and it thrives regardless of age, gender, Arendt's Jewish heritage, or Jaspers' German nationality. Together they reveal their own natures and uncover lasting truths.
- "The Centaur" by May Swenson. This poem is in her collection *Cage of Spines.*
- *Joyful Noise, Poems for Two Voices* by Paul Fleischman.
- *Horton Hatches the Egg* by Dr. Seuss.

RESPONSIBILITY

A pressing need calls up an immediate
obligation to care for; roles and
responsibilities call up an obligation
to respond in a caring manner.
—RITA MANNING, "Just Caring"

THE TOPIC

Often when I arrive in a new classroom, I will see the word
responsibility displayed somewhere prominent. It may be in bold
letters over the doorway or at the top of a short list of "musts"
noted on the chalkboard. Children are told repeatedly that they
must be responsible for this and that or there will be consequences. At what age do we become responsible for our actions?
How can we determine what is and what is not our responsibility? Do most people figure this out on their own? Why do some
people have more obligations in their lives than others? How
often do adults as well as children hear that so many of our problems today result from a failure to assume personal responsibility?
There is much guilt and blame attached to this apparent failure,
but *why* should we fulfill our obligations?

Many adults longingly recall carefree childhoods, forgetting that memories can cast a rosy glow on our youthful days. But children will tell you that they are far from free of responsibility. Parents and teachers regularly remind kids of their obligations both as students and as family members. It is important that a heavy, punitive air does not hang over the concept of responsibility. Without knowing precisely what responsibility is, yet understanding that it is undeniably a part of our lives, we may desire to avoid it automatically. Children (and adults!) can develop elaborate strategies to escape from responsibility.

Philosophy asks that we stop and think, that we first become very clear about what responsibility means, in order to determine its place in our lives. Defining responsibility is not as easy as it may seem. You will find that it is one of those words, like *fun* or *good,* that we use all the time without really stopping to think what the idea means. After some careful thought, most kids define responsibility as essentially "what you have to do." Among the one-word definitions I often hear: chore, job, task, work, duty, obligation.

Once I have listened to kids tell me what they think about responsibility, I explain to the child philosophers that the root of the word responsibility, *response,* holds the key to my definition. The phone rings and we answer it because we know that our caller expects a *response.* I tell the kids that I think responsibility begins when pieces of the world dial my number and ask for me by name. Some pieces cry out, some whisper, and some signal to me silently. They call to me from far and wide, demanding that I answer. My responsibilities come from my living in the world. My responsibilities are the dues I pay to be a member of the universe.

As adults in the lives of children, we have the opportunity to guide little big minds toward seeing the positive side of responsibility: the invitation to help sustain the world and to express caring. You will be amazed to watch children's perspectives on their actual responsibilities shift once they see how wise and honorable assuming responsibility can be. I have found that kids are drawn to the thoughts offered by Albert Camus (ahl-BAIR ka-MOO) and Rita Manning on the subject of responsibility. For Camus, taking responsibility for your life is the only way to make your life belong to you. If I'm not responsible for my life, who is? Camus wonders. Seeing clearly that we are, each of us, connected to everyone else, Manning reveals the powerful truth that we are responsible for these connections. We must care for our relationships because we are part of the world, and we must act on our caring. For both philosophers, assuming responsibility comes naturally when we understand and accept its relevance to our lives.

 TEACHING TIPS: THE TOPIC

- Be sure to write the word *respons*ibility on the board and underline its root: *response*. This is the key to your discussion of the meaning of responsibility.
- Search for a one-word definition of responsibility and have the kids do the same. They will remember the word they choose.

 DISCUSSION QUESTIONS: THE TOPIC

- What are your responsibilities?
- In what specific ways do you feel responsible for your own life right now? Where does your responsibility end and an adult's begin?

- Where do you see a need for people to talk about the meaning of responsibility? (In a hospital? At the zoo? Umpiring a Little League game?)
- How can adults improve *their* response to *their* responsibilities? Be specific.

 EXERCISES: THE TOPIC

- Look through Demi's collection of tales, *Buddha Stories,* for lessons in responsibility, particularly "The Clever Crab," "The Cunning Wolf," and "The Black Bull." The gold and black illustrations are lovely and inviting. When read slowly and with animation, the fables make delightful listening. They are usually no more than a page, and the moral of each story is stated at the end. Don't reveal the moral until the children work to figure it out for themselves. Then have a good discussion about how each tale relates to responsibility.
- A look at Aesop's fables is a great complement to Demi. I read and discuss "The Two Dogs" with children. It is an important realization and a huge relief for kids to understand through this fable that one thing in their lives is definitely not their responsibility: the shortcomings of their parents. Take time to talk about other things that are not their responsibility. It is valuable to learn when young not to take on problems that are clearly the responsibility of others. Watch children's faces relax when they learn that a parent's yelling, a teacher's ridicule, or a friend's cruelty is not their responsibility. Have the children make two lists in their philosophy journals: a list of things that they think are clearly *their* responsibilities and a list of things that they think they aren't responsible for. Talk with children individually about their distinctions,

followed by a group discussion of some discoveries concerning responsibility.

THE PHILOSOPHERS

In the ideal caring society with sufficient resources to meet needs and to provide for some sort of flourishing, each of us would spend roughly the same amount of time being cared for. We would experience this as children and as adults.

—RITA MANNING, "Just Caring"

Rita Manning draws on her experiences as a parent, a teacher, a political activist, and a volunteer to show us why it is so crucial that we act responsibly toward our world and the people with whom we share it. Her most famous work, *Speaking from the Heart,* looks at her central concern with an ethic of caring action. Whether she is addressing air pollution, the ethical treatment of animals, or land use and its relationship to poverty, the ideal of responsible action is at the heart of Manning's philosophy.

Manning maintains that simply by virtue of the fact that we are caught up in an interwoven network of relationships, we are under a general obligation to care. Every day we form connections as we interact with one another and our surroundings, and these connections extend in every direction, one link to the next. One broken connection can cause the whole to come apart. We therefore must acknowledge the delicate ties that we have to one another and never let them loosen. Chains in a chain-link fence and bricks in a building serve as examples of individual pieces tightly connecting to make the whole. You can look around your classroom or outside for numerous examples of links in a chain. My favorite example is a hand-knit sweater that I pass from one child to another for a close look at the importance of the connection between each thread, each knot.

Manning's philosophy of responsible action hinges on awareness of our relationships. For her, our responsibilities lie in the existence of these relationships and our various social roles. "Social roles . . . commit us to some responsibilities to care" ("Just Caring"). In introducing Manning's take on responsibility to kids, I first look with them for the roles and relationships they see in their lives. Kids usually begin with their most familiar examples: parent-child, teacher-student, friend-friend, sister-brother, coach-player, neighbor-neighbor. They then branch out: minister-congregation, customer-salesperson, worker-worker, driver-passenger, dentist-patient. It is interesting for the children that I repeat some of their examples of relationships as my own: student-teacher, mother-daughter, brother-sister, citizen-country. We chat about the responsibilities that come with these relationships, and I begin with some questions. What responsibilities do both the passengers and the driver have while in a moving car? What do the salesperson and the customer owe to each other? What does my mother deserve from me, and what can I expect from her?

While acknowledging these relationships and the responsibilities that come from them, the child philosophers admit that knowing your responsibility and living up to it are two different things. Manning agrees with her young students. While we should anticipate and embrace our responsibilities, quite often we fail to do so out of carelessness. Manning reasons that rules and rights are needed to sketch a moral minimum below which no responsible person should fall. "We can reason in the language of rules with those who lack a sufficient degree of caring" ("Just Caring"). She provides as an example the necessity for rules in a hospital emergency room to ensure that the needs of the first patients to arrive do not cause the staff to neglect later arrivals. I work with child philosophers to come up with situations in our world that *should* be handled responsibly without the need for rules but in which rules seem to be necessary. It helps to begin with the question: "What needs *should* we, as caring people, have anticipated on our own?" I offer the example of the necessity of building codes to force the accommodation of people who travel by wheelchair. Surprised to learn that this regulation is even required, some fourth-graders offer examples quickly: "It's too bad that we need fines at our school to make students return library books." "It seems crazy that there has to be a smoking section in restaurants." "I guess some people won't think twice about littering unless they see an ugly road sign telling them not to."

Truly following an ethic of care means reaching out and antic-ipating the needs of others without being told to do so. Manning insists that meeting the bare minimum of essentially doing no harm does not take us to the heights of responsibility. She envi-sions an ideal, caring society in which we would be so keenly aware of our connections that our responsibilities would be an unquestioned part of our lives. Manning's hope is for an interre-lated world in which caring is reciprocal, a pendulum on which we are all invited to swing responsibly. "In addition to being sen-sitive to my place in the world and to my general obligation to be a caring person, I am also obligated to care for" ("Just Caring").

> All I maintain is that on this earth there are pestilences
> and there are victims, and it's up to us, so far as possible,
> not to join forces with the pestilences.
>
> —ALBERT CAMUS, *The Plague*

Born in Algeria in 1913, Camus grew up poor and fatherless. He worked his way through university with stints as a journalist, a weatherman, and an auto-parts salesman. His admiration for simple folk handling hard lives stemmed from his youth and student days in Algeria. He was active in the Resistance in occupied France during the Second World War and was a vigorous participant in Parisian intellectual and civic life afterward. Camus wrote short stories, plays, and essays in addition to his novels. A recipient of the Nobel Prize for Literature in 1957, he died in an automobile accident in 1960.

Camus saw all humans engaged in the same struggle to find meaning in their lives. He believed that although we can't make sense of the world as a whole, each of us has the task of making sense of our own existence. We must be responsible for the lives that we create, and this responsibility for our own lives extends naturally to accepting responsibility for one another. Camus felt a strong sense of solidarity with his fellow humans, and he believed that our banding together could help us find the strength to handle our responsibilities in better ways. If we feel supported by a strong awareness of fraternity, the question of whether we deserve the challenges life brings us becomes irrelevant, and we can take pride in our shared triumphs along the way.

The theme of responsibility runs throughout Camus' works. Learning philosophical theories through an engaging story delights child philosophers, and they love his two stories that I use to examine responsibility: *The Plague* and "The Myth of Sisyphus." In *The Plague,* Camus tried to come to grips with the Nazi occupation of France and the spiritual plague of isolation and loss of human solidarity that resulted. The book is also a perfect vehicle to showcase the rewards made possible through the virtue of responsibility. A completely unforeseen outbreak of disease closes the town gates of the city of Oran, and both friends and strangers find themselves trapped within its walls. The epidemic they face is deadly and alarmingly contagious. Although the signs of plague are obvious, its prisoners' first challenge is to acknowledge that plague is there to stay and that they must respond to it. Each "hostage" must then decide whether to respond by skulking in isolation or working side by side to fight the terrifying sickness as the death toll relentlessly rises. Most townspeople pitch in with determination and extend themselves as volunteers in ways that were previously unimaginable. The character Cottard, a criminal, stands out in his refusal to volunteer for work with the sanitary squads or take responsibility for his own health or the health of others. A visiting journalist, Rambert, waffles between his indignation that he does not belong in Oran and his instinctive feeling of responsibility to join in the fight against the plague. Camus' model of fearless responsibility, Dr. Rieux, persists in his duties and never turns away from the bleak reality he shares with those around him.

The plague gives the citizens who were sleepwalking through their lives the opportunity to respond with courage and dogged endurance. The victory lies not in abolishing the plague but in their heroic effort to fight for their own lives and the life of every member of the community. In the end, many of the townspeople's passionate acceptance of the bonds that link them to one another saves them from Camus' spiritual plague of irresponsible isolation, leaving them with the unforgettable experience of close kinship.

I find it intrigues children to imagine their school as the setting for their own interpretation of *The Plague*. Before I talk to children about the novel itself, I ask them to imagine that a lot of kids have been coming down with the flu and that everyone must stay at school until the threat of spreading the flu is over. They immediately want to tell me of times that "*everybody* got the flu one day," and their identification with the outbreak of a contagious disease prevents *The Plague* from shocking them. Indeed, their experience with the flu and other contagious diseases at school and at home helps them understand Camus' story and the predicament of the people in the town. The gory details of Oran's bubonic plague are irrelevant. What matters is the understanding of responsibility kids can glean from imagining how *they* would respond, what *they* would do, either in Oran or at their school. "Plague is here and we have got to make a stand, that's obvious. Ah, I only wish everything were as simple!" (*The Plague*). Kids come up with a variety of ways to assume responsibility for their unexpected captivity: "I could help set up cots where we would sleep." "If I get the flu, I'll stay in the contagious room to keep others safe." "When I realize that people are sad, I will try my best to keep their heads up." Many realize one advantage they have that the residents of Oran could have used well: "I can keep connected with my family and friends by e-mail so that they don't worry about me."

Camus makes the point throughout the book that responsibility comes with being human and is a part of *every* life, however we choose to deal with it. Before the arrival of the plague, the people of Oran distanced themselves from responsibility in their lives. Ironically, Dr. Rieux remarks at the book's end that in an important way the people of the town were fortunate to be awakened by plague. "But what does that mean—'plague?' Just life, no more than that" (*The Plague*). Camus invites every reader as well as our child philosophers to use the responsibilities that are part of every life to enrich one's own humanity.

☑ TEACHING TIPS: THE PHILOSOPHERS

- When you read *The Plague,* look for characters that you think would be most interesting for your particular group of child philosophers' examination of responsibility. For example, the three characters Cottard, Rambert, and Rieux are mirrors that reflect Camus' perspective on responsibility. Cottard is the antithesis of a responsible individual, denying responsibility for his own life as well as the lives of those around him. Rambert is like most people, both aware of the value of responsibility and tempted to flee this same responsibility in his current situation. Dr. Rieux assumes responsibility as naturally as a swimmer glides through water. Camus suggested that he would like to come close in his own life to the ideal of Dr. Rieux.

- When teaching Manning's interconnections, pass around a loosely knit handmade sweater for close inspection. The children can see that each thread matters and works to keep the whole together.
- An enlarged photograph of a spiderweb, intricate and strong, shows interwoven connections that will fall apart if a piece pulls away. Kids like this familiar observation in nature as an illustration of Manning's theory.

DISCUSSION QUESTIONS: THE PHILOSOPHERS

- Why do you think Manning says that the best way to teach students about responsible action is to work in a soup kitchen?
- Why do you think it was so hard in the beginning even to admit that plague had come to Oran?
- How can you explain in Camus's philosophy that the plague provided an opportunity to the people of Oran?

EXERCISES: THE PHILOSOPHERS

- Set up a long, winding chain of dominoes with the children. After setting it up, discuss connections between one caring action and the chain of positive results. For example, if you keep track of your coat and don't lose it, then a smaller child can be warmed by it when you outgrow it. And picking up the trash at your feet will allow people to see a clean park and inspire them not to litter. Have a child tap the first domino and watch the rest tumble. Talk about the ripple effect that one seemingly small responsible action can set in motion.

- Read Mary Oliver's "The Summer Day." Through her poetry children can understand human nature better as they see that their lives are woven into the earth and all that lives. If we don't wake up to our responsibilities, what would happen to the grasshopper that is featured in this poem? After talking about the poem a bit, focus on the last two lines: "Tell me, what is it you plan to do / with your one wild and precious life?" Ask the children to write a poem that begins with the words "With my one precious life, I . . ."

    Oliver connects her admiration for the natural world to human responsibility in her poem titled "Lead." Lead that leaked into a harbor is responsible for the death of a once beautiful loon lying on the shore. Oliver wants our hearts to break so that they remain open to assuming responsibility for the lives around us. This "speckled and iridescent" loon had "a plan to fly home." The poem's power is that it doesn't end in sadness but rather in a call to spread our arms wide to embrace this big world. Have the kids write a poem that tells a different story of the loon's life. Ask the kids if they can think of a connection between their lives and that of the loon. How about the grasshopper from "The Summer Day"? Help them trace possible connections.

BURDEN
Rita Manning describes the world in which we live as a "pre-caring world." She does not see a world in which responsibility is

assumed willingly, but rather responsibility is a burden to be borne with reluctance. "We don't live in a caring world. By that I mean that not everyone recognizes his or her obligation to care. Our society does not encourage the flourishing of this capacity, but undermines it in various ways" ("Just Caring"). Manning observes that looking out for one's own needs is a higher priority in our consumer society than caring for others. She recognizes that responsible caring does not appear attractive to a large number of people and wonders how to develop an ethic of care in a society that looks at caring as a burden.

It is important to let children talk about the various ways that responsibility feels like a burden to them. Chatting at length with kids about this very human feeling paves the way for them to appreciate fully the transformation of responsibility from a burden to a welcome invitation to do their part. Most child philosophers tell me that thinking of responsibility as anything *but* a burden is a new thought for them. A frequent refrain is that "responsibilities get in the way of my free time." Sometimes I am reminded that there is a reason that "responsibilities are called chores." Far from seeing the relationships that Manning emphasizes in their families, kids insist that it is just *too* much to have to "keep picking up my Legos," "remember to close the refrigerator door," and "take out the gross stuff to the compost pile." When I ask them whose responsibility it *is* to do these things, the children sheepishly realize that someone else must be picking up their slack.

The responsible caring that Manning advocates is reciprocal and "sustains all parties in the relationship." One unfortunate result of our failure as individuals to take care of our responsibilities is the "total caring burnout" suffered by caring persons. As children take an honest look at their perception of responsibility as a burden, they become increasingly aware that this mind-set puts even more responsibility on the shoulders of those willing to bear it.

Work with your children to link their lack of responsibility to its repercussions in the relationships in their lives. As they warm begrudgingly to our topic, I take a look with them at their participation in Manning's "pre-caring world" in their interactions with their classmates. I ask them to imagine that Manning is planning to visit their classroom and to foresee any examples she might find of this pre-caring world. Many kids claim to have been on one side or the other of an imbalance of responsibility in a "group" effort. "Whenever we're split up in groups of three for projects, I end up doing all the work while my partners sit around and talk." Another sixth-grader volunteered that he walked away at "just the right time before the other kids had to pick up the sports equipment at the end of recess." In these two examples, Manning's reciprocal responsibility is missing from the group project and on the playground. The burden falls on the conscientious student and the rest of the gym class.

By talking with your young philosophers about how they burden their classmates by their failure to care, you can help them make the connection as well between their avoidance of responsibility and the impact of this behavior on the grown-ups in their lives. Kids struggle first to understand and then to explain their sense of themselves as a burden to those who are responsible for them. But they can understand that while their childhood calls to their parents and teachers to care for them, *their* own actions can turn adult responsibility, lovingly undertaken, into an uncalled-for burden. Kids know that their parents are responsible for them financially, often facing difficulty as a result, yet I frequently hear that still doesn't "keep me from asking for more." One eleven-year-old expressed empathy for the constant worry that her parents had for her safety, amazed as she wondered if she could have been a burden "when I just forgot to call and say I was at my friend's house." And on several occasions, kids described how sad their parents seemed "whenever I fight with my sister." The child philosophers can see the burden they can create for the teachers responsible for educating them, as well. "We keep talking when he's trying to teach, no matter what." Also, "I go off alone at recess and don't hear the bell when it's time to go in."

I have yet to encounter a child who enjoys the thought of being a burden. Accepting the philosophical invitation extended by Camus and Manning to be responsible members of the human community seems more and more attractive to kids. You will find that your discussion of viewing responsibility as a burden, though it may have a negative feel, can yield positive results. Little big minds understand that if they face their current shortcomings honestly, they will be able to make improvements. Slowly, many realize that running from responsibility "doesn't ever work," because the world you live in "catches up with you." Children of all ages tell me that they make excuses because they find it hard to finish anything. "Admitting that I threw the ball through the window was not what I planned to do." It comes as no surprise to their teachers, who hear their students say that "I try to get away with stuff until I get caught." As they listen to themselves and one another, their past behavior strikes them as embarrassing and careless. As you discuss avoiding responsibilities, the child philosopher's perspective on duties gently twists from ambivalence to opportunity.

? DISCUSSION QUESTIONS: BURDEN

- Have you ever run away from a specific responsibility? Why?
- How is it possible to avoid responsibility and be a happy person? Do you think that you can be a happy person surrounded by irresponsible people? How?

EXERCISE: BURDEN

- Watch Ravel's fifty-minute opera with a libretto by Colette, *L'enfant et les sortilèges* (*The Bewitched Child*), featuring an irresponsible and self-absorbed boy. He is intentionally destructive, damaging many things, including a grandfather clock in the house and a tree in the garden. One day all the things in the house and the garden that have suffered his abuse come alive. They appear life-sized! The objects and animals sing their complaints loud and clear, and in all the commotion a squirrel hurts his paw. The boy has hurt this squirrel before, but this time his heart is touched and he bandages the wound. The creatures now see the potential for caring in the child and take him home to his mother. After enjoying the opera, the child philosophers can talk about the reasons for the boy's behavior. Ask them if and how they relate to both his irresponsible *and* his responsible behavior.

A UNIQUE OPPORTUNITY

In "The Myth of Sisyphus," Camus introduces us to a man who finds the meaning of his own life through his determined and loving acceptance of his one unique responsibility. This short tale sheds light on several of Camus' central theories. For example, he is acutely conscious of the indignation that humans feel at our inability to grasp the ultimate meaning of life, yet he vehemently denounces suicide or apathy as a response to life's difficulties. For our purposes, the essay tells a story that children ask repeatedly to hear again, and it celebrates the benefits of taking responsibility for our lives. Though Sisyphus's responsibility is dramatic in its eternally relentless nature, Camus intended it as a comparison to the day-in and day-out handling of responsibility that occurs in every life.

"Myths are made for the imagination to breathe life into them" (Camus, "The Myth of Sisyphus"). I invite the child philosophers to draw the picture in their imaginations of Sisyphus as I tell his story, from Camus' perspective, in the following way: "Sisyphus loved his life so much that he forgot to pay proper attention to the gods. The gods were not pleased, and they decided to punish him. He was made to push an enormous rock up a mountain, over and over, only to have it roll back down to the foot of the mountain *every single time* he made it to the top. And Sisyphus had to do this hard work forever! Yet as hard as this may be for you to believe, he didn't think of it as a punishment. Sisyphus responded to his predicament honestly. He accepted the rock as his responsibility. He never complained about getting a day off, or pretended that he was going to get out of this situation somehow, or moaned that it was just not fair. He chose to love his rock because it was *his* rock.

"Picture him wedging his foot under it, the way he wraps his arms around it as far as they will go, and the way he presses his cheek against it. This is his life. His life belongs to him and he takes responsibility for the way he lives it. Sisyphus's burden lifted as soon as he took charge of his situation." Children agree with Camus that his Sisyphus is amazing. Often they draw the connection between their everyday lives and the rock, realizing that *everyone* has rocks to push. A young artist in one group pictured Sisyphus going back down the mountain to face his responsibility "skipping and whistling." A number have sketched him with his head unbowed and his chin up. Many notice his refusal to "jump into some fantasy escape." Sisyphus is realistic, knowing that his rock is not going to stay at the top of the mountain; nor is it going to go away. If he can hug his rock, the child philosophers realize that they can take charge of their lives. They are especially encouraged by the last lines of Camus' myth: "The struggle itself towards the heights is enough to fill a man's heart. One must imagine Sisyphus happy."

To Manning, moral theory is meaningless unless it motivates us to act without needing to be reminded. For Camus, acting responsibly gives us the opportunity to experience personal growth and shared harmony. For both philosophers, if you care about your life, other people, and the world itself, responsibility can be a welcome part of being on the planet. Kids' points of view broaden in all directions. Teachers and parents alike tell me that children become kinder and happier as this new look at responsibility honors their humanity. They really are important!

With their new understanding, the child philosophers warm gradually to their opportunity to play an active part in the world. They become more aware that each of us chooses, as a way of life, either caring involvement or uncaring irresponsibility. I ask the children what it would be like to turn their backs on the relationships in their lives. Kids love to act out what it would be like to try to turn their backs on the world! As one child spun in a repetitive, giggling circle around the classroom, she announced that "you just go around, but there is nowhere to hide." Gladly sitting among her classmates again, she concluded that "trying to turn away from responsibility just made me dizzy!"

I see children feeling important when they think that they have much to offer as a member in full standing of the universe. They sit up taller when I remind them that they've received a phone call from the universe that is just for them. The world is counting on them to be part of it. Many kids say that thinking about responsibility in this way helps them "do things they might not want to do" and teaches them simply "to do what needs doing." "My day-to-day interactions with other persons create a web of reciprocal caring" (Manning, "Just Caring"). Children see that they will give and get, and it sounds like a good deal.

TEACHING TIPS: A UNIQUE OPPORTUNITY

- Before you tell Sisyphus's story, be sure to spell his name quite clearly on the board. Otherwise, I guarantee that at the sound of his name the children will blurt out "Sillyfuss" and laugh at their repeated pronunciations of his new name.
- Try to find an artistic representation of Sisyphus for the children to enjoy. I bring in a small gold statue of him and his rock so that they have a lasting image of him and his responsibility in their minds.
- Children concentrate well, and sometimes better, if their hands are busy. Drawing is especially effective. Hand out paper before telling Sisyphus's story and ask the kids to illustrate it as you tell his tale. The kids will concentrate hard when listening to the story of the rock pusher in order to get their sketches just right.

 DISCUSSION QUESTIONS: A UNIQUE OPPORTUNITY

- How is responsibility an opportunity? How is it an invitation? How does thinking about your responsibilities as opportunities and invitations change the way you feel about them?
- How can accepting your responsibilities change your life in good ways?
- How does it feel to contribute to a better world?
- Would you care about an injured driver of your school bus or about school library books that are damaged and never returned? What can you do to take responsibility for these two situations?

- Why does Camus admire Sisyphus? What are his best qualities, according to Camus?

 EXERCISES: A UNIQUE OPPORTUNITY

- Listen to selections from Sweet Honey in the Rock, an a cappella group accompanied by a rhythmic beat rooted in African chant. "In This Land" and "Trying Times" point to hunger amid plenty, homelessness, drug abuse, and despair—all a result of people's refusal to accept responsibility for others. The comfort of "I Be Your Water" balances these harsh truths. These are big problems, so share what's appropriate for the age and experience of your children. Reflecting on this music, ask the kids if anyone they know has a very heavy rock to push. Have them write in their journals about this person's rock and how they can respond helpfully.

- Read Robert Frost's mainstay, "The Road Not Taken." This is an excellent poem for examining both our choices and our responsibility for them. Ponder the lines "Two roads diverged in a wood, and I— / I took the one less traveled by." Frost reminds us that the road we choose to take makes all the difference. Have the children draw a picture of two roads diverging in different directions, and write a poem to go with the drawing that describes the road that they want to travel in their own lives. What's on this road? Who is responsible for it? What were the two possible roads to take in Oran?

- Find out how many children are staying at a local shelter and then have your class pack lunches for them to take to school. This combines both active caring and pushing the rock. If you leave it to the children to decide what should go into the lunches, their efforts will expand, as they complete each bag, to include gifts like small notepads decorated with stickers and glitter, pencils, or a tiny sharpener. One eight-year-old philosopher I worked with was struck by her sudden realization that some of her classmates could be living at the shelter without her knowing it. The day after the lunches are delivered, have your children reflect in their journals on the connection they see between their project and the philosophies of Camus and Manning.

- There are rocks to push in every life. Have the children write about their very own "rocks" in their philosophy journals. They can share with the rest of the class if they like. Sharing is often a source of comfort as they realize they are not alone. Have them write a paragraph about how they think Sisyphus would push *their* rock if he were around.

How well I remember the expression on a child's face as he quickly asked the first question on my first day in his classroom. "Are you ever not going to show up when you say you are?" His question is a reminder of how frequently adults reduce the importance of their obligations to children simply because they are children.

At first kids appear bored and a bit resistant to the familiar chore of hearing about responsibility. Soon Camus and Manning give responsibility a simple meaning that makes sense to them. The idea boils down to giving what you can because you can. The kids remind me that assuming responsibility is not easy at any age, but that satisfaction and joy can be found in pushing our personal "rocks" with devotion. It turns out that a responsible life is a happy one.

Children are experts at hearing the call for a response from the environment as well. Toward the end of a lengthy discussion about responsibility and the environment, one child's excitement propelled her from the floor to her feet. This third-grade environmentalist proclaimed that recycling isn't the answer, even though everybody thinks it is. "Landfills are overflowing and you can't keep recycling forever, can you?" Her solution came to her immediately. "The next time, and every time from now on, when I go into a store, I am going to stop myself and ask if I really need that or that or that. If everybody did this, too, what would be in the landfills?"

Resources

- "The Summer Day" by Mary Oliver. This can be found in two of her collections, *House of Light* and *New and Selected Poems.*
- "Lead" by Mary Oliver. In *New and Selected Poems,* volume 2.
- "The Road Not Taken" by Robert Frost. An excellent source is *The Road Not Taken: An Introduction to Robert Frost,* with commentary by Louis Untermeyer.
- *In This Land,* by Sweet Honey in the Rock.
- *L'enfant et les sortilèges (The Bewitched Child)* by Maurice Ravel. On CD, André Previn conducts the London Symphony Orchestra, and on DVD the Netherlands Dance Theater joins the French National Orchestra, treating the children to dance and song. There is also a wonderful children's chorus in the opera.
- *Buddha Stories* by Demi.
- *The Fables of Aesop.* The Aesop collection illustrated by Edward J. Detmold makes a fine presentation.
- *The Fairy Tales of Hermann Hesse,* translated by Jack Zipes. Middle-schoolers love this collection.
- *Existentialism from Dostoevsky to Sartre,* edited by Walter Kaufmann. This includes "The Myth of Sisyphus," as do many of Camus' collections.
- *The First Man* by Albert Camus. In this intimate autobiographical look at his childhood, children can see the philosopher as a soccer

goalie who loves his mother and is influenced by a wise school-teacher. His boyhood clearly planted the seeds of his commitment to taking personal responsibility for his life. The children can compare Camus' childhood to their own.

- *The Fall* by Albert Camus. The narrator takes no responsibility for his life. The pivotal event in this novel is the night he ignores a woman's cry as she jumps from a bridge. Here, as elsewhere, he keeps walking and offers nothing but excuses.
- *The Plague* by Albert Camus. Note especially the character of Joseph Grand, who does all he can with all his might, and is the character most admired by the narrator of this story.
- *Speaking from the Heart* by Rita Manning.
- "Just Caring" by Rita Manning. This article can be found on pages 44–54 in *Explorations in Feminist Ethics: Theory and Practice*, edited by Eve Browning Cole and Susan Coultrap-McQuin. It is also in *50 Readings in Philosophy*, edited by Donald C. Abel.

HAPPINESS

We learn in our guts, not just in our brain,
that a life of joy is not in seeking happiness,
but in experiencing and simply *being*
the circumstances of our life as they are;
not in fulfilling personal wants, but
in fulfilling the needs of life . . .

—CHARLOTTE JOKO BECK, *Everyday Zen*

THE TOPIC

Caught up in our busy lives, so many of us forget the reason for our striving. What is the longed-for goal of our day-in, day-out efforts? Isn't it all so that we can ensure our happiness and that of our loved ones? Why do we veer off course and fail to make the choices that will actually lead to this happiness? Human forgetfulness of something so essential to our lives intrigues philosophers. How do we become so shortsighted that wealth or social stature often become poor substitutes for a happy life? From ancient to modern philosophy, the drive to understand what truly makes us happy and how we might obtain such happiness circles the globe.

Children know that life comes with difficulties, and they accept this reality. They also sense that both kids and adults devote considerable energy to pursuits that don't really matter. In my conversations with kids about the importance of having a clear understanding of the meaning of happiness and what the actual opportunities are in their lives to find it, I have benefited from their wisdom. By following their lead, I can guarantee you a fresh perspective!

We will approach our search for an understanding of happiness in two philosophical steps. To begin our analysis, we will look for the heart of its meaning. What are the ingredients of a happy life? Aristotle drew a distinction between pleasure and happiness that remains a focus for many philosophers. We must be clear about the difference between short-term fulfillment of desires and the long-term activity of a happy life because, Aristotle reminds us, some joys are fleeting while others have staying power. Quite often, apparent pleasure drags along with it unfortunate consequences for kids as well as adults. The pleasure of avoiding homework abruptly ends with a morning quiz, and the memory of an extravagant meal loses some of its savor with the arrival of the bill. What about those joys that provide lasting happiness *without* any negative consequences? What *is* happiness?

With just a bit of thinking, children are quick with their definitions of happiness. Happiness is "feeling okay about everything and being satisfied no matter what." It is also the "feeling that you belong somewhere," a definition that one child philosopher quickly amended to belonging *anywhere*. It makes a person happy to "feel good about how they're living," and this satisfaction makes them feel light. If you are able to "trust because you're not afraid, then you can be really happy."

I define happiness for them as a certain way of being in the world. It is a way of feeling and thinking about life that leaves you, deep down, full. Quite frequently a child will ask immediately if I think that everybody can be happy. My answer is that each of us makes the choice whether or not to be happy, and people go about it in their own way once they make this decision.

After our search for the meaning of happiness, our next philosophical step is to uncover the countless things that we mistake for happiness. As we continue to peel back the layers of our errors, the sources of happiness appear in bold outline. As we realize that possessions and societal approval still leave us surprisingly restless and unfulfilled, the essential ingredients of a happy life emerge. Ah, look. Peace of mind, security, unconditional love, the appreciation of little things. Of course.

Making partners of Epicurus (eh-pih-KYOOR-us), strolling in ancient Greece, and Charlotte Joko Beck, sitting in traffic in sunny California, is an ideal approach for an honest inspection of our lives and fresh insight into happiness. Together they offer specific characteristics of a happy life and practical advice on how to become a happy person. Beck, an American teacher of Zen Buddhism, lives in the world we know. Stop, be still, and breathe, says Beck. Epicurus unveils the abundance of simple pleasures right before his eyes as well as ours. Stop, look around, and pay attention, he says. They give us the map. People plot their own courses.

✓ TEACHING TIPS: THE TOPIC

- Much to the children's delight, I like to play different versions of "Here Comes the Sun" before embarking on our discussion of happiness, during a snack, or at the end of the session. Children are intrigued when they hear the same tune sung by various artists. There must be something important about that sun coming out! Watch it appear with the Beatles, Richie Havens, Nina Simone, and with Rockapella.

- Remember that having children write down their ideas about the meaning of happiness in their philosophy journals before a discussion prevents their imitation of what others say and gives them confidence when it's their turn to speak. Seeing their own words in print validates their thoughts.

 DISCUSSION QUESTIONS: THE TOPIC

- What is your definition of happiness? Does your definition satisfy you?
- How do you distinguish between pleasure and happiness?
- Picture yourself sitting in a rocking chair on your front porch, one day a long time from now, perhaps when you are your grandparents' age. What will you want to look back and see? What do you think you'll remember with pleasure?

 EXERCISES: THE TOPIC

- Read e. e. cummings' "who knows if the moon's / a balloon . . ." The children thrill at the possibility in this poem. Display the poem so that the children can enjoy a temporary reprieve from the rules of grammar! Have the children write a poem that begins "who knows if . . ." and fill in the possibilities. The "balloon" is number 13 in his *100 Poems.* "When faces called flowers float out of the ground" of course "the mountains are dancing." In number 97, cummings's joy at the arrival of spring fills the listener's heart. Ask the young poets to write their original version of number 97 that ends with mountains dancing.
- Read in a hushed voice Edna St. Vincent Millay's "The Fawn." She invites the listener to take part in her joy in coming upon

a fawn in the woods. Listening to "The Fawn" read aloud, children hold their breaths so that the baby deer can't hear them. Seeing him stand on brand-new legs, shaky in his thinness, is a simple pleasure. Have the child philosophers write a poem describing a time that they came upon something in nature that touched their hearts. Millay's "Recuerdo" is an escape to ride on a ferry and be quite merry. Buy the children a ticket for the ferry, take them on a field trip, and have them point out all the simple pleasures on their journey. Ask them to write a poem in their journals that begins, "We were very tired, we were very merry . . ."

THE PHILOSOPHERS

Let no one when young delay to study philosophy, nor when
he is old, grow weary of his study. For no one can come too
early or too late to secure the health of his soul. And the
man who says that the age for philosophy has either not
yet come or has gone by is like the man who says
that the age for happiness is not yet come to him . . .
—EPICURUS, "Letter to Menoeceus"

Epicurus was born an Athenian citizen on the island of Samos in 341 B.C.E. He grew weary of political turmoil and public life and established a house and garden on the outskirts of Athens that was the center of life for followers of his simple philosophy. His commune included women and slaves as well as free men. Along with his students and friends, Epicurus lived quietly and by all accounts quite happily.

Epicurus's work is a celebration of simplicity. Throughout his writings, he assures the reader that life's basic pleasures are many and easily obtained. The absence of pain, both physical and mental, *is* pleasure. A luxurious lifestyle leads to the loss of tranquillity and to budding anxiety. The physical needs of hunger and thirst can be met without competition, whereas desire is never satisfied. The good life is blessed by friendship and grounded in a sense of security.

Epicurus is the most requested of all the philosophers I teach. Children hurry home to discuss him with their parents and the word spreads. He provides a practical approach to lifting the baggage that modern life leaves at our doorstep, and therein lies his appeal. "Prudence," or common sense, is the chief virtue for Epicurus because it helps us to distinguish between the things that are important and the things that are irrelevant to human happiness. He unveils a "new" way of looking at how we live today and suggests a thorough examination of our priorities. From ancient Greece he promises that happiness comes from simple living because streamlining our lives is the cure for stress and misery. Modern child and grown-up philosophers alike appreciate his awakening of what we once knew instinctively but forgot unknowingly. It might amuse Epicurus to find that his view of good living and how to achieve it is considered profound.

Let's look at Epicurus's secret. The good life is one that consists of "freedom from pain in the body and trouble in the mind." Happiness is within reach because "the limit of good things is easy to fulfill and easy to attain, whereas the course of ills is either short in time or slight in pain" ("Letter to Menoeceus" [meh-NEE-see-us]). Spiritual repose and contentment come from the satisfaction of basic needs. Extravagance is unnecessary. Acquisition of possessions is not the path to happiness. Confusion and accumulation go hand in hand, and "stuff" exerts increasing control over human life. Daily living needs reshaping by using the tool of practical philosophy. Common sense tells us to prune back our lives.

Mental fear is the worst pain and a result of the victory of complication over simplicity. Everyday life surrounds us with innumerable simple pleasures. A conversation with a friend, a long walk, and the flight of a butterfly can fill our hearts with joy. But if our minds and hearts are too crowded, simple pleasures elude us. The birds can't sing over the noise. Philosophy can show us once again how to distinguish between what is necessary and unnecessary. Determining what is unnecessary in our lives and clearing it out soothes us mentally.

Children immediately understand this Epicurean distinction between basic and frivolous needs. They think it's odd that "the things that you don't really need cost money that you don't really have" and then you worry how to pay for the . . . TV, fancy car, and "popular shoes." With a slight bit of resistance at first, kids acknowledge that neither a microwave nor a dishwasher is essential. It is highly entertaining to watch the predictable response when a child suggests that video games also go in the unnecessary file. There is an initial outcry punctuated with groans, then a mixture of denial, rejection, and complete agreement all at once. The discussion of the importance of video games is a good one to highlight the children's concern that it is not always easy to live simply. Many insist that they want what the people around them have, even if they know better. Sadly kids report that not having what's fashionable makes you feel like something is wrong with you. Epicurus reminds them to join him in his garden when they feel left out or alone. "We must then meditate on the things that make our happiness . . ." ("Letter to Menoeceus").

Prudence! Pleasure is the key ingredient of human happiness, but we must be sensitive to the consequences that come with pleasurable activity. "No pleasure is a bad thing in itself: but the means which produce some pleasures bring with them disturbances many times greater than the pleasures" (Epicurus, "Principal

Doctrines"). Mental pleasures rarely have painful consequences and are abundant. Pleasure that comes from material possessions is short-lived, but the worry over hoarding these items comes with a lifetime guarantee. Memory—of a laugh or a scene or a fragrance—is the source of countless treasures that cost nothing. Epicurus maintained that remembering a conversation with a friend negated his own chronic physical ailments because "the acutest pain is there for a very short time . . ." ("Principal Doctrines"). Today this might be called mind over matter. Epicurus calls it common sense: "It is not possible to live pleasantly without living prudently."

> If I were to tell you that your life is already perfect, whole, and
> complete just as it is, you would think I was crazy. Nobody believes
> his or her life is perfect. And yet there is something within each
> of us that basically knows we are boundless, limitless.
>
> —CHARLOTTE JOKO BECK, *Everyday Zen*

Charlotte Joko Beck was born in New Jersey and attended public schools. She studied at the Oberlin Conservatory of Music. A divorced mother, she supported her four children as a teacher and a secretary. She began her study and practice of Zen Buddhism in her forties. Her studies with Maezumi Roshi culminated in her selection as his third Dharma heir. She lives and teaches at the Zen Center in San Diego.

Beck merges Japanese spirituality with her life as an ordinary woman living in the United States today. She addresses universal human concerns. She applies Zen practice to anger, despair, fear, love, suffering, hope, and the challenge of making commitments. Beck's words are neither fancy nor self-important, and her practical approach to realizing happiness in our lives draws students to the Zen Center and readers to her works.

Each of us has an inner life of the spirit that by its very nature is a place of clarity, simplicity, and peace. This Buddhist belief shows that the potential for happiness lies within us and that each person has the power to realize happiness in life. Happiness comes from a unified life without fragments and distractions. This unified life *is* a simplified life.

Beck is well aware of the fast-paced American lifestyle in which multitasking is an achievement. But is it? What about the peace that comes from calm? Similar to Epicurus, Beck calls her practical advice concerning happiness "nothing special." We need to work on ourselves to reduce the physical clutter in our lives and the confusion in our minds as well. Each of us must find our own way to happiness. The good news is that "every moment offers us a wealth of opportunities" (*Everyday Zen*). We must be patient and not expect an immediate overhaul of our way of life. It takes effort to train ourselves to need less so that gradually we can stand up straighter as we reduce the weight that we carry on our tight shoulders. This progression from the life of multitasking to one of simply doing is a slow one. Being mindful is an integral part of Buddhist practice. Mindfulness has a better chance in a mind emptied of preoccupations.

Everyday life itself is wondrous. In our whirring around, our lives become like the spin cycle of a washing machine, and we fail to see that "life is a second-by-second miracle" (Beck, *Everyday Zen*). Children see this miracle in a blade of grass. How many blades are there in the world? They experience it when they encounter by surprise a friend from their old neighborhood. It's miraculous when the training wheels come off their bikes. And who can forget the magic of the letters of the alphabet becoming words that you can read!

Beck encourages everyone, regardless of age, to find happiness in *full* commitment to the only project any of us really owns, and that is the project of our lives. Happiness comes from full-bodied and full-spirited living. If we can find balance and live our lives from the center of our being, happiness is ours.

So, how do we find this center within? Joko tells her students to *just sit*. Meditation is at the heart of Buddhist practice. With her background in carpooling, Beck knows that *just sitting* poses tremendous difficulty. A zigzag of emotions and random thoughts flood our minds, making restless limbs want to move. Here is her response to her students' complaints that meditation is too hard and its rewards uncertain: *Just sit*. Beck can tell them from her own experience that "gradually our life settles down, becomes more balanced. Our emotions are not quite as domineering. As we sit, we find that the primary thing we must work with is our busy, chaotic mind" (*Everyday Zen*).

Children not only see the benefits of meditation in their own lives but also select candidates whom they would like to learn this practice. Whom do they want to tell about centering? Many kids want the principal and their teachers to enroll in a class quickly. Come to think of it, the secretaries and cafeteria workers, as well as the nurse and the school bus drivers, can sign up. Perhaps their family should *just sit* before gathering around the dinner table. Maybe coaches would lower their voices if *they* sat on the bench prior to the game. Kids can see the value *for themselves* of adult serenity.

Patience is essential in the Buddhist approach to happiness. Joy comes from within, and "to look outside of ourselves for true peace and satisfaction is hopeless." We must be content with a slow turning away from a dizzying world toward a simple life that is anchored in our true natures. Life isn't meant to be a chore. "Our body has its own wisdom; it's the misuse of our brain that screws up our lives" (Beck, *Everyday Zen*).

TEACHING TIPS: THE PHILOSOPHERS

- I like to open a discussion of Beck's philosophy by asking children if any of them know what meditation is. One confident child announced that he most certainly did know and that he took it twice a day. Well, meditation is medication in its own way! Write the word on the board and define it clearly for your kids. Again, meditation is *just sitting,* sinking into steady, calm reflection. *Nothing fancy.*

- In your discussions of Epicurus's philosophy, take the time to define *commune* clearly. It's fun to hear the kids' preconceptions on this one. ("Did you know that a commune is where hippies hang out?") My definition is a gathering of like-minded people living together in a community, sharing chores and rewards.

- Children love to have a grown-up play the part of the philosopher. When I become Epicurus, I can count on them to ask me if I knew him. Don't worry, you'll get used to being twenty-five hundred years old.

- Children hear the term *common sense* a lot, but make sure that everyone shares the same meaning during your discussion of Epicurus. I use a child's definition: "regular thinking if we only stop for a minute."

 **DISCUSSION QUESTIONS:
THE PHILOSOPHERS**

- Give some examples of apparent pleasures that can turn out to have painful consequences.

- Choose just one very specific reason that you are happy.
- Describe times when you are unhappy. What are the causes of your unhappiness?
- Do you know anyone you would describe as a happy person? How do you think this individual became happy? Are you happy?

 EXERCISES: THE PHILOSOPHERS

- Join a bored Milo in the tollbooth that appears in his room in Norton Juster's philosophical fantasy, *The Phantom Tollbooth*. Sharing Milo's adventures is a fun way to learn new lessons about happiness. Milo slowly realizes that the things we need, like caterpillars and clouds, are right before our eyes and are a source of constant wonder. The last chapter, "Good-by and Hello," is lovely. Written in 1961, the story of Milo's journey points a finger directly at so many mistaken notions about the pursuit of happiness. Note Jules Feiffer's black-and-white sketches scattered throughout the book, and ask the children how the drawings convey so much so simply. Kids enjoy all the plays on words. Saying *balderdash* for the first time feels important. Ask them what they learn from Milo. Tell them something that the young boy makes you realize. With Sheldon Harnick, Juster wrote the libretto for a musical adaptation for his book that premiered in 1995. If you are lucky, a production may come your way.
- Listen to *You're a Good Man, Charlie Brown*. This is a perfect way to hear simple pleasures in song. The finale, "Happiness," celebrates "climbing a tree, catching a firefly and setting him free, . . . coming home . . ." Charlie Brown and his friends realize it's just the little everyday things that bring happiness.

Have the children draw their own comic strips, complete with captions, that depict the simple pleasures of a balanced life. What are the titles of their comic strips? You can paste their comics on a large poster board and put them on display.

SIMPLICITY

Understanding the concept of simplicity and actually paring down our lives are two different things. Children feel the rush of daily life and are willing to sort through the confusion and slow down. Kids know they are caught up in the world of things, but they do not think this snare is inevitable or hopeless. They want to direct their energies toward a happy life of enduring satisfaction. So many lament that there is little time to do nothing, and on more than one occasion children have compared their lives to their "hamster running on a treadmill." Epicurus and Beck have some ideas.

Epicurus knows from his own experience that we can teach ourselves to need less. It is not so much just minimizing our needs, however. Better still, simplicity lies in truly perceiving what our needs really are. First, we must distinguish between vain and natural desires. Discard vanity's needs. The desire for clothing is natural, but the name on the label provides no warmth. "Among desires some are natural and necessary, some natural but not necessary, and others neither natural nor necessary, but due to idle imagination" (Epicurus, "Principal Doctrines"). Now, our job is to uncover the distinction between natural desires that are trivial and natural desires that are essential for good living. Friendship is necessary, but the number of friends is irrelevant. "Of all the things that wisdom acquires to produce the blessedness of the complete life, far the greatest is the possession of friendship" ("Principal Doctrines"). The gifts of philosophy, such as sound judgment and practical reason, are basic needs. Play and relaxation are necessary gifts from life. On the other hand, toys are not us.

Children are eager to tell anyone who will listen about the value of simple pleasures. Some of the simple pleasures they've described to me are the following: having a lazy day, sleeping well without loud noises outside the window, going barefoot, finding an old bird's nest, feeling the way an old baseball hat fits, eating watermelon and having a seed-spitting contest, leaving the doctor's office without a shot, and hearing that school is closed due to snow. As they begin to name such basic sources of happiness, they marvel that they ever neglected these joys. Simply relaxing is such a treat.

Beck could have been one of the female participants in Epicurus's community. She insists that it is impossible to be centered and have a stable life without simplicity. "I begin to strip my life down to what my life truly needs. I no longer find suddenly that I absolutely *have* to have that, or that, or that. It's not that I give them up, it's just that I don't really need them so much. Most people who sit for years find their lives considerably simplified—not because of some virtue, but because, needing less, desires naturally drift away" (*Everyday Zen*). Desire buffets us indefinitely from one temporary satisfaction to another.

Beck knows quite well that very few have Epicurus's opportunity to retreat from the world to the security of a protected home and garden. The question for this American Zen master living in San Diego is the question for everyone: How can we simplify our lives today?

 TEACHING TIP: SIMPLICITY

- Show the children some photographs of Zen gardens. Explain that these plants are pruned so that unnecessary bulk does not inhibit new, healthy growth. You can compare this to stripping away the nonessentials from their own lives as recommended by Epicurus and Beck. Kids feel the peace in these gardens, and you can encourage them to find a quiet outdoor place of their own.

 DISCUSSION QUESTIONS: SIMPLICITY

- What are some things in your life that you thought you had to have, but when you gave it some thought, they turned out to be unimportant? Do these unnecessary things have anything in common?
- How can you prune your life? Do you think you will enjoy your simpler life after your pruning work?
- Imagine a fruit tree with a thousand oranges hanging from it and that each orange is a simple pleasure waiting to be picked. What simple pleasures will you pick to put in your basket?
- Why do we forget about simple pleasures and how much they mean to us? What are some simple pleasures that are missing from your life?

 EXERCISES: SIMPLICITY

- Ask the children to make two columns on a clean sheet in their journals. One column has the heading "Necessary/Happiness" and the other "Pleasure/Wants." Ask them to do an inventory of their homes and to put items in the column in which they think they belong. Have them explain their reasoning in some cases. Why is the trampoline or the poster a necessity? Narrow the focus a bit and ask them to put the items in their bedrooms under the same microscope. Next, do an inventory of the kitchen for the two columns. If you have a credit card, get out the most recent statement and continue your discussion of necessities versus wants, happiness versus pleasure. Many kids have not seen a credit card statement, and now they can connect future purchases to receiving a bill in the mail. Hmmm . . . What did we eat at that restaurant? What did you buy at the toy store?

• Gather around a piano or keyboard. Ask someone to play the authentic Shaker song "Simple Gifts." Join with the children in learning to sing this melody, harmonizing altos, sopranos, and any and every voice. Elder Joseph Brackett, author of this lively Shaker tune, would appreciate the children's voices singing in praise of "true simplicity" and coming "round right." The children could perform "Simple Gifts" at a nursing home, for emergency workers on their lunch break, or at the neighborhood center closest to their school. Ask the children for any other suggestions for an impromptu concert.

• Listen to the "Queen of Soul." As a child in Detroit, Aretha Franklin spent happy times with her siblings singing gospel music on her front porch. Join your kids as they "run for the bus" with her in "I Say a Little Prayer." Let the children dance any way they want wherever they want. Watch them become a dancing "See Saw" as they bounce along with her voice. One behind the other, they can form a gyrating "Chain of Fools." Ask your dancers why people of all times and places prize dancing. Do they think that dancing and happiness are twins? Ask them to explain why people find music and dance among life's greatest simple pleasures. Once when I did this exercise with a group, a pigtailed nine-year-old sang out to me as she danced by, "I love feeling all the dancing in my life."

CREATING BALANCE
Meditation can clear out an even path to take us through life. We can bring balance and calm to our lives through quiet. "All we

must do is constantly to create a little shift from the spinning world we've got in our heads" (Beck, *Everyday Zen*), and silence fosters this gradual change. *Just sitting* opens the core of our beings to a center that is unmoved by events. *Just sitting* awakens a serene inner sanctuary of balance. As a math student uses a protractor to locate the center of the circle, each of us can find our center to ground us in all we do and, perhaps more important, to ground us in all that we don't do. The willingness to sit still in silence eventually slows down our lives to their natural rhythm. Meditation is this practice of *just sitting*: sinking into steady, calm reflection. Nothing fancy.

I have great fun introducing children to the practice of meditation. I explain to them that by *sitting quietly* on a regular basis they will become more relaxed and gain the ability to reduce any confusion in their lives. Here is my set of instructions that you can give to your children: "Sit with your spine straight and your head up as if there is a string connecting the top of your head to the ceiling. Your shoulders should be so even that an arrow could pass straight through one and then the other. Your spine becomes the vertical part of a T, and your shoulders are the horizontal part. Both feet need to be flat on the floor. Place the back of one hand in the palm of your other hand and rest them in your lap. This position will eventually feel natural to you. It allows your breath to flow easily in and out of your body. You can close your eyes or, if you like, focus them on a spot in front of you on the floor. Little by little, breathe in through your nose from the bottom of your stomach to the count of one-two-three-four. Hold your breath for the same four-count. Last, push your breath out through your mouth, slowly, one-two-three-four. And then repeat, over and over. When we go outside to meditate, your string will connect the top of your head to the sky!"

The making of this vertical and horizontal T is brand-new for most people. A slump that forces us to catch short breaths from the chest area has become standard posture. Sometimes children associate being asked to sit up straight with discomfort or a reprimand. It's important to circulate among the children and silently help and encourage them to adjust to this new position. Soon slow exhales will be the only noise. Repeat particular instructions as needed.

Kids' descriptions of their experiences after meditating for the first time are quite vivid. Some have called it "kind of scary" because they had never been so still. Others have said that they felt as if they didn't know what was going to happen to them but decided later that "it felt cool." Often child meditants have remarked that they heard certain sounds for the first time. Although she was unable to explain the experience itself, whatever it was, one child announced with conviction that "everything was real and clear." Her twelve-year-old classmate Cory provided a very powerful description that is also an accurate portrayal of formal Buddhist meditation: "I was really concentrating. I looked and listened and then everything started to blend together, including me. When I blended in, it was like *I* wasn't looking at anything at all. Everything felt near and far, odd but interesting."

Children are meditation's best advertisement. They tell me that when their minds are clear, they are rarely angry because they are not confused. What a powerful realization! Just sitting opens their young lives to the good judgment and discretion that Epicurus recommends to "avoid pain and fear." They enjoy less commotion and say, "It feels great to feel like myself." It's nice "not to be all crazy or way happy and then way sad." If you are quiet on the school bus or before starting your homework, it seems that "you can concentrate on everything better."

Learning to appreciate a balanced life when young is an experience that can stay with children all their lives. The ability to be steady in the midst of a busy world will serve them well. And *just sitting* brings unexpected pleasure here and now. I remember so well nine-year-old Keyona's arms stretching with dancing upturned palms after her first try at meditation. Shaking her head from side to side to a beat all her own, she made the following proclamation: "I feel jahhhfulll!"

When our minds settle, like muddy water becoming clear when it is still, our true natures can revel in the simple and ordinary joys that are always present. It is as though we need to take the trash out to make room for our lives. Epicurus agrees that this "independence of desire we think a great good . . ."("Letter to Menoeceus"). It is within our power to create an inner life through meditation and an outer lifestyle through self-imposed discipline that leads to happiness. We need to make the effort to understand what happiness is, and then to decide to make happiness a reality in our lives.

 TEACHING TIP: CREATING BALANCE

- Use a Frisbee and mark the very center of it for your discussion of balance. Meditation can help us reach our own center. The center is the point of balance in the Frisbee as well as in the human being. Ask the children how they can pinpoint *their* center. Another helpful image is a perfectly even seesaw that doesn't move. You can imitate this balanced seesaw by straightening your hands with your middle fingers touching tip to tip. Ask the children to do this with their hands, as well, and to look at the balance.

DISCUSSION QUESTIONS: CREATING BALANCE

- Which grown-ups in your life would you like to have *just sit* and enjoy a quiet time? Why?
- Is it hard to *just sit,* and if so, why? Does quiet time get easier? What benefits can you see as a result of meditation?
- Do you think your life is too busy? Are there too many things going on in your life? How did this happen?

 ## EXERCISE: CREATING BALANCE

- Find time each day for quiet reflection. The children will reap more benefits from meditation when you include it as a regular part of the day. This slowing down and settling gently seeps into other aspects of their lives. Talk to them about the ways you can see their behavior and attitudes changing as a result of sitting quietly. Be sure that you or a volunteer demonstrates the proper posture for meditation to let the children see breath flowing freely. Go through the instructions slowly. I ask the children, for once, not to ask questions so that silence can grow.

Children's longing for happiness is apparent not only in their words but also in their voices and facial expressions. Too many children are unhappy and endure hard lives. Some are lured by consumerism and at the same time are confused and distracted by it. Almost all kids take immediately to Epicurus and his life of simple pleasures. But they also think that a simple life is not so easy to create in today's frenetic world. Unless adults work with children to scale back the stress and confusion that threatens people of all ages, it will be impossible for children to be free of the trap. They are truly grateful to learn how to *just sit*. As I open the door to many classrooms, I am greeted by happily meditating little big minds.

When children examine their young lives, they put on display the countless wrong turns that one can take in the pursuit of happiness. They freely admit that we make ourselves unhappy but point to the unlimited possibilities that remain open to all of us. Even grown-ups can empty their minds and find new ways to play.

Resources

- "who knows if the moon's a balloon" and "when faces called flowers float out of the ground" by e. e. cummings. You can toss syntax out the window with these and other delights in *100 Poems*.
- *Everyday Zen* by Charlotte Joko Beck. "My dog doesn't worry about the meaning of life." How can anyone resist turning the page of a book that begins this way? It's all here, but the one must is "The Parable of Mushin." He lives in a town called Hope, spending time at the train station and taking care of the kids. There are chocolate bars and a swing set as well as a baseball team that plays in the back of the train station. You and the children will remember your trip on Mushin's train.
- *Nothing Special* by Charlotte Joko Beck.
- *Zen in America,* edited by Helen Tworkov. Zen meets and mixes with life in the United States through a look at five American Zen masters.
- "Letter to Menoeceus" by Epicurus. In this actual letter, Epicurus explains the heart of his central ideas. The letter, as well as his other work, can be found in *Classics of Western Philosophy,* edited by Steven M. Cahn. This collection contains the works of several of our principal philosophers.

- "Principal Doctrines" by Epicurus. This consists of forty short statements. Numbers IV, V, XV, XXI, and XXIX are perfect for our look at happiness. Numbers XXVII and XXVIII celebrate friendship. This also is in the Cahn anthology *Classics of Western Philosophy.*
- "The Fawn" and "Recuerdo" by Edna St. Vincent Millay. Both are included in *Collected Poems,* edited by Norma Millay.
- *The Phantom Tollbooth* by Norton Juster.
- *You're a Good Man, Charlie Brown,* music, lyrics, and book by Clark Gesner, based on Charles Schultz's comic strip *Peanuts.* Both original cast albums, 1967 and the 1999 revival, are available on CD.
- "Simple Gifts" by Elder Joseph Brackett. Aaron Copland includes several variations on "Simple Gifts" in *Appalachian Spring.* Children enjoy William Warfield's baritone rendition that is included on *A Copland Celebration,* volume 2.
- "I Say a Little Prayer" and "See Saw" by Aretha Franklin. These are on the *Aretha Now* CD, as is "Hello Sunshine."
- "Chain of Fools" by Aretha Franklin. This is on the CD titled *Lady Soul.* Also included is "Money Won't Change You," but we know better.
- "Here Comes the Sun" by the Beatles. You can find this on the *Abbey Road* CD as well as in other Beatles collections.
- "Here Comes the Sun" by Rockapella. This is on the CD titled *Smilin'.* Perfect for a peek at happiness are "Shambala," "Lazy River," and "Smile in My Heart."

JUSTICE

Act in such a way that you treat humanity,
whether in your own person or in the person
of another, always at the same time as an
end and never simply as a means.
—IMMANUEL KANT, *Grounding for
the Metaphysics of Morals*

THE TOPIC

In talking with children about the idea of justice, I find that it is
a concept that eludes my grasp. Central to the concept of justice
is the notion of equality. But is equality a real possibility given the
unique circumstances of every life? Perhaps true justice lies in
acknowledging and attempting to make less dramatic the differences among human beings. Most of us treasure the comfort that
comes from living in a society that values justice. But what *is*
justice? Has there been progress in understanding its meaning? Is
any society close to experiencing the reality of justice? Would
there be fewer social problems if there were a better grasp of
the idea of justice? Oppression and justice appear to be polar
opposites, so is it futile to think that oppression can be overcome
without clarity concerning the nature of justice?

Philosophical and religious texts are full of explorations into the many issues involved in justice. Plato spent considerable effort on the development of a template for a just society that could be used by Greek city-states. Aristotle looked at the differences among distributive, compensatory, and retributive justice. Confucius sought to return justice to China by using traditional values, such as respect for family and social propriety, in order to end centuries of brutal civil warfare. Old and New Testament concepts of justice—seeking retribution, or "an eye for an eye," and turning the other cheek as a response to injustice—are clear and contrasting. An evolving sense of justice based on the unyielding laws of karma unfolds in Hindu and Buddhist scriptures.

Children come quickly to crisp definitions of the concept of justice. They tell me it means "even," "equal," "balanced," and "fair." Though the definitions come easily, kids immediately intuit that somehow they didn't quite get all of it. When I probe the source of their uncertainty, they advise me that "things that seem unfair may be fair," and vice versa. For example, some students get more help in math because they really need it, and some get in trouble for things that they didn't do. Not all water fountains have to be the same height because the short ones are good for kids. "I can use the stairs, but somebody on crutches needs the elevator." Kids know that whether something is "equal" or "fair" quite often lies in the eye of the beholder.

In an effort to help us broaden our definition of justice, I present the kids with this possibility: Justice is protection of the opportunity to live to your full potential, whoever you may be. I then ask them, "What are some things that need protection to grow?" Their answers vary: "young trees," "puppies," "campfires," "friendships." As the dialogue progresses, a number of child philosophers simultaneously realize that they are a special group requiring protection to grow to their potential. Who else needs protection? "We do!"

Children have a strong sense of justice and an even stronger sense of injustice. Many claim they have experienced teachers who favor some children and who fail to apply standards consistently. Unwarranted differences in parental treatment of siblings is another frequent complaint. Coaches must watch their behavior, since it is monitored closely by their young players. Children also admit that they sometimes call an event unjust when they know better: "It wasn't fair that I was put in time-out just because I happened to eat Sam's lunch." Kids have many examples such as this one of fair treatment that they simply didn't like at the time. Their instincts, however, alert them to unjust treatment as if they have radar. They may not be able to articulate the problem, but they sense something is amiss.

In many ways children are *the* most vulnerable members of our society. Short in stature, with smaller voices, children suffer if adults fail to bend down and listen. It's important that as grownups we work with kids to develop an expansive and inclusive understanding of justice, and that we treat them as members of society in full standing. I find through discussions with them that parents and other authority figures don't always treat them justly. As the kids and I work together, we come to a better understanding of justice in the life of a child, who, though dependent on adults, is a person with full humanity.

Immanuel Kant (cahnt) and Paulo Freire (POW-lo freh-EE-reh) create an excellent partnership with the children in getting to the core of justice. Kant seeks to make the concept of fairness and dignity applicable to all. Freire looks at the link between poverty and oppression, and the role that education should play in breaking this bondage. Kant counts on the human ability to reason to make just decisions, and Freire posits a just theory of education that honors human dignity.

 ## TEACHING TIPS: THE TOPIC

- The temptation to tell a story *about* the topic or to give examples *of* the concept, rather than defining the idea, is especially appealing when discussing justice. Sadly, we all know one too many stories about people who have been treated unfairly. Keep bringing the kids back to a one- or two-word definition.
- If the meaning of justice feels out of the kids' reach, you can look first at examples of injustice to help shed light on its opposite.
- Remember to look out for large, sweeping statements. In their enthusiasm to point out injustice, children can fall into generalizations such as *people, teachers,* and *coaches.* Remind them to catch themselves when making broad statements that suggest "all _____." If you should lapse into such generalizations, it's a great lesson for the kids to watch you correct yourself.

? DISCUSSION QUESTIONS: THE TOPIC

- What are some of the ways that you hear the word *justice* used?
- Are all people equal? Are all people the same? Can you explain your reasoning?
- What are some examples of injustice both in your life and in the larger world?

EXERCISE: THE TOPIC

• Listen to Aaron Copland's *A Lincoln Portrait.* Selections from Lincoln's speeches and letters mingle with songs from his day. Have the children pretend that Lincoln is speaking to them today, and ask them for specific ways that they can use his ideas. For example, he says that the old ways of thinking in the past are no longer adequate. We need new ideas and fresh approaches to correct our problems and to create better lives for all. Ask them for examples of old ways of thinking that have proven inadequate. Were schools that were segregated by race a good solution for racial tension, for example? Does violence provide a permanent solution to conflict? If you ignore injustice, will it go away? After the child philosophers listen to the recording at least twice, let them share with you, as you represent Lincoln, any questions or observations. Listen to their concerns.

THE PHILOSOPHERS

> I should never act except in such a way that I can also will
> that my maxim should become a universal law.
>
> —IMMANUEL KANT, *Grounding for the Metaphysics of Morals*

Immanuel Kant lived his entire life in Königsberg, East Prussia, never straying farther than the surrounding countryside. His career at the university began as a student and culminated in a prestigious professorship in logic. Through his *Critique of Pure Reason,* published in 1781, Kant joined Plato as a cornerstone of Western philosophy.

As a logician with complete faith in the power of reasoning, Kant presented a framework for resolving moral dilemmas based on reason alone. He insisted that emotion and concern with outcome prevent objectivity and impartiality. The influence of Kantian ethics on our legal system and contemporary moral reasoning cannot be overstated. With its appeal lying in its reliable filtering of impure motivation to illuminate what is fair for all, this ethic promises equality and impartial justice.

Kant believes that ordinary folks, sitting with him on a park bench in Königsberg or at a baseball game today, have in their consciousness the knowledge of what it means to do the right thing, even if they can't articulate it. He guarantees that every human being with the power of reasoning has the ability to create a moral theory that never admits an exception. What's fair for you is fair for me and for all others. It's his task in *Grounding for the Metaphysics of Morals* to bring this absolute morality to light for all to see clearly. At the heart of his moral theory lies the rationale that you can't ask of someone what you are not willing to ask of yourself. For example, when I allow myself to be dishonest to you when it is convenient for me, I shouldn't count on your honesty at all times in our relationship. When I ask you to care for my animals in my absence and rely on your sense of duty, it is unfair for me to refuse to care for your pets when you go on vacation.

I ask the kids to point out exactly what's wrong in my previous examples, according to Kant's theory, and they immediately say, "It's *just* not *fair.*" The child philosophers follow with numerous examples of their own unfair behavior. They agree with Kant that they are quick to "make an exception just for me this one time." Several friends admitted together that "I hate it when the jump rope is twirled so fast that I can't skip, but I do it anyway, because it's funny when my friends' feet get all tangled up." And one entire class agreed that the essential rule of hide-and-seek is "no peeking," but every hand went up in acknowledgment of their "*occasionally* taking just a quick look around." Given the obvious natural tendency to make excuses for ourselves, the child philosophers are eager to see what Kant's suggestions for improvement might be.

Kant sets forth a logical structure with which the human mind can sift through an issue objectively by using the filter of reason to purify motivation. After the dilemma passes through the sieve of clear thinking, what remains is the solution. The motivation of right action must be a "good will," a will that rises above selfishness, personal feelings, and concern with the consequences of the act. "A good will is good not because of what it effects or accomplishes, nor because of its fitness to attain some proposed end; it is good only through its willing, i.e., it is good in itself" (*Grounding for the Metaphysics of Morals*). When I explain to the kids that Kant's good will implies that what *you* get out of being fair is irrelevant, they assure me that they know what he means: "I don't help out in the cafeteria just because the principal is taking names. I do it because everyone should help out." "I take the time to help my friend find his coat because that's what any friend should do." You do the right thing *only* because it is the right thing to do.

This logical framework that makes it clear what the right thing *is,* Kant calls the *categorical imperative.* When you introduce the categorical imperative to your child philosophers, it is helpful to explain the two words, *categorical* and *imperative,* separately. A *categorical* statement is one that is absolutely, universally true and i s applicable to all people. A good substitute for the word *categorical* is *unconditional*. There are no conceivable situations in which an unconditional statement could possibly be untrue. I remind the children frequently that Kant is looking for a way to make decisions that will be true for *all* people, for *all* time. An *imperative* sentence, back to English grammar, is a sentence that issues a command. "Jump!" "Keep trying!" "You must respect others." An imperative statement tells me beyond a doubt that I *ought* to do something.

Once the kids understand the meaning of the two words, you can put them together to make Kant's meaning clear: *The categorical imperative is a universal command that applies equally to all.* I find that the phrase *categorical imperative* does not roll easily off the tongues of child philosophers, and after learning its meaning, they enjoy using *cat* as their personal shorthand for this important theory.

For Kant, the categorical imperative, with its reliance on objective reasoning, ensures that the fair decision will be obvious. He provides two statements of the categorical imperative that he maintains are identical despite their very different wording. First, "Act only according to that maxim whereby you can at the same time will that it should become a universal law" (*Grounding for the Metaphysics of Morals*). Because moral decisions have universal meaning, they promote a just society. While for Kant tough moral choices are few and far between, the demands of justice require impartiality when one faces such a dilemma. To make your choice impartially, you must be able to will that everyone make the same choice. If I choose not to pay my taxes, I thereby will that everyone do the same. If I choose to be generous even in tough financial circumstances, I will, then, that generosity be a universal law.

Each person's "pure heart," by which Kant means "good will," commands categorically that one never make an exception of oneself. Kant recognizes that the answer produced by the logic of his imperative may not be the one you want, but the logical command tells you what is universally fair. In his famous "false promise" example, he asks if you can borrow money with no intention of paying it back. While there may be many practical considerations relevant to *your* case (the lender is wealthy, and it's only twenty dollars, and so much good could come from the purchase, etc.), the question is whether or not you can will lying to be universal law. Well, can you? Kant's categorical imperative, with its emphasis on the unbiased use of reason, answers "absolutely not." Unintentionally, many child philosophers have reiterated Kant's belief that the categorical imperative resides in our ordinary understanding: "Now I know the *reason* that it's wrong if *I* pick flowers from the park. Because what if everybody did?"

The second statement is to "act in such a way that you treat humanity, whether in your own person or in the person of another, always at the same time as an end and never simply as a means" (*Grounding for the Metaphysics of Morals*). Human beings have dignity and are ends in themselves, not pawns in a chess match to be moved around at the whim of another. In this account of the imperative, Kant insists that an action that involves using people *only* to suit your needs is never acceptable. Plagiarism, for example, uses the author, the teacher, and the other students *only* for the purposes of the plagiarist. I ask the children to think of times that they may have used another person as a tool for their own needs. Using another as a means to an end is not a difficult concept for kids. Actually, they understand how easy it is to do this, even though it doesn't "feel right": "I distracted the teacher so we wouldn't have to do math." "I only sit with Sara at lunch because she gives me her cookies." I ask the children how they would explain what's unfair about using a human being in this way. Their answers have been numerous and varied, among them: "Other people are people, too." "People aren't like money that you trade for something." "Everybody ought to be respected, I think."

Though Kant suspects that the categorical imperative is not the language that ordinary folk would use to describe what it means to do the "right thing" for all, it is what he maintains we know to be true in our hearts. He admits that human motives are very complex and that perhaps some trace of selfishness remains in all endeavors, yet he has tremendous faith in a reasonable person's capability to operate within the just framework of the categorical imperative. The world that Kant envisions through use of his imperative is one in which agreement on large issues is possible through the meeting of rational minds cleansed of personal considerations. It is a balanced world in which justice thrives.

> Another testimony that should not be missing from our relationship with students is the testimony of our constant commitment to justice, liberty, and individual rights, of our dedication to defending the weakest when they are subjected to exploitation of the strongest.
>
> —Paulo Freire, *Teachers as Cultural Workers*

The Brazilian educator Paulo Freire brought his passionate enthusiasm for education to bear on the problem of adult illiteracy. The aim of his life's work as professor of the philosophy of education at the University of Recife was to challenge the oppressive effects of poverty through learning. His efforts to educate Brazilian peasants threatened the Brazilian military and resulted in fifteen years of political exile. Freire was a visiting scholar at Harvard in 1969, and in 1989 he was named education secretary of São Paulo.

His years in exile confirmed Freire's suspicion that his radical demand for change in educational policy and practice would "probably arouse negative reactions in a number of readers" (*Pedagogy of the Oppressed*). He is sure that if you are comfortable with the status quo, then you will be uncomfortable with his revolutionary voice. But his philosophy breaks new ground, probing the recesses of societal complacency. No sincere investigation of justice can avoid an honest look at *injustice*. Freire holds oppression up to the light, baring its gnarled roots, and shows that part of the dark tangle of the injustice of poverty is made possible and supported by suffocating teaching methods.

Freire's lifelong empathy with the plight of the Brazilian masses began because he was one of them. He grew up poor and never lost his identification with those who were powerless to combat unrelenting poverty. Freire knew that oppressed individuals lose the power to control and direct their destiny independent of economic constraint. The poor endure marginalized lives of constant struggle on the fringe of the society that exploits them. Inequity appears to them to be the way of the world, and the thought of taking political action to change it never occurs. "Liberation doesn't take hold of people's consciousness if they are isolated from the world" (*Teachers as Cultural Workers*). Thoroughly dehumanized, the oppressed assume the image that the oppressor has of them. This pitiless image of the oppressed in the mind of the oppressor is of ignorant people who are to be kept at a distance from members of normal society. Without any empowering resources, never knowing or imagining another way of life, the oppressed internalize the notion that their poverty is warranted and that *they* did *this* to themselves.

Freire perceives that oppressors see no need for changing a system that fulfills *their* needs so well. The oppressor benefits from cheap labor and services—a real-life example of using human beings as means to an end. Oppression silences the voices of the exploited, and those who exploit them enjoy the obedient, unquestioning compliance of the uneducated masses. "Oppressors . . . care neither to have the world revealed nor to see it transformed" (*Pedagogy of the Oppressed*). Oppressors do not think of themselves in this way, and oddly they exhibit indignation at what they see as unfairness directed at *them*. What have *they* done? Domination by the powerful is the natural order, so privilege is their due! There is no concept of justice for *either* the oppressed or the oppressor. The dehumanization caused by oppression circulates throughout all levels of society.

Freire takes a hard look at the role of accomplice that institutional education can play in perpetuating oppression through a repressive educational practice that he labels the *banking method*. The banking method deposits the values of the status quo into students who are seen as no more than passive receptacles. No questions asked; no action taken.

Freire knows the futility of breaking the cycle of poverty without educational reform. He challenges educational practitioners everywhere to rethink critically both the method and the content of their teaching. At the heart of his rebellious, activist philosophy of education is *conscientizacão* (cone-see-ehn-tee-zah-SOW). Conscientization is the process of becoming aware of social injustice by understanding its causes and developing skills through education to resist and overcome oppression. Freire demands that educational theory come alive through dynamic communication in the classroom and that it support students as they make their way in the world.

I have found that Freire gives me new ways to talk about the very delicate topic of poverty with kids. Socioeconomic inequality is a subtle and sometimes overt force in the lives of the child philosophers. It is clear which students are trying to shield their reduced-price meals from students enjoying packed lunches from home. A child's journey to a seat on the bus in a patched coat can be a walk of shame. Freire's life and philosophy make it possible to talk about poverty in a room filled with children from different economic realities. I save my discussion with the children about the injustice that comes with poverty until we have talked about Freire's views at length. The fact that he himself was poor makes him the champion of *every* child in the room, especially those who know firsthand how lonely it can feel. "I had to do a project and used cardboard from a dumpster, and my work looked terrible compared to the other kids' new poster board." This example from a ten-year-old emboldens a classmate: "Computers cost too much money for my family, so what happens is that I have to use the school computer at recess or stay after school to use it, and all the other kids know it's because I'm poor." Freire empowers children who have been too embarrassed by the circumstances of their lives to speak up, and I find almost all their classmates to be sensitive and receptive to their remarks. "I'll ask my mom if you can come home with me from school, and we can use my computer together." Child philosophers learn together with Freire's help that poverty is not a source of shame and that education focused on equality is the way out. The opportunity for any adult in the life of a child "is not exhausted in the teaching of math, geography, syntax, history. . . . It also requires . . . involvement in and dedication to overcoming social injustice" (*Teachers as Cultural Workers*).

Liberating education exposes the vile nature of oppression and stimulates burgeoning critical thinkers to fight for their lives. Oppressive structures crumble as a world of possibility opens for individuals.

☑ **TEACHING TIPS: THE PHILOSOPHERS**

- It helps kids to understand Kant's concept of universal law to explain that it means "if *I* ought to do it, then *everyone* should do the same thing in the same situation."

- Be sure that you have explored Freire's philosophy to the point that the child philosophers understand that poverty is not somehow *their* fault. When you discuss Freire's view of poverty, some children will learn to get past their sense of blame or guilt for the first time.
- *Clean* is a helpful synonym for Kant's concept of a *pure* heart. A pure heart has gotten a thorough cleansing of any selfish motives.

 ## DISCUSSION QUESTIONS: THE PHILOSOPHERS

- What do you think about the two statements of the categorical imperative? Will you use Kant's suggestions in your life? Why or why not?
- Why do some kids have good health, fun, and opportunities whereas others suffer? Do you believe in luck, and if so, is luck fair?
- What are some examples of unfair situations that do not affect you right now but could show up later in your life? For example, if someone in a wheelchair can't get into a building, when do you think you would *really* notice this lack of access?
- What is oppression? Where do you see it? What can you do about it?
- What is power? Why do some people really want it? Why would a person want to control others?
- How did things become uneven? What created the gap between rich and poor, and why do some people have an easy life while others struggle?
- What can your teachers learn from Freire that would benefit you? If he were your teacher, what do you think your school day would be like?

- What would Freire think if he visited your classroom for a week? Would he see the banking method or the problem-posing method of teaching?

 EXERCISES: THE PHILOSOPHERS

- Listen to Bob Dylan's "Blowin' in the Wind." The lyrics provide many fruitful topics for your examination of justice. Dylan's harmonica and guitar accompany his desperate plea "how long?" He questions how long caring people will continue to ignore serious social problems. Invite the children to join him in wondering how many people will die before everyone can agree "no more." Let the kids tell Dylan why they think it is so hard to recognize the humanity of each person. Talk about how people can prevent themselves from being part of the problem of injustice. Ask the children to write down, in their philosophy journals, any solutions they can share with Bob Dylan. Kids enjoy listening to other recordings of this song by different artists as well.

- Read *Beatrice's Goat,* a lovely picture book that shows the changes in the life of a nine-year-old girl in Uganda when the sale of her goat's milk and offspring allows Beatrice to go to school. She and the goat, Mugisa, show the child philosophers the importance of learning and encourage them to look at the meaning of their own education. Through this book kids can see how oppressive and undeserved the poverty in this village was, and that providing basic resources can help alleviate this unjust burden. The gift of the goat comes from a project sponsored by Heifer International. This organization is an excellent resource for learning about global issues and motivating philosophers of all ages to act. Mugisa affects the entire community by making a huge dent in poverty in Beatrice's village. Look at the variety of excellent educational programs designed by Heifer International for both schools and communities. Teach the children that they are neither powerless nor too young to take an active interest in the world community. Help them choose one project sponsored by this organization and guide them in making their project a reality.

- Read Seamus Heaney's three-line poem "The Strand." Explain to the kids that an "ashplant" refers to a walking stick in this poem. Ask them to picture themselves many years from now as they walk along a beach, resting on a walking stick as the poet's father does. The walking stick makes a line of dots that the water will not wash away. Remind the child philosophers of Kant's moral theory that attempts to make rules that apply to everyone, always. Ask the children to write in their journals some moral rules that they think should last forever no matter what, rules just as permanent as the marks made by the walking stick in "The Strand."

DIGNITY

"Treat others as you would want to be treated." Kids hear this reminder repeatedly. In looking at the concepts of justice, fairness, and equality, this sentence that implies the path to respectful treatment of others warrants further philosophical analysis. In my experience, a rich discussion results from asking children: "How *would* you like to be treated?" Their answers shed more light, not only on the "golden rule" but also on kids' sense of their dignity as human beings. "I like to be treated like I am worth something, like I am worth a whole lot." "I want people to think I'm my own person." "Even if I'm still young, I would like to be talked to like I'm smart." Kids like learning about human dignity, especially when they realize that dignity applies to them as well.

For many young people the thought of their own dignity is new, and they think hard about what to make of this concept and how to fit it into the reality of their lives. You will find that Kant's categorical imperative and Freire's advocacy of critical thinking both lead to productive talk about human dignity's central place in the concept of justice.

Many kids I've met can describe what it's like to "go to school at a bank." Elementary and middle school students alike have examples of how the banking concept of teaching criticized by Freire can degrade students and diminish their human potential: "Being forced to memorize tons of stuff is busywork." "I have to hold my pencil just *one* way." "Math papers should look like *that*." "Here's how *we* walk in the hallways." "Yes, that's a creative answer, but not the one you're *supposed* to give." "Unfortunately, those who espouse the cause of liberation are themselves surrounded and influenced by the climate which generates the banking concept, and often do not perceive its true significance or its dehumanizing power" (Freire, *Pedagogy of the Oppressed*). When the children and I discuss the banking concept of education and its connection to injustice, several have told me in many classrooms that "that way of teaching is not how I like to be treated because it makes me feel stupid."

Children's ignorance is assumed by banking methodology. Preserving their self-respect often becomes "counterproductive" for a teacher pressured to deposit established information as efficiently as possible into what is seen as the empty vessel of a child's "mind." "The more completely he fills the receptacles, the better a teacher he is. The more meekly the receptacles permit themselves to be filled, the better students they are" (*Pedagogy of the Oppressed*). In some classrooms, if children misbehave or fall behind in their work, they are deprived of "extras" such as recess, music, and art. These activities are important opportunities for self-expression, and without them children can lose their sense of self-worth. Numerous kids are eager to give me examples of times during the school day when they feel they have been treated with disrespect: "In the front of the classroom there is a slot with my name on it for different colored flags depending on how bad I've been. When I'm bad, I have to get up in front of the whole class and change my color to a worse one." "We have a lot of times during the day when we can't talk, even at lunch, and kids really like to talk." I've been taken aside to listen to children's stories of times they felt ashamed when their way of talking was "corrected" because it was "wrong." "Only as learners recognize themselves . . . and see that their right to say 'I be' is respected will they become able to learn the dominant grammatical reasons why they should say 'I am'" (*Teachers as Cultural Workers*).

The children and I connect Kant's second statement of the *cat*—never to use another person merely as a means to end, nor let yourself be used—to the concept of dignity. Kids have concerns to share with Kant about how this second statement can help them be their own person with dignity. Some have expressed worries about how they can keep themselves from being used . . . for grown-up convenience, for a group laugh at their expense, as a scapegoat, and by one parent against the other. They want to know what a kid can do. I examine the second statement with them more closely. Not only does this command negate using another, but it also forbids allowing yourself to be used. *You*, a rational human being, have dignity. What are some possible applications of this statement of the categorical imperative? I ask the kids what they owe themselves as human beings with dignity. How can they treat themselves justly? Kant insists that the requirements of justice imply that we have moral duties to our*selves* as well as to others. The kids explore their duties to themselves: "I won't let somebody copy the answers off my test." "I'll ask the gym teacher to please stop yelling at me when I can't do something." "When a teenager tells me they'll give me money to do something really wrong, I'll walk away fast." Little big minds have "the dignity of a rational being" (Kant, *Grounding for the Metaphysics of Morals*).

 DISCUSSION QUESTIONS: DIGNITY

- When do you lose your dignity? How do you feel when you are treated with dignity?
- Do you know anyone who isn't treated with dignity, but ought to be?

 EXERCISE: DIGNITY

- Introduce the children to Nina Simone as she plays the piano and sings with unforgettable emotion "Why? The King of Love Is Dead" and "To Be Young, Gifted, and Black." In the first song Simone grieves over the death of Martin Luther King, Jr., and insists that we better stop and ask . . . did he die in vain? Ask the children what they imagine King would think about justice in America if he were alive today. In the second song you can feel Simone's experience of discrimination as a talented, black musician. She begs young people to keep their "soul intact." Explain to the children that by an intact soul Simone means that kids need to stay strong inside and keep the sense of dignity that they deserve no matter what. Talk to the children about ways to keep injustice from crushing their souls. Ask them to write the lyrics of their original song called "My Soul Is Intact." Simone's piano sounds like no other with its mix of classical, jazz, and the blues. Let her music play as the children compose their tunes. She will inspire their songwriting.

CHILDREN'S RIGHTS

From the time I began my study of philosophy as an undergraduate and through my current teaching profession, I have been struck by how few philosophers address the issue of children's rights. Many philosophers mention children in passing, and some contemporary philosophers delve into specific areas of interest. But I see more philosophical energy expended on such issues as artificial intelligence and cloning, for example, than the urgent subject of justice for children. The child philosophers, however, have plenty to say about their rights.

Kant's quest for a moral theory with universal application surely implies that children be included in the determination of what constitutes impartial and fair treatment of humanity. Failure to consider children robs his categorical imperative of the fullness of its meaning. This is *not* to suggest that kids are fully independent moral agents capable of making major moral decisions on their own. Rather, it is to suggest that if you can will an act to be universally applied to all humans, then children as part of humanity deserve inclusion in your thought process.

In many classrooms, after discussing Kant and Freire, I have asked the kids if they would like to create their very own Children's Bill of Rights. They jump for the nearest writing utensil. We work together until the time comes when they are satisfied with their list of rights and ready to commit the list in permanent marker on a large poster. These are some of the children's rights that make it to the poster every time: Children have a right to: "breathe fresh air," "be respected as individuals," "be listened to," "drink clean water," "play unless we're sick," "be safe and protected by grown-ups," "have food to eat," "feel secure and not afraid," "get an *excellent* education."

We must ask if these children's rights are included in our current philosophy of education when the circumstances of any life can be dictated by economics and politics. The path that a child will travel is preordained in many ways from the start. A particular school district is directly tied to income level. There is a link between academic performance and the economic circumstances of a child's life. Freire's "problem-posing" approach to education is one way to address injustice and give every child the tools to overcome both current and future forms of oppression.

In stark contrast to the banking method, Freire's problem-posing educational alternative opposes rather than reinforces societal oppression. In his mind, schools must never reproduce social injustice but must protect and empower learners. Educators must be agents of change and vigilant against their own indirect participation in an unjust social order. Freire encourages teachers to "challenge their students, from an early to a more adult age, through games, stories, and reading so that students understand the need to create coherence between discourse and practice" (*Teachers as Cultural Workers*). He proclaims that the teacher's authority and expertise ought to be on the side of the students, who can then become active participants in the experience of transforming their lives. There must be time for discussion and reflection to decide what knowledge means and why it matters. Teachers should honor students' perspectives and varied life experiences. "Educators need to know what happens in the world of the children with whom they work. They need to know the universe of their dreams, the language with which they skillfully defend themselves from the aggressiveness of their world, what they know independently of the school, and how they know it" (*Teachers as Cultural Workers*). Freire envisions educational practice in which teachers and learners investigate the world together in heartfelt dialogue. There is no substitute for this animated interaction and communication of ideas. Agreement and disagreement, questions and further analysis all have a place in this give-and-take dialogue that creates critical thinkers. "Let us fight, day and night, for a school in which we talk to and with the learners so that, hearing them, we can be heard by them as well" (*Teachers as Cultural Workers*).

Philosophy provides both children and grown-ups with the means to broaden our concept of justice to include full consideration of children. As philosophers, we can ask ourselves difficult questions about justice in the lives of youth. Each of us needs to be on the lookout for our cultural blinders. "I hardly believe that the fair sex is capable of principles . . ." (Kant, *Observations on the Feeling of the Beautiful and Sublime*). Kant's brilliance did not preclude his exclusion of women from use of his categorical imperative. He missed his own contradiction. What are *we* missing?

". . . with liberty and justice for all." *For all?*

 TEACHING TIP: CHILDREN'S RIGHTS

- Talk of justice leads many children to dream of fixing the world. Make sure that you have suggestions ready for doable fixes.

 DISCUSSION QUESTIONS: CHILDREN'S RIGHTS

- What would be on your list of children's rights?
- Will you give a full description of your picture of a just world? What do you see and hear and what are people talking about? Is your world a possibility?

- How can you teach yourself to recognize injustice better? How can you keep from being part of the problem of injustice?

 EXERCISES: CHILDREN'S RIGHTS

- Work with your child philosophers to create a Children's Bill of Rights. Make sure that they can list their rights in clear and brief statements after your lengthy discussion of justice in a child's life. Ask them where they would like to display their colorful poster and if they would like to make reproductions to post elsewhere. Ask them to explain their reasons for wanting to put a poster listing children's rights in the places they choose. For example, kids have suggested to me that we take their posters to the recreation center and several particular restaurants.

- Recite slowly and with feeling Maya Angelou's 1993 inaugural poem, "On the Pulse of Morning." Young ears perk up and eyes brighten when they hear her invite *children* to a new day in her poem. *All* the many individuals who make up this one country must join together, she pleads, and look into one another's eyes. Help the children take the poem apart and define and explain for them as needed. Angelou looks at some groups that have suffered injustice in our nation's past, such as "The African and Native American." As you look with the child philosophers at the wide variety of cultures represented in this poem, ask the children how the United States can become *everyone's* country, "your country," as Angelou hopes. What steps can the child philosophers suggest to combat oppression of any group? Invite them to create an original poem based on Angelou's words: "I am the tree planted by the river / which will not be moved." In their poem, have them describe the principles of justice they would want to plant, like a tree that grows by the river forever.

※
※

Children impress me with their natural dignity. They are young and dependent, but their humanity is full-blown. I see their innate abilities and desire to be part of the world. It is painful to realize how easily children become the helpless victims of injustice.

Listening to stories about their lives inspires me to try to teach better, to be more vigilant about what I may be missing, and to guard against any assumption on my part that I can be fair and respectful without continual effort. I admire them.

Resources

- *Teachers as Cultural Workers* by Paulo Freire. In a series of letters to teachers, Freire puts both authoritarian and permissive methods of teaching to the test. You can feel his passionate advocacy for democratic learning.
- *The Politics of Education* by Paulo Freire. This is a formal analysis of the cultures of power and liberation.
- *Pedagogy of the Oppressed* by Paulo Freire. The "banking" concept of education gets Freire's full attention in the second chapter.
- *Grounding for the Metaphysics of Morals* by Immanuel Kant, translated by James W. Ellington. Here is an excellent, reader-friendly translation of this work. Kant's look at purity of motivation is at margin numbers (mn) 393 and 394. The first statement of the categorical imperative, universal law, is at (mn) 402 and 421. You can find his famous "false promise" test in the last few pages of section one (mn 402–404). Section two opens with the threat posed by self-love in all of our decisions. A call to cultivate our natural talents and to practice generosity can be heard at (mn) 422–424. Toward the end of section two (mn 429), he issues his moral command never to use another person.

- *Observations on the Feeling of the Beautiful and Sublime* by Immanuel Kant. In the second section, "Of the Attributes of the Beautiful and Sublime in Man in General," Kant describes the ways in which he makes a case for women's inferior logic that precludes their use of his categorical imperative.
- *Beatrice's Goat* by Pat McBrier and Lori Lohstoeter.
- "The Strand" by Seamus Heaney. This is included in *The Spirit Level*.
- "On the Pulse of Morning" by Maya Angelou. Here is her poem recited for the inauguration of President Clinton in January 1993.
- *Bob Dylan and Philosophy,* edited by Peter Vernezze and Carl Porter. This features eighteen different analyses of Dylan as a philosopher.
- *The Essential Bob Dylan.* This CD salutes many of his classics, leading off with "Blowin' in the Wind," which he wrote and sang in 1963.
- *Anthology* by Nina Simone. In addition to a soulful rendition of "Blowin' in the Wind," this is where you will find "Why? The King of Love Is Dead" and "To Be Young, Gifted, and Black," as well as "Here Comes the Sun."
- *In the Wind* by Peter, Paul, and Mary. This CD includes their vintage recording of "Blowin' in the Wind."
- *At the Close of a Century* by Stevie Wonder. This boxed set of CDs includes his version of "Blowin' in the Wind."
- *Lincoln Portrait* by Aaron Copland. James Earl Jones narrates an excellent recording of Copland's work on a fine CD titled *Portraits of Freedom* by the Seattle Symphony Orchestra.

TIME

If we try to think of the speed at which time
is passing or at which things are changing our
minds are set in a whirl, for it is a speed which
can never be calculated. The harder we try to
catch hold of the moment, to seize a pleasant
sensation, or to define something in a way
which will be satisfactory for all time,
the more elusive it becomes.

—ALAN W. WATTS, *The Spirit of Zen*

THE TOPIC

"What time was it when time began?" I've felt my mind bend and
flip just hearing child philosophers ask this question! And their fol-
low-up questions aren't any easier. Just one example: "When I first
started to count, I thought I could count all the way to infinity, but
what is infinity?"

Do you remember when you were first learning to tell time? Was
it a process of simply learning how a clock works, or was it somehow
more than that? From a ve ry early age we are aware of time's movement in our lives. It takes time for a tree to grow, for snowflakes to
gather themselves for sledding, for the moon to become full. But

what do we really know about time? What is it? Further investigation reveals even more questions. Does time exist separate from our world or only in reference to it? Does it have meaning for anything other than human beings? Is it something that the human mind invented, a tool that we designed for arranging reality and making sense of it? Do we rely on the structure that time provides because we can't handle everything coming at us at once?

Humans are rather preoccupied with time. Being too busy and not having enough time are common complaints. We are made to understand from a very early age that time should be used well and never wasted. Time makes a lot of demands and it never lets up. It crawls at an agonizing pace when we ache with physical pain or emotional grief, and it speeds by while we are in the presence of those we love. Perhaps as adults we feel much more acutely longings for the past and anxieties about the future. Yet, in the end, our adult feelings and questions about time aren't so different from those of children.

Around the world, seemingly *forever,* philosophers have yearned for a glimpse of an eternity beyond the grip of time. But what, if anything, exists untouched by time? Children dance to this topic. Up and down, in and out, minds tango as one question leads to another. And yet as attracted by the mystery of time as they may be, they remain laughingly suspicious of it. After all, it's always stalling and stopping their fun. They run out of it at recess. As they wait and wait for their birthdays, it stands stubbornly still. Yes, children, too, feel the limitations imposed upon them by time as they race to catch the bus for school or take a timed test that may affect their future.

The elusive nature of time rules out the possibility of a clear definition. Perhaps Stephen Hawking's incredible scientific analysis of time can help, but that's a story for another (long!) day. When exploring the subject of time, the human mind retreats even as it creeps closer. A child explained to me that the best thing to do with this mystery is to "hug it and not to squeeze it to bits." You might want to begin your philosophical conversations with kids on time by saying that this is one concept for which they may never find a satisfying definition.

For our discussion of time we will draw from the writings of a Christian bishop who lived during the fall of the Roman Empire and a man who helped to make Buddhism accessible to Americans in the twentieth century. Saint Augustine (AW-guh-steen or aw-GUS-tin) stretched toward a comprehension of the infinite while Alan Watts strove for awareness of each instant. Together they kindle the wonder of time for little big minds.

 ## TEACHING TIPS: THE TOPIC

- Wait and hear what your kids have to say! Children love talking about time, playing with it, and laughing about it. Just asking them what time *is* gets them going. I follow their lead and tailor my questions and comments to suit their curiosity.
- Scatter a number of clocks about the room and set them to the time in different places around the world. Add a sundial for Augustine, take them outside to learn to use it, and be prepared for their question: How do you tell time at night? When it is 11:00 A.M. here, it is _____ in Budapest, Beijing, Anchorage, Sydney. This is a great way to begin your look at the wonders of time.

 ## DISCUSSION QUESTIONS: THE TOPIC

- What is one question you really want to ask about time? Just *one* question!

- How does it feel when you learn to tell time? What are you doing exactly?
- Have you ever been so caught up in the flow of life that time passed and you didn't notice it? What were you doing? How can an activity absorb you so completely?
- Would your life be confusing without time? Do you need time to sort things out?
- Is it possible to count to infinity? Can something go on forever without an end? Does everything have a beginning?
- Can you make more time in your life? Does everyone have the same amount of time in a day?

 EXERCISES: THE TOPIC

- Interacting with people of different ages is a subtle but enduring lesson in time's movement. Involve the children in activities with seniors as well as with children who are younger than they are. Check with your local senior center and ask if some experts will volunteer to give sewing lessons or do some gardening with the children. Helping a younger sibling or student learn to read (or tell time!) shows the older children their own faces at that age. The experience of learning to knit with a seasoned pro or playing with a beginner a familiar game they thought they had outgrown gives child philosophers more insight into the passage of time.
- Madeleine L'Engle's timeless *A Wrinkle in Time* is exciting reading and packed with philosophical curiosity about time. Join Meg Murry and her brother Charles Wallace Murry as they travel through space and time and question the world. Invite the children to trade places with either Meg or Charles Wallace. In their philosophy journals, have them write a short

adventure of their own to add to the story. Ask them to write a list of new questions about time that this book evokes. If they reach a better understanding of time with the Murrys, have them describe their insights thoroughly.

- Modern American composer George Crumb finds the notes to express his fascination with time in his *Echoes of Time and the River.* Children are open to music that is new to them and enjoy getting into Crumb's mind. Have them listen to the four movements of his work consecutively, then separately for analysis, and then as a unit again. Watch their facial expressions change with the music! Have a conversation about the titles of each movement: "Frozen Time," "Remembrance of Time," "Collapse of Time," and "Last Echoes of Time." Is frozen time a present moment? Do the last echoes of time whisper or thunder? Music has often been referred to as "time art," which means that it exists in time as it moves from one sound to the next sound. As they listen to Crumb's sounds, ask the children to write their thoughts about time. Encourage them to use his music as their inspiration.

THE PHILOSOPHERS

We are forever talking of time and of times.

—AUGUSTINE, *Confessions* BOOK XI

Augustine is by most accounts the most influential theologian of early Christianity. He shaped Christian doctrine with a Platonic flavor for at least a thousand years. He died in 430 as the bishop of Hippo in Roman Africa as the city was under attack by the Vandals.

In his *Confessions,* his autobiography, Augustine lures readers with his vigorous intellectual and spiritual thirst for knowledge of the Truth. Spanning his life, this renowned work details Augustine's transformation from man-about-town to his conversion to Christianity in 386. Book XI is his famous look at the baffling concept of time. Augustine was haunted by the disconnect between the abstract notion of eternity and time as we know and experience it in our everyday lives. He humbly admitted his perplexity. In *The City of God,* Augustine spends considerable time on the thorny question of the existence of human free will, given an all-knowing God. He concludes that God's foreknowledge does not rule out free will because *humans* don't know the future. This apparent conflict and the Augustinian resolution remain part of a theological debate to this day.

Augustine believed that God's eternal being exists outside the bounds of human time. God's essence is timeless, and Augustine longs for eternity because it is God's "home." Still, he longed to know God in his life on earth despite being constrained by time. While his faith in the timelessness of God's divine nature never wavered, Augustine still struggled to make his intellect grasp the concept of eternity. Yet after much searching, he discovered that even his powerful mind was no match for this task.

"Grant me to hear and understand what is meant by *In the beginning, You made heaven and earth*" (*Confessions,* Book XI). Time has a beginning, and with this as his starting point, Augustine turns his mind loose on the effort to grasp its slippery nature. It seems that time begins with creation and did not exist until God made the world. Augustine even manages a sense of humor. To those who would ask what God was doing *before* creation, he refuses to reply, using the standard joke of his day, that God was getting hell ready for those who push their probing questions too far.

As Augustine embarks on his roller-coaster journey through time, children eagerly strap themselves in for the ride. His questions and temporary solutions, followed by more questions, both intrigue and amuse young minds. His preliminary analysis of the present is strenuous mental exercise. "If we conceive of some point of time which cannot be divided into even the minutest parts of moments, that is the only point that can be called present" (*Confessions,* Book XI). So the present moment has no duration because it is a momentary flash, like the clap of a hand. How can you measure something that doesn't stand still? The present, an undivided moment, is therefore unfathomable. But when Augustine looks backward and forward, he is really in a quandary. If the past is gone and the future is not yet here, does either past or future exist? Is time real or not? Does "in the beginning" mean anything?

As the roller coaster slows and begins its smooth descent, Augustine gradually reaches an understanding. He realizes that everything happens in the present. Humans remember the past in the present moment and anticipate the future in the present moment. That's it! Time passes from the future into the past through the gateway of the present. The human mind constructs time to sort life into manageable bites, past—present—future. "There are three times, a present of things past, a present of things present, a present of things future. For these three exist in the mind, and I find them nowhere else" (*Confessions,* Book XI).

Eternity is nothing but the constant present. The concept of *constant present* was hard for Augustine to hold in his mind, and the kids and I glimpse the notion in brief, wordless flashes. The heart of the difficulty lies in the impossibility of understanding the vast difference between the constant present and time as humans use it. A present moment that is constant removes awareness of both past and future "time." Human time has nothing to do with this infinite moment. The difference between eternity and time is qualitative rather than quantitative, so that adding up every moment in time does not equal eternity. Augustine states that "in eternity nothing passes but all is present, whereas time cannot be present all at once" (*Confessions,* Book XI). For him, there is absolutely nothing on earth to which to compare eternal life.

Kids thrive on Augustine's dilemma. They also think that time is *weird.* "When you're bored, it goes too slow, when you are happy, it goes too fast." It "stops when you are scared and is totally crazy in your dreams." When you are doing "something you love, you have no clue what time is doing." They identify with Augustine's longing for eternity in their desire to have a play day last forever. The unmanageable distance between time and eternity was too much for Augustine, but the children want to bounce on that distance like a trampoline. Kids do not internalize Augustine's feeling of failure in resolving time's mystery. Many are delighted by the notion that time is something the human mind creates. "If we can make it up, then we can do anything we want with it," they tell me. I hear tales of kids delightedly dropping back into the Middle Ages and pulling on dragon tails, while others zoom forward in their self-constructed time machines to explore infinity.

> It has been said that to define is to kill, and if the wind were to
> stop for one second for us to catch hold of it, it would cease
> to be wind. The same is true of life. Perpetually things and
> events are moving and changing; we cannot take hold of
> the present moment and make it stay with us . . .
>
> —ALAN W. WATTS, *The Spirit of Zen*

Born in England in 1915, Alan Watts was a philosopher, a prolific writer of some twenty-five books, and an entertaining speaker. He served as a bridge between East and West through his work in comparative religions. Frequently pointing to the many complementary beliefs shared by Christianity and Asian religions, he interpreted and presented Eastern philosophy in a way that made it accessible to Western cultures. *The Spirit of Zen*, written early in Watts' career, is perfect for our look at time as he examines both time and eternity from a Buddhist perspective.

In *The Spirit of Zen*, Watts uses the perspective of Buddhist theory as a lens through which to see clearly into the nature of time. "Briefly, this doctrine is that man suffers because of his craving to possess and keep forever things which are essentially impermanent." Watts suggests that time is like the wind, which cannot be grabbed and held. Misery comes from the human desire for things to stay the same in life's whirl of perpetual movement.

It is in the life of the spirit, however, that unchanging eternity exists. Spirit lives in the present moment. That's the key: The present moment is eternal. When people become absorbed in their lives, they lose the sense of time. Focus on the present moment requires undivided concentration on what is immediately before you. This one-pointed, focused attention on experiencing the present moment directly springs the trap of time and frees the human spirit. Time vanishes through one's total involvement in this very instant right now. The fog of a life divided into past, present, and future lifts. There is no longing for permanence or Augustine's eternity here or elsewhere. Eternity is within every present moment.

In your discussions with children about time, suggest to them, as Watts does, that the solution to time's mystery just might be within them. Ask them: Is our true nature timeless? What if we can develop the ability to concentrate, to focus all our energy on what is immediately before us? Paying attention to each moment, we become one with the "changing stream of events which is flowing past us all the time" (Watts, *The Spirit of Zen*). Ask each child to tell the group about a day that just flew by. Why do they think it felt that way?

It is a treat to share the Buddhist concept of real time with children. Kids love the idea of living in the *now,* only and forever *now.* Life is constant movement *now.* And yet they decide that this intense focus on the present moment will take some getting used to. "If the hands of the clock no longer move, how will I be on time?" They are sure that they will be in trouble for showing up late. With more discussion, however, kids find it "very cool" when they realize that they can lose their sense of time for extended periods—"free time" takes on a whole new meaning! Before philosophizing about time, two children agreed that they "didn't know what to call swimming all day" or "looking out the window on the train." Now these sixth-graders describe these experiences as "freedom from time's chains."

TEACHING TIPS: THE PHILOSOPHERS

- Looking at the Christian and the Buddhist approaches to time is a fine occasion to remind the children of how often different religions share similar ideas.
- Write "constant present" on the board. The present moment is a concept that dangles eternity within kids' reach. By referring to this phrase as you question the reality of time, you will make it easier for them to think about the difference between human time and eternal timelessness. Another technique that is helpful to me is to put this simple equation in (Buddhist) subtraction on the board: Life – Time = Now. Without time's limitations, life is lived in the constant present.
- Watts has many audio recordings available. You can make him a passenger on a class field trip or on a leisurely drive in your family car.

DISCUSSION QUESTIONS:
THE PHILOSOPHERS

- When you think of the concept of *constant present,* can you imagine living moment to moment to moment? Is it possible to become so absorbed in the moment that you have no awareness of either the past or the future?
- What would it be like to have a watch that was always set on *now*?
- Do you think that it is possible that only the present moment really and truly exists, and if so how would you explain it?

 EXERCISES: THE PHILOSOPHERS

- Sit with the children as each of you looks at one thing, and one thing only, for ten minutes. Concentrate on a blade of grass, a leaf, or a bird's nest. Listen to the sound of crickets. Savor the fragrance of hyacinths. Touch the bark of a tree. Slowly taste an apple one small bite at a time. Afterward, ask the children if they can describe what those ten minutes were like. Have them tell you whether they prefer to talk about this experience or not and why. Do they have any idea how much time went by as they were sitting? Did it seem like a long or short period of concentration?
- Read Wu-Men's poem from thirteenth-century China titled "Best Season of Your Life." This poem is an excellent example of Watts' one-pointed look at life. If our minds are clear and focused, we can take the time to experience the moon, flowers, everything. Ask the children if it is possible to pay such close attention to their lives that every day can be the best day.

Have them describe in their journals a day that they can imagine when every moment contributes to a best day. Do they agree with Wu-Men that every season can be the best season of their lives?

• Introduce them to artwork that is an exercise in discipline. Calligraphy is the art of pen-and-ink drawing requiring one-pointed attention. Concentration on calligraphy negates the sense of time. Watts eagerly gave himself to the study and practice of this art. Place on each child's desk a black crayon and one piece of white paper. Make sure to have characters from the Chinese alphabet in full view. You can use prints of artwork or books on Asian art. Thumbing through a book written in Chinese is a treat. Ask them to choose any one character and try to copy it precisely. Join the children in trying your hand at calligraphy. Doing activities along with them makes a huge difference. Explain that even the slightest alteration in the outline or shading of the figure changes the character and therefore its meaning. Smile when they complain that they don't have an eraser and need more than one piece of paper. Remind them that they are developing their ability to focus, and it requires complete attention to get it just right. "If the artist were to stop and think in the middle of his stroke the result would be an ugly blot" (Watts, *The Spirit of Zen*). Why be careful if you can do it over and over again? A long-term project, such as calligraphy, makes the lesson on keeping a one-pointed attitude a lasting memory. Children remember taking the *time* to understand *time*. And maybe one day they will be ready to graduate to the use of black ink and a paintbrush on white parchment paper.

CHANGE

We live in a world in which everything seems to change, where all too often we are unable to stop the passage of time. There is no lockbox that is out of time's reach for safeguarding life's treasures. Time eventually leads to loss, the loss of innocence, health, and those we love. Time closes in and ends every life. It can be difficult to discuss this aspect of time with children, and some of what we know as adults is perhaps better left unsaid. But you will find that they are very excited at the opportunity to discuss change. Ask them to tell you about things in their lives that they miss, people or places that once gave them pleasure that now they can only remember. Kids are enthralled by what was before and is no longer. They are equally intrigued by the many promises that the future holds.

Peter, a second-grade scholar, explained to me time's damage in this breathtaking way. "Time is the creator and the destroyer of everything. It is about beginning and ending. Every single one of my problems is right there, in the beginning and at the end and everything in between. I don't want to leave town when my family moves at the end of the year." These reflections reminded me of Augustine's lament that "I am divided up in time" (*Confessions,* Book XI). Peter continued to dissect the turmoil time causes with his observation that everything changes and nothing stays the same. "Nobody can stay the same age and it is too confusing to keep up with all the changes. I'm not like I was last year or at my old school or even yesterday. And *you* are not the same person either." Young Peter recognizes "the illusion that a continuing ego survives from moment to moment, to feel that I who sit here am truly I who came in at the door ten minutes ago" (Watts, *The Spirit of Zen*). Time is an oddity, indeed. How can a seven-year-old possess such wisdom?

Many children I have spoken with have told me that they can remember, though somewhat dimly, a period in their lives when they were unaware of time. Close enough to such timeless absorption that they can describe the transition away from it and into the world where time triumphs, they have spoken of this as a painful change in their lives. Many of them recall with longing doing one thing contentedly for long periods of time. Oh, for those timeless days . . . playing on the floor in a make-believe world while their father worked at his desk in the basement; simply sitting on the back stoop watching birds; riding their bikes well past dark. Talk to your child philosophers about these times. Help them figure out how they can continue to enjoy timeless pleasures. Remind them that the Buddhist suggestion is to make peace with the continuous flow of time and to stop creating discontent by craving permanence. "The fact that man notices and regrets change shows that he himself is not moving with the rhythm of life" (Watts, *The Spirit of Zen*).

 ## TEACHING TIP: CHANGE

- Place a plant in a window so that the children can keep an eye out to see *when* it grows. This plant can be your invitation to look back at the topic of time as weeks and months go by.

 ## DISCUSSION QUESTIONS: CHANGE

- How long can you concentrate on any one thing without becoming distracted? Is it hard to keep your mind focused on what is right before you? Why?
- How can you use what you learn from the past as an incentive to make improvements in the future?
- Use your five senses for exploring time. What would a photo-

graph of time look like? Would time feel more like water or like a rock?

 EXERCISES: CHANGE

- In a strong voice, read the poem "Women" by Alice Walker. Walker looks at the women who have gone before her with admiration and gratitude. They worked so hard, without complaint, and unknowingly paved the way to a big world for her. She wonders "how they knew what we / must know." Ask the children how they are connected to the past. Who do they think made their opportunities possible? I offer them the example of my grandmother, who raised two girls as a single mother during the Depression. Ask the children to name someone they feel connected to but never knew and to explain this connection in a poem. This thought process pulls the past into the present like magic. Kids love to trace their lives backward and meet new/old people.

- Listen to Joni Mitchell's "Big Yellow Taxi." You and the children can sing along with her that "you don't know what you've got till it's gone." Ask them why they think we realize our mistakes *after* we make them. Do we only miss the trees after the parking lot is paved? Next, have the children look at their childhoods by listening to "The Circle Game." A young child finds the seasons have passed ten times and looks forward to sixteen summers. Mitchell sings poignantly that this child who now wants time to hurry up will beg it soon enough to slow down. The seasons go 'round and 'round, and we are riding on time's carousel. Ask the children to become songwriters and compose the lyrics of a song about time for Joni to sing.

PERMANENCE

In my conversations with children on the subject of time, I have found that they have a strong belief that time can't change what is truly beautiful. Their examples of unchanging beauty include love, trust, and ideas. Some things in life are so perfect that not even time can hurt them. A couple of kids have even expressed to me their desire to tell Augustine he doesn't have to wait for heaven, he can have a taste of the timeless on earth. One of my favorite insights from an eight-year-old philosopher is the following: "I wish he knew we were studying him *after all these years.* He beat time and didn't even know it—we're listening to him *now.*"

Augustine asks in his *Confessions,* "But the two times, past and future, how can they *be,* since the past is no more and the future is not yet?" Then, unknowingly mirroring Buddhist thought, he reasons, "On the other hand, if the present were always present and never flowed away into the past, it would not be time at all, but eternity." The present isn't time, after all; it *is* eternity. The present moment is as close to God's eternal nature as he can ever hope to come on this earth. With a sunset as your backdrop, ask your little big minds what the word *eternity* means to them. Are there really only twenty-four hours in a day?

Watts suggests that if we train our minds to have a one-pointed attitude, constantly focusing on the present, we can live unhindered by time. If our minds create the notion of a life divided by time, then our minds can also undo the damage. Children know that having this one-pointed focus is no easy undertaking. They tell grand tales of the enormous difficulty of concentrating and the giant obstacles that prevent them from paying complete attention *ever.* One first-grader told me his mind was "like a grasshopper," carrying him always one leap ahead of time. A classmate expressed regret that she had been put in time-out, but it was really hard to "settle myself." For children as much as it is for adults, time is a big tease. Try as hard as we like, time refuses to be mastered.

With some help, however, kids begin to realize that in some ways they already have this one-pointed attitude and can work to bring it more into their lives. With a little thought, their examp les of timeless experiences pour out one after another: splashing in the bathtub, practicing piano or violin, reading a good book, watching my cat, doing ballet, staring at fish in an aquarium, making pies with my grandma. It turns out that they can concentrate well and, surprisingly, somewhat effortlessly. This realization is most encouraging. Quickly they can imagine the beneficial results of living with full awareness of what is immediately before them. They envision less pressure in their lives and not being in a hurry so much. They could "listen better" and "not wiggle around like a worm going crazy." They could "do homework *and* have time to goof off." You can be "like a wizard and make time go poof." Goof *and* poof! Some seventh-graders have an inkling that if they take good care of the present, that then the future will take care of itself. They trust that time will prove this is true. This is an incomparable relief for the ones who believe it.

In a distracted life, going in many different directions, time takes over. Putting all your energy into what is going on, ahhh . . . it is not so much time that changes. When an individual experiences life just as it is in Augustine's undivided moment, there *is* no time. Just living life. "Calmness is the result of a one-pointed attitude of mind . . . avoiding all the useless running backwards and forwards, worrying about the past and future" (Watts, *The Spirit of Zen*).

TEACHING TIP: PERMANENCE

- Responding to particularly insightful comments with silence lends importance to children's ideas. They soon realize that a wordless response is an indication that you are thinking hard about their insights.

 DISCUSSION QUESTIONS: PERMANENCE

- What are some things that time does not change? Does time affect Mozart's music? Do we still love people after they die?
- In as few words as possible, describe *forever*.
- What does it mean to waste time? What does it mean to use time well?
- If you take good care of the present, the future will take care of itself. What does this mean to you? Do you believe it?

 EXERCISE: PERMANENCE

- Look at Chinese landscape painting either in art books or, better still, on an excursion to a museum. Watts was captivated by the spaciousness in these paintings that makes the observer feel somehow suspended above space and time. Have the children contemplate these works of art in silence. Later, ask them how they feel looking at the empty space. Does space appear still and permanent like a present moment? Limiting themselves to the use of as few colors as possible, have the children draw their very own landscapes on large pieces of white paper. Do they want to give their paintings names? Why or why not?

※

Children remind you how much fun philosophy can be as they romp through the maze of time. Kids make it clear that they are keenly aware of the problems associated with this thing called time despite its questionable reality. Why do they "have so much more time than grown-ups"? Children feel a tug between their wish for permanence on some occasions (an unending weekend) and their acceptance and excitement at the prospect of change (a new teacher next year). They laugh at themselves and at time but grow weary of hearing the phrases "Not now" or "Wait till later" from adults.

For you as their guide in a philosophical conversation about time, well, time itself will disappear when you watch their moment-to-moment absorption in this topic.

Resources

- *A Wrinkle in Time, A Wind in the Door,* and *A Swiftly Tilting Planet* by Madeleine L'Engle. These three books complete *The Tesseract.*
- "Best Season of Your Life" by Wu-Men. This is in the Stephen Mitchell anthology of poetry *The Enlightened Heart.*
- "Women" by Alice Walker. Among other collections, this is in *Words with Wings,* which features fine artwork.
- *Echoes of Time and the River* by George Crumb. This is on the CD *Complete Crumb Edition,* volume 6.
- "Big Yellow Taxi" and "The Circle Game" by Joni Mitchell. These songs are available on her CD *Ladies of the Canyon.*
- *Confessions,* Book XI, by Augustine. His autobiography captures his relentlessly curious intellect from boyhood through his conversion to Christianity. In Book XI each section has questions and ideas for playing with time.

- *The Spirit of Zen* by Alan Watts. Children will enjoy the simple legends and anecdotes as well as the sense of timelessness that Watts conveys in his look at judo, fencing, and music. I find especially useful the chapters "The Secret of Zen" and "Zen and Civilization of the Far East." There are samples of calligraphy and Asian art to enjoy as well.
- *Tao: The Watercourse Way* by Alan Watts. Watts presents the Taoist perspective on change and permanence that heavily influences the Buddhist view.
- *A Brief History of Time* by Stephen Hawking. Traveling through time with this brilliant physicist is not for the faint of heart, so you may want a lighter trip. Try *A Briefer History of Time*, edited by Stephen Hawking and Leonard Mlodinow, for easier reading.

COURAGE

When anything happens to you, always
remember to turn to yourself and ask what
faculty you have to deal with it.

—EPICTETUS, *Enchiridion*

THE TOPIC

What is it that allows us to meet life's many challenges? Courage. The questions tumble forth immediately. Do people possess courage naturally? Is it possible to increase our reserves of it if and when they are lacking? Does courage have the same meaning for everyone, or is it defined within the unique circumstances of every life?

Through the ages and across cultures, philosophers have contemplated the entwined connection between courage and fear. Possessing courage, they insist, includes acknowledging our fears. The courageous person confronts fear head-on, uncovering sensible approaches and practical solutions even in the direst circumstances. Still, many of us know all too well how easy it is to allow our fears to grow and multiply, how we even create imaginary worries lest we run out of things to fear.

But what *is* courage exactly? Both Aristotle and Confucius deemed it the ability to choose a moderate course of action despite extreme stress or pressure. The courageous act, therefore, is neither rash nor cowardly but somewhere between the two. And how do we cultivate the virtue of courage? Aristotle maintained that we become courageous only by *acting* courageously. The Buddha and the Dalai Lama bridge the years between them with their emphasis on training oneself to become courageous by using the many opportunities that each day presents. For example, overcoming shyness and speaking up for one's beliefs or standing up for a friend in a tough situation can serve as preparation for more serious challenges. Buddhist philosophy asserts that we cannot acquire courage on demand or in a crisis, but must nurture it in ourselves slowly and gradually until it becomes our tendency to respond to challenges directly and with a steadfast spirit. Courage becomes a reliable, habitual response to difficulties both large and small.

The young philosophers I have worked with demonstrate strong convictions in their own definitions of courage. They've told me that courage means that you "keep bouncing back up because you are strong inside yourself." When you have courage, you "always find a way to hold on." "Courage makes you do your best even when life is way hard."

In order to drive our conversations further, I often tell kids that I'm sure they see and hear tales of extraordinary courage in the news: the firefighter who brought the family pet to safety, the pilot who landed the plane in a violent storm, or the child who saved her mother from choking by calling 911. But what about the plain old courage that happens every day, rarely noticed by those around us? Well, many ask me in response to my question, how would I describe this "everyday" courage? I share with them that, for me, some of my most courageous moments have been when I was willing to admit that I made a mistake or, at other times, when I held fast to my values even if no one else agreed with me. By taking a look at my life, the child philosophers are encouraged to look for courage in their own lives. I will never forget one fifth-grader who described how hard it was to admit that she couldn't swim when all her friends were jumping in the deep end of the pool, how "walking away took more courage than diving in." Didn't I know, her friend continued, that "you have to be pretty strong to admit that you are scared?"

When you talk to kids about courage in the face of fear, you immediately sense what a relief it is for them to voice their feelings and to find that they are not alone. It is heartening to watch them slowly realize that courage is available to everyone, that it's not just the exclusive possession of astronauts and mountain climbers.

In your discussions with kids about courage, Epictetus (eh-pic-TEE-tus) and Mary Wollstonecraft (WOHL-ston-craft) are the perfect guides. Their theories give the child philosophers the balance of two very different yet complementary perspectives. While strength of spirit grounds both philosophers, Epictetus resolves to endure the world as it is, and Wollstonecraft fights for the principles that will liberate her world. Epictetus focuses on addressing difficulty with steadfast rationale, whereas Wollstonecraft's courage is viewed as anything but rational by the male-dominated society that seeks to force its limitations upon her.

✓ TEACHING TIP: THE TOPIC

- Remember to involve *every* person in the room. One passive bystander, a teacher's aide or a visiting student who looks on without participating, gives a potential child philosopher

permission to withdraw. For whatever reason, this unwillingness to join in as an "outsider" is especially common when discussing courage.

 DISCUSSION QUESTIONS: THE TOPIC

- At what times in your life have you been courageous? Had you
  recognized your own bravery before?
- Who is someone you know personally who is courageous? What
  is this person's story?

 EXERCISES: THE TOPIC

- Read William Armstrong's classic *Sounder,* which paints a multi-
  faceted portrait of courage. In Louisiana in 1933, members of
  a sharecropper family somehow survive unthinkable circumstances while increasing their capacity to trust and to love.
  Have the children choose their favorite character and write
  a back-and-forth dialogue about courage between them and
  this character. The kids can ask, "Were you scared when . . . ?"
  "Where did you find the courage to . . . ?" "What was it like to
  realize that . . . ?" This can be their first original screenplay.
  For a treat they can get comfortable with popcorn and pillows
  and watch the 1972 film, starring Cicely Tyson and Paul Win-
  field. Tell them that the music is by Taj Mahal, who plays Ike
  in the movie. Cheer for Sounder!
- Listen to *Hansel and Gretel,* or watch on DVD this opera that
  Engelbert Humperdinck wrote for his sister's children in 1893.
  This brother and sister display abilities that enable them to
  survive that scary woman with the oven. Although the child

philosophers can count on never facing this particular predicament, ask them if they share some of the same qualities as Hansel and Gretel. Let them list different facets of courage the siblings portray. Complement the opera by reading aloud this fairy tale by the Brothers Grimm. Have the children write a short story about a courageous escapade that they would like to see become an opera. Have them read their stories to the class.

THE PHILOSOPHERS

Everything has two handles, one by which you can carry it, the other by which you cannot. If your brother wrongs you, do not take it by that handle, the handle of his wrong, for you cannot carry it by that, but rather by the other handle—that he is a brother, brought up with you, and then you will take it by the handle that you can carry [it] by.

—EPICTETUS, *Enchiridion*

Epictetus was an exemplar of Stoicism, a practical philosophy that had its prime for approximately five hundred years, beginning around 300 B.C.E. Born of a slave mother and himself a slave until his release after the death of Nero, Epictetus lived from 50 to 130. He began his education and study of Stoicism in Rome shortly after he was freed. He taught Stoic philosophy there and later in Greece.

It is not surprising, given his lameness as a result of being shackled and mistreated as a slave, that Epictetus was drawn to the Stoic emphasis on using reason to deal with any hardship. Stoicism provided for him the courage to handle a difficult life in a very challenging period of western European history. The Stoic manual *Enchiridion* (EN-kih-rid-e-on) is a straightforward guide to coping with the circumstances of *any* life, regardless of its difficulties. Dictated by Epictetus to one of his students, the handbook uses as its foundation the Stoic belief that the universe operates according to rational principles and that human life, as well, should operate according to reason. Each individual life should be a replica in small print of the larger logic of the universe itself.

Often when people today first encounter Epictetus, they are struck most by the lack of optimism and joy in his outlook. It becomes clear upon closer inspection, however, that his is a philosophy that is extremely valuable when one requires a shot of strength to deal with a problem, and Epictetus is quickly forgiven for his neglect of life's thrills and passions. At the heart of Epictetus's brand of Stoic philosophy is his conviction that courage comes from the realization that it is within our power to handle *everything* in our lives. There is a handle for lifting every burden, as well as a handle that is sure to fail. An emotional response to fear and difficulty is the handle that *worsens* the problem by creating additional worry.

Attitude is key. Reason's major revelation is that while most events lie outside our control, we worry about these things anyway. Reason guides us in distinguishing between the things that are in our power and the many things that are not: We control our thoughts and actions but not our height or others' behavior. Although we cannot control the circumstances of our lives, Epictetus's huge consolation is that we can manage our *response.* "What disturbs men's minds is not events but their judgments on events" (*Enchiridion*). How we choose to look at *any* situation is always within our power, and human will is strong enough to take us beyond our fear and anxiety regarding things outside "the region within your control" (*Enchiridion*). For Epictetus, choosing to take a reasonable perspective on the events of our lives guarantees tranquillity. For instance, we know that it is in the nature of a clay pot to break and so we do not weep when one shatters. "When you are about to take something in hand, remind yourself what manner of thing it is. If you are going to bathe put before your mind what happens in the bath" (*Enchiridion*). Were you prepared to be jostled and splashed? If someone can treat you unjustly, is it wise to expect fairness at every turn? Attitude is key.

Security and self-sufficiency result from expending our energy on appropriate issues in a smart way. Epictetus recommends, therefore, that we get to know our strengths and weaknesses. "You can be invincible, if you never enter a contest where victory is not in your power" (*Enchiridion*). With this understanding we can engage in satisfying work and avoid activities in which we over-reach and disappoint ourselves. Understanding both our abilities and our limitations prepares us for a calm, composed response to difficulty. Did someone make you angry? Never, answers Epictetus, because no one has that kind of power over another's emotions. The most we can say is that we allowed ourselves to become angry, and Stoic awareness that we have control over our thoughts and actions serves us well. And can a physical ailment deprive us of strength of spirit? Absolutely not, says the experienced Epictetus. "Lameness is a hindrance to the leg, but not to the will" (*Enchiridion*).

I have taught the Stoic philosophy of courage in many classrooms filled with children enduring extremely difficult lives. I have never heard a child voice, either as a statement or as a question, the notion that Epictetus's philosophy of endurance excuses adult abuse or neglect. This take on his philosophy simply does not occur to them. The conclusion that I hear struggling child philosophers draw from Epictetus can be summed up in this remark made by an eight-year-old boy: "He just means for me to be reasonable how I handle my problem, like who to tell about it, and when, and maybe what exactly I should say. I like him because he gives me the courage to deal with it."

Regardless of the circumstances of the lives of child philosophers, they almost always intuit the heart of Epictetus's message
and how to use his philosophy. There is a handle that is within
their reach with which to carry life's hardships, and carry them
courageously. Kids say that "he's the best if I'm in a jam," "he helps
me get out of being *dis*couraged," and "his philosophy shows me
that I can get past my problem by changing how I look at it."
Epictetus "is cool because he shows *me* how to be cool under
pressure."

Epictetus's approach to courage is neither showy nor dramatic.
His vision of courage is that of self-possessed individuals in charge
of their lives and directing their efforts only at the possible. Children love Epictetus's assertion that they can manage difficulty by
realizing that it is up to them how they look at it. Many say that
it gives them the courage to resist peer pressure and to stand tall
when left out or bullied. Kids know the sting of gossip too well,
and they cherish Epictetus's suggestion that when you hear that
people are speaking badly of you, say to yourself that they must
not know you very well or they would have mentioned many of
your other shortcomings. They *love* this!

I think Epictetus would have admired an animated dialogue I
witnessed between two students who were discussing Stoicism.
Marcus mumbled that he was afraid of sharks. His friend Peter
replied that he needed to be reasonable and not swim in the early
morning or evening when sharks are eating. Marcus reasoned as
well as he could and came up with a final question. "Do sharks
eat lunch?"

I earnestly wish to point out in what true dignity and human
happiness consists—I wish to persuade women to endeavor
to acquire strength, both of mind and body . . .

—M ary Wollstonecraft, *A Vindication of the Rights of Woman*

Mary Wollstonecraft was born in London in 1759 and died in 1797 as a result of complications during childbirth. This author of twelve books, written while raising a family, had the gumption to have those books published more than one hundred years before women could vote in the United States. Wollstonecraft looked at her society, and in particular at the status of women in England, and sighed with a resounding "What nonsense!" She championed the creation of a new concept of woman, with education and autonomy for women as her goal. Wollstonecraft sought improvements in the legal system to serve women's equality, especially economic equality within marriage and professional opportunities. In her writing she challenged well-known philosophers of her day such as Rousseau, Gregory, and Burke. Despite her youth and gender, Wollstonecraft's thorough analyses were well received because of her educated understanding of their works. Perhaps she would not be surprised that her landmark *Vindication of the Rights of Woman* is not included in the canon of Western philosophy, but having read her work, I find this glaring omission preposterous.

Through the years, many of her readers have marveled that such a forward-thinking philosophy came from a woman during a period in history when women were severely marginalized within society. On top of these limitations, Wollstonecraft had very little formal schooling and grew up in an abusive household. But against all odds, Wollstonecraft educated herself and in so doing not only enlightened her contemporaries but continues to be a progressive voice to this day. Her advocacy for women remains a part of modern activism's ongoing demand for women's equality in public and private life.

"The fear of innovation, in this country, extends to everything. This is only a covert fear, the apprehensive timidity of indolent slugs, who guard, by sliming it over, the snug place" (*A Vindication of the Rights of Woman*). Wollstonecraft's philosophy of courage begins with her definition of cowardice. Cowardice is feeble submission to a restrictive status quo, going along with an unjust social system because it requires too much effort of will to campaign for innovative ideas. Cowards lack the strength to rise above the lives that were dictated to them. "The mind must be strong that resolutely forms its own principles; for a kind of intellectual cowardice prevails which makes many men shrink from the task, or only do it by halves" (*A Vindication of the Rights of Woman*). Courage is neither lackluster nor halfhearted.

In contrast to cowardice, courage is stamina of will. It is the source of fierce determination to overcome one's predicament by *changing* it. Understanding the situation and enduring it are not enough. Wollstonecraft asks first of herself and then of all women that they have the courage to find "the vigour necessary to enable them . . . to find strength to recur to reason and rise superior to a system of oppression . . ." (*A Vindication of the Rights of Woman*). It is here that Wollstonecraft takes Epictetus one step further, encouraging women to be assertive and to rise above others' discomfort or outrage at persistent challenges to a preestablished order.

Every woman must have the courage to lay out a course of life to suit her character. Equality for women must be achieved *by* women. It is a show of weakness to expect to receive it as a gift from men. It's up to each woman to refuse the dictates of social expectations and to issue a forceful personal challenge to the status quo, for "how can a rational being be ennobled by anything that is not obtained by its *own* exertions?" (*A Vindication of the Rights of Woman*). It is cowardly to participate in a system that subjugates you because of your fear of change. To dream of a better future that you have no intention of actualizing is to give up.

The tone of Wollstonecraft's major work is serious, demanding, sometimes mocking, sometimes playful, and always passionate. She argues for full human rights for women based on a rigorous education that matches educational opportunities for men. Her call for the reform of education for girls has as its eventual goal active citizenship that includes the right to vote. Public coeducation for girls and boys will serve the larger good of a prospering society filled with thriving individuals. "Girls and boys, in short, would play harmlessly together, if the distinction of sex was not inculcated long before nature makes any difference" (*A Vindication of the Rights of Woman*).

Young children are aware, some more than others, of girls not being passed the ball at recess or being expected to lower their voices. Wollstonecraft heightens kids' awareness of uneven treatment and expectations. She lives in the children's memories as proof that you can pull yourself through difficulties and that hardship doesn't doom your life. She also leaves children with the courage to be feisty and to have the conviction of their own ideas. Over the years a number of kids have expressed regret that Epictetus didn't know Wollstonecraft. They wish he could see that she discovered that "a whole lot more was in her control" than any reasonable person could have guessed. "I may be accused of arrogance" (*A Vindication of the Rights of Woman*), but not by the children.

Mary Wollstonecraft was the consummate adventurer. She had the nerve to leave her society and her century behind. She did not become society's victim or use the severe limitations imposed upon women as an excuse. Corseted at the waist just as Epictetus was shackled by the leg, she found the courage to free herself.

 TEACHING TIPS: THE PHILOSOPHERS

- Remember to find the homes of the philosophers on a map or a globe. Mark the distance between Greece and England.

- Make a bit of a game out of doing philosophy, especially when discussing a difficult topic. Type statements for eve ry student from Epictetus's handbook on pieces of brightly colored construction paper. Put them in a canvas bag to pass around so that the children can pick their very own colorful quotes. After they read their tips to the class, the kids can tack their statements on the bulletin board. They can look for help from Epictetus when there is a problem in the classroom or difficulty in their personal lives.

DISCUSSION QUESTIONS: THE PHILOSOPHERS

- What are your three favorite pieces of advice from Epictetus? What specific situations in your life can be handled better by applying these suggestions?
- Do you agree with Epictetus that there is a handle by which you can carry absolutely *everything* in your life? Explain.
- How well can you distinguish between the things in your life that are in your control and the things that are not? Do you think people worry a lot about things over which they have no control?

EXERCISE: THE PHILOSOPHERS

- Invite a local person whose life embodies courage to talk to the students. The more they can identify with this person, the better. Have them learn about people in their own community who soar above hardship every day—the blind college student . . . refugees from the brutality of civil war who are making new lives . . . participants in the Special Olympics.

FACING YOUR FEARS

You will find in your discussion of courage with your children that, as one child philosopher explained to our group, "Admitting your fear takes the most courage of all." A number of kids have labored to put into words that I can understand that being "unable to say what it is keeps you scared." At the beginning of our conversations, they do not look for solutions, but they seem sure that facing their fears together is better than facing them alone. This is a big start. It makes them "feel less pressure because it's a relief just to say I'm afraid," and they agree that it is "awesome to know that other kids have the same worries as me." How do the child philosophers express the difficulty in meeting fear face-to-face? "It's scary because I have to be honest about me, but also tell the truth about people I really love." As I watch them delve into a topic that I know is hard for them, I can feel the mood in the room lighten as the kids find the confidence to unveil the things that frighten them. They see much that is positive in admitting fear because they feel that they are actually working toward a solution.

The kids I have worked with can put to rest any grown-up assumption that their lives are easy. In every classroom I find children from all backgrounds coping as best they can with real problems. Here are some poignant examples: "It's really scary when Daddy starts yelling and acting crazy and puts me in his car and drives too fast." "Mad voices make me shake." One third-grader whispered for the class to hear, "It's dark when my mom makes me walk to the store before school to get stuff for her, like cigarettes." Many children in his class identified with Patrick's admission that he "needed courage when I went to the hospital because it's a place for sick people and I thought I might not get well." "It takes courage to fix problems with a friend instead of acting mean." While one child expressed anxiety over choosing which parent to live with, her classmate responded to her that his biggest fear was that "my parents *won't* get a divorce." And "if you have a stutter ... like me ... it takes courage ... every ... time ... you ... speak." Facing their fears makes the child philosophers eager to understand courage. Courage ceases to be an abstract concept and becomes a desirable asset.

Kids also anticipate things in their future that may be hard to handle. A lot of children have an uncanny inkling that life will surprise them. The first problem many foresee is the very real difficulty of "growing up." Not having a job and being unable to get one loom large. The prospect of becoming sick worries quite a few, as does the fear that people they love will die. One child expressed the daunting notion of "moving to a new place and being unable to speak the language." To be unable to go to school because you can't afford it is an unsettling prospect for children of all ages. It is also a heartfelt anxiety that the world could "make me false." Their faces are evidence that thinking honestly about their lives opens up places that are sore and sometimes chronically painful.

Epictetus provides a huge relief by helping children discriminate between manufactured, unnecessary worry and a valid assessment of difficulty. "And if it is concerned with what is not in our power, be ready with an answer that it is nothing to you" (*Enchiridion*). Fear that comes from a horror movie or a Halloween costume can be eliminated, whereas erratic driving or an invitation from a stranger remain legitimate concerns. With confidence that everything has a handle by which to carry it, kids can gain a new perspective on a forgotten birthday or being ignored by adults. With courage children can take charge of their outlook on life. The Stoic approach encourages them to forget about a test when it is over, or to keep talking even if others stare as they stutter, stop, and start again. Epictetus and Wollstonecraft give kids some new ways to handle fear. Courage is in their reach. Fear cannot be eliminated, but it can be faced successfully. Obstacles can be "hopped over and blown past." Children feel powerless before so many of the events in their lives. Having a measure of control at their fingertips is liberating.

 ## TEACHING TIPS: FACING YOUR FEARS

- Because fear so often creates a sense of isolation, tell the children as you open your discussion that all people have trouble in their lives. Remind them of this universal predicament throughout your dialogue.
- Give lots of examples of being reasonable in facing our fears. I tell them that if I'm afraid of heights, then I should not plan on becoming an astronaut.
- Be sure to talk about your own fears. Children jump right in as you admit your worries.

 ## DISCUSSION QUESTIONS: FACING YOUR FEARS

- Do you anticipate something that will be hard for you to face in the future?
- What are some fears that weighed you down previously, which, after our discussion of courage, you can now let go?
- What are some simple ways you can develop courage every day so that it will be there whenever you need it? Can you say that you don't understand something without being ashamed? Does it take bravery to admit that you're afraid?

EXERCISES: FACING YOUR FEARS

- By befriending someone older with broad experience, children discover the courage needed to endure physical pain and loneliness. This lesson helps them gain valuable perspective on their own young lives. Establish a line of communication between the children and residents of the veterans' hospital nearest your town. Select patients who would like to hear from the children. Each child can write letters and create works of art to send to an unseen friend. You can mail a video of a class poetry reading or the spring concert to entertain a group in the common area of the hospital. With the veterans' permission, a child philosopher can learn about their backgrounds, experiences, and daily lives in the residential part of the hospital. Help the children think of overlooked populations, such as the residents of the veterans' hospital, as well as people they know who are grieving or recovering from injury, whose courage may need a boost.

- Work with the children to distinguish between unnecessary fear and fear that is sensible. Have them title one page in their notebooks "Groundless Fear" and the page across from it "Sensible Concern." Each child will then fill in the two pages honestly. Here are some common examples that are candidates for the "Groundless Fear" page: sharks, ghosts, and roller coasters. Help them work through their thinking by asking whether they have ever seen a shark or a ghost, and how they can opt to decline a ride on a roller coaster if they find the prospect scary. Here are a few items that often appropriately appear on the *Sensible* page: dogfights, guns, and traffic jams. Yes, it is smart never to get "smack in the middle of a dogfight."

FINDING YOUR VOICE

I learn from children over and over how critical it is for them to find their own voices. When I introduce the child philosophers to the world of ideas, to wonder, to delight in asking questions, in every classroom at least one child has responded with the following statement: "No one ever asked me what I thought before." In addition, numerous children find it hard to articulate the difficulty of "speaking up," and tell me privately that for some reason they are too afraid to speak in class. When I ask them to explain their difficulty in saying what's on their minds, some answers I have received include: "It's hard to keep your voice firm." "As soon as I get ready to open my mouth, I decide to give up because whatever I say is stupid." "Some kids do all the talking and I can't push myself to join in." These disturbing comments come not always, but mostly, from young girls.

Some parental concerns expressed to me echo the same requests from teachers everywhere I travel to share philosophy with kids. "Is there some way you could talk to my class about girls feeling excluded and being dominated by the boys?" Similar to the need to discuss the damage done by cliques and bullying, I can count on the request to look at the unfolding of restrictive gender roles in the very early lives of children. There is no reason to downplay the seriousness of this problem, any more than inequality based on race or economic disparity. I see the problem firsthand. Boys' hands often go up first and seldom come down, while girls' raised hands frequently go unacknowledged. Certain behaviors, expected and sometimes tolerated in boys, would rarely be accepted in a female student: horseplay and classroom interruptions, for example. A boy is more likely in my experience to question his teacher than a girl is, "without considering whether he steps out of his sphere by indulging such a noble ambition" (Wollstonecraft, *A Vindication of the Rights of Woman*).

Girls testify to the damage that comes from feeling less important than boys. They begin to feel that there are "things I shouldn't even try to do because girls can't do them." Some girls assume that they are weak physically and that certain activities are off-limits: climbing trees, throwing a football, moving the desks for the teacher in class. These perceived physical inabilities are unfortunately complemented quite often by feelings of intellectual inferiority: "Girls aren't good at math," "Girls shouldn't even take shop class," and "Only boys have been presidents so they must be smarter."

With Mary Wollstonecraft's philosophy in my pocket, I am confident that I can address the issue of all children—girls especially—finding their voices. Every adult in the life of a child needs to ask to hear her voice, to listen to her voice, and to create a climate that *encourages* her to discover it perhaps for the first time. In the spirit of philosophy, we can ask individual children more questions: "Do you want to . . . ?" "Are you interested in . . . ?" "What would you like to know about . . . ?" "What would you like to try for the very first time?" As you wait for many answers to such simple questions, you can savor a child finding her voice and exclaiming, as several have exclaimed to me, "I love to hear myself talk!"

I take philosophy to a middle school for girls that was established to encourage girls' unhindered development in math, science, and technology. Too many previous teachers assumed that the girls lacked interest in these subjects, although there was no proof of their lack of inquisitiveness or ability. The two experienced teachers who founded this school also created a liberal arts curriculum that showcases women writers, artists, and inventors.

When I talk with some of these students on an individual basis, they express their joy in the kind of education that Wollstonecraft envisioned for them. "It puts spunk in me." "The more I study," one comments, "the better I can defend what I think in my own words." "I can hold my own" is followed by the quick disclaimer "but that doesn't mean I'm stubborn!" "I . . . will venture to assert that till women are more rationally educated, the progress of human virtue and improvement in knowledge must receive continual checks" (Wollstonecraft, *A Vindication of the Rights of Woman*).

Wollstonecraft's gift of courage is a many-colored prism. Her life and philosophy paint a lifestyle of weakness in cowardly colors. She insists that all students ask hard questions of themselves and of everyone and that they seize the courage it takes to make a problem better. Through the philosophies of both Epictetus and Wollstonecraft, more children feel that in some important ways they are able to take care of themselves. They can be "true to their hearts." Also, they can find the strength to address things they know are wrong and be smart enough to figure out how.

"I must be allowed to ask some plain questions . . ." (Wollstonecraft, *A Vindication of the Rights of Woman*). Having the permission from her to ask questions and to disagree is huge in the life of a child. One liberated second-grader announced that she could go through life with her hand raised to ask questions.

✓ TEACHING TIP: FINDING YOUR VOICE

- Talking about courage is an ideal context in which to teach the children that saying *I don't know* or *I don't understand* is not a sign of weakness. Tell them that, instead, these words will indicate to the people around them that they have a strong desire to learn.

DISCUSSION QUESTIONS: FINDING YOUR VOICE

- Are you interested in an activity that seems off-limits to you because you are a girl? Because you are a boy? Do you have the courage to overcome these limitations as Wollstonecraft did?
- Do you have the courage to be yourself?
- Do you think that it was hard for Mary Wollstonecraft to speak her mind loud and clear? Why didn't she tell herself that life was too hard and give up?

EXERCISES: FINDING YOUR VOICE

- Imagine the courage it takes to make the world that John Lennon "imagines" a reality. Play his song "Imagine" for the kids several times. Children get new ideas every time they hear this tune. Kids agree that the world Lennon pictures is most desirable, and they ponder the line "It's easy if you try." They question why we don't have the courage to try. Have them write their own songs titled "Imagine." Now ask them if *they* will have the courage to try.
- Read John Masefield's enduring invitation to adventure in "Sea-Fever." Let the children share their dreams of future travels and explorations. "I must go down to the seas again, to the lonely sea and the sky, / And all I ask is a tall ship and a star to steer her by . . ." Have them describe in detail what calls to them as the sea does to Masefield. Ask the kids to explain the connection between courage and adventure. Their assignment is to compose a poem titled "I Would Give Anything to . . ."

Real difficulty weighs on narrow shoulders. When the child philosophers voice their fears to me, it is always a sad realization that their problems are so often in their classrooms, in their homes, or on their teams. As eight-year-old Martesha promised, "I'm also trying to keep my courage up when I'm left alone," a fear that this small child mentioned in every session. The little stout hearts want to be strong and smart, and they have taught me over and over that sometimes courage "just means trying again." They have made me ever mindful of the courage that it takes to admit fear and its cause. And it has become very clear to me just how much kids will face difficulty squarely or, in contrast, claim they are powerless, depending on the grown-up behavior they observe around them.

I can also count on lightness and optimism from child philosophers even in a session that includes tears and frustration. Young Jermaine, who had decided to become a full-time philosopher when he was old enough, feared that one day he would need to know how to spell the word *philosophy*. I applauded his first courageous attempt: "F-O-L-L-O-S-O-F-E." One of my all-time-favorite exchanges on courage keeps Miriam's truly miserable face before me as she bemoaned her lack of courage. Apparently she was "foolin' around with something that belonged to my sister" but denied to her mother that she had been using it. As I groped for just the right words of encouragement, Miriam confessed. "I did it. I shaved my legs with my sister's laser." Truth-telling aside, *that* shave of the leg took some courage.

Resources

- *A Vindication of the Rights of Woman* by Mary Wollstonecraft. Miriam Kramnick is a fine editor of this work, written in 1792.

- *Thoughts on the Education of Daughters* by Mary Wollstonecraft. Mary Shelley, author of *Frankenstein,* was her daughter. It seems that Wollstonecraft knew something about her topic!
- *Enchiridion* by Epictetus. He divides this manual into fifty-three very short, numbered sections. Numbers 1, 10, 19, and 43 showcase his core beliefs. The significance of our own attitudes and our responsibility for these attitudes constitute the challenge in numbers 5, 12, 23, 35, and 48. Arrogance is defused in numbers 6 and 33. The mind's ability to overcome illness is shown in number 9. Number 25 reminds us that everything has a price, and number 20 rules out whining if we come up short on payment. Number 20 also places the responsibility for anger on the shoulders of the angry person.
- *Sounder* by William Armstrong.
- *Hansel and Gretel* by Engelbert Humperdinck. CDs are available in both English and German, and there is an inviting performance on DVD with the Metropolitan Opera, Chorus, and Ballet.
- "Hansel and Gretel" by the Brothers Grimm.
- *Lennon Legend: The Very Best of John Lennon* and *Imagine/Give Peace a Chance* by John Lennon. "Imagine" is included in these two collections, among others.
- "Sea-Fever" by John Masefield. This poem is featured in, among other collections, *Sea-Fever: Selected Poems,* edited by Philip Errington.

DEATH

There is nothing to lose.

—SHUNRYU SUZUKI, *Zen Mind, Beginner's Mind*

THE TOPIC

Is there a "right way" to discuss death with a child? Because each child's life is different, you need tremendous flexibility in how you choose to engage kids in dialogue. The most important thing is to listen to the children. As you pay attention, you will be able to adapt to their particular circumstances and concerns. As I listen to the child philosophers talk about their thoughts and emotions concerning death, it feels as if they are moving through a heavy thicket to an open space. Shoulders relax and brows lose their furrows. Kids welcome the opportunity to try to get a grip on death, and they're adamant that it is much more frightening to try ignoring death or wishing it away.

On my last day with any group of child philosophers, each child has tucked into the bottom of a deep pocket the one question for which he or she would most like to have an answer. Regardless of age or locale, by far the most asked question involves the inevitability of death. When will I die? How? Why can't we stop it? What happens? Does anything really die at all? Why won't anybody talk with me about it?

Kids are well aware of different religious perspectives on death. Some accept the views on death that they have been given, and I make sure to create an atmosphere in which these beliefs will be respected. But many of them long to go beyond rehashing familiar explanations. The children as well as innumerable philosophers keep returning to two central concerns: First, how does anyone handle the unbearable grief that loss brings and cope with the longing for one more look? Second, what in the world, or oddly out of the world, happens after death?

Get over your fear of death and live well, the Greek chorus of Socrates, Epicurus, and Epictetus sings. Facing your mortality gives your life passion and urgency, existentialists claim with gusto. End the illusion of being an isolated individual and lose yourself in life, Eastern philosophers invite. Of course, the Dalai Lama laughs, the source of *all* life is nonmaterial and unavailable to our senses. Can matter or energy be created or destroyed, and if not . . . ?

What is the heart of the matter? Is death really a problem or is the problem merely anticipation of it? What survives death? How? In order to help children address these questions, I introduce them to Zen Buddhist master Shunryu Suzuki (shun-REE-oo suh-ZOO-kee), who will point them to the waterfall as a metaphor for the unity of life and death. Our other guide in this exploration of death will be the classic Hindu text the *Bhagavad-Gita* (BAH-gah-VAHD GHEE-tah), which takes us inside ourselves to behold our eternal spirit.

☑ TEACHING TIPS: THE TOPIC

- Let the kids know that it's likely that an analysis of death will lead neither to certain conclusions nor to permanent solutions. Together your goals are to ask good questions, to explore this many-sided issue, and to express ideas and feelings.
- Although with a bit of initial hesitance, children glide willingly into a philosophical discussion of death. Death becomes another subject for their review. However, admit that it can be hard at times for any of us to talk about a topic so close to our hearts. Assure the children that everyone grapples with the confusion and hurt surrounding death. I frequently remind both child and grown-up philosophers that showing emotion is appropriate and, indeed, quite healthy. Your dialogue may stall without this support.
- Be prepared to talk about your own feelings. As you begin your first session, you may want to acknowledge that you have been touched by the sorrow that death brings. You needn't go into detail. Kids appreciate the solidarity they feel with the adult taking them through sensitive issues. Reinforce your identification with the children's experiences as they share them.

? DISCUSSION QUESTIONS: THE TOPIC

- Why do you think many people refuse to talk about death?
- What are some of the ideas that you have heard about what happens after death? What are your very own ideas?
- What is your philosophy about death? What does death mean to you?
- If you think of death as a teacher, what can it teach you?

EXERCISE: THE TOPIC

- Listen to a recording of Samuel Barber's Adagio for Strings. Although Barber did not compose this piece with death in mind, it is played at funerals as well as memorial celebrations. Its solemn beauty wraps its uplifting and comforting notes around you. You can show the children a clip from the funerals of Franklin D. Roosevelt or John F. Kennedy, and they can experience the reverence that the music inspires. At the Kennedy funeral they can see two small children who lost their dad. Ask them why they think the music is such a popular choice to celebrate life and death. Have the children make a list of other compositions that they think would be good choices.

THE PHILOSOPHERS

The light of a lamp does not flicker in a windless place.

—*Bhagavad-Gita*

The *Bhagavad-Gita,* literally "Song of God," was composed by Hindu seers independently of the world's longest epic poem, the *Mahabharata,* into which it was incorporated. It is a perfect fit. Both works were written between the fifth and second centuries B.C.E., and the *Bhagavad-Gita* continues to hold relevance for contemporary Hindus. Its illumination of immortality provides consolation in the face of the inevitability of physical death.

The two central characters in the poem are Krishna, the human incarnation of the divine, and Arjuna, a confused warrior lamenting death on the battlefield. Krishna explains in many ways to Arjuna what he should already know: There will be no death in battle or anywhere else. The soul is infinitely far from death's reach.

The pure light that is the essence of human nature, the Atman, is deathless. The Atman is identical with Brahman, the divine source of being and the infinite ground of spiritual reality. Brahman = Atman, meaning "Thou art That," is the heart of Hindu philosophy. The human spirit is eternal because there is no distinction between the human and the divine. The physical world is a veil that covers the spiritual essence that unites all. Atman = Brahman. You are immortal *now.*

Think of peeling back the layers of an onion, back and back, until you arrive at the invisible center. Human beings have layers as well. Peeling back from external physical appearance to the layers that lie behind, one after the other, takes us to our true nature. This true nature is the Atman, our eternal soul, that always was and always will be. Because death makes its home in the physical world, we *will* fear death if we focus our attention on the body. Arjuna does not experience Atman within himself, and he surely cannot see past the physical manifestation of his kinsfolk and comrades preparing for war. His questions for Krishna help anyone struggling with human mortality. He worries as he looks upon the battlefield at beloved faces in both armies and sees the impending death of teachers, uncles, and friends. Krishna's task is to convince the reluctant warrior that "the truly wise mourn neither for the living nor for the dead" (*Bhagavad-Gita*).

While the physical world is ultimately unreal, it is nevertheless a powerful attraction. Material attachments cling to us, and physical concerns become paramount. By far *the* biggest preoccupation is anxiety over the death of the body. The irony is that the very thing humans desire is in our possession already. "Not wounded by weapons, not burned by fire, not dried by the wind, not wetted by water: Such is the Atman, not dried, not wetted, not burned, not wounded, innermost element, everywhere, always, being of beings, changeless, eternal, for ever and ever" (*Bhagavad-Gita*). What defines each of us never dies. Krishna explains this good news to Arjuna until its truth takes hold.

Each of us must work to evolve spiritually in order to experience the reality of our true self. As we grow in spirit, death slowly and quite naturally leaks from our being. Death becomes irrelevant when its true impotence becomes clearer. "Bodies are said to die, but That which possesses the body is eternal. It cannot be limited, or destroyed" (*Bhagavad-Gita*).

Hindu belief emphasizes that one of two things happens upon death of the physical body: The Atman will be reincarnated and have infinite opportunities to evolve further. Or if the highest state of evolving in the material world is reached, the soul is released from the bondage of thoughts of death and returns to its original fullness within spiritual unity. "Before birth, beings are not manifest to our human senses. In the interim between birth and death, they are manifest. At death they return to the un-manifest again. What is there in all this to grieve over?" (*Bhagavad-Gita*).

Child philosophers are part Krishna and part Arjuna, understanding but not quite, thinking yes and then no. One child compared the Atman to an energy body that "goes along with his physical body." Basically, he explained, that means that "I'm *already* alive forever." On a number of amusing occasions, kids talk about "improving inside themselves," and they act out how hard it would be for death to squirm or wriggle into their full lives. In their twisting and turning, they look much too quick for death. What they like the most is the idea that you can live so that death will be less and less on your mind. "Just as the dweller in this body passes through childhood, youth and old age, so at death he merely passes into another kind of body. The wise are not deceived by that" (*Bhagavad-Gita*).

You may think that when you die, you disappear, you no longer
exist. But even though you vanish, something which is
existent cannot be non-existent. That is the magic.

—SHUNRYU SUZUKI, *Zen Mind, Beginner's Mind*

Suzuki is a spiritual descendant of the legendary Zen Master
Dogen. Already famous in Japan for his wisdom and effective
informal teaching, Suzuki came to the United States for a short
visit to give a series of talks in 1958, a visit that lasted until his
death in 1971. He found Americans eager and receptive to Zen in
his meditation sessions at the Zen Center in San Francisco. The
center expanded in a number of directions, including the Zen
Mountain Center, the first Zen training monastery outside Asia.
Suzuki served as its first abbot.

Suzuki was a marvelous listener and was always available for
question-and-answer sessions with his students. Like Krishna with
Arjuna, Suzuki was patient as he answered the same questions in a
variety of ways until he found an analogy or a description that
rang true for each pupil. Whether in Japan or in America, Suzuki
could count on his students' lingering concerns over death, and
he explained the Buddhist response with endearing humor and
unfailing encouragement.

Acceptance of impermanence is the focal point of Buddhist
theory. The reality of the constantly changing flow of life makes
no exception for the human being. Our names are practical des-
ignations and should not imply a permanent personality that survives moment to moment, much less death. "Every existence is
a flashing into the vast phenomenal world" (Suzuki, *Zen Mind,
Beginner's Mind*). There is no individual *you* or *me* that will experience death. Reality is an everlasting spiritual union in which
everything participates. It is a paradox that defies language and
logic that *you* exist but not as a distinct individual. This Buddhist

truth makes death a meaningless term, but at the price of one's sense of personal identity. Suzuki promises his students, however, that "no matter how you feel about this teaching, it is very important for you to change your way of thinking and a c c e p t the truth of transiency" (*Zen Mind, Beginner's Mind*). Relax, he winks.

The Buddha insists that life in the physical world is characterized by suffering due to separation that begins at birth. Departure from the original bliss of spiritual unity into the solitary experience of life as an isolated being is painful. Our true identity is within the world of the spirit. It requires "big mind" to experience this true nature of unlimited, eternal being. "Big mind experiences everything within itself" (*Zen Mind, Beginner's Mind*). Suzuki calls this big mind a "beginner's mind." With this open, inclusive, embracing mind one can experience life as it *is* without separating from it as an individual. Big mind absorbs the unity of all without distinctions, fully appreciating that there is no *me* to die but only *life to live. All* lives eternally.

Let's accept Suzuki's invitation to go to Yosemite National Park and view from a distance a 1,340-foot waterfall. From this distance we can see the waterfall as one whole curtain of water, and no separate drops of water are discernible. As we hike closer to the waterfall, however, it is possible to see tears in the fabric of the falling curtain. Water sprays in many directions as it hits rocks, shifts with the wind, and splashes in cliff crannies. If we return to our original vantage point from afar, we see once again that there is simply one whole, flowing sheet of water. Our birth as individuals is like becoming a separate drop of water, and all difficulty begins here.

Suzuki's assurance is that death means "to join" again, no longer to be a drop alone, and to return home to live as an indistinguishable part of the larger waterfall itself. Water is made of water. Drops of water are water. Spirit is spirit. Big mind grasps the waterfall from a distance, never getting soaked in the confusion of the splashing and spraying. Our fear of our mortality and the unthinkable loss of who *we* are is nothing compared to the joy of belonging again. "How very glad the water must be to come back to the original river! If this is so, what feeling will we have when we die?" (*Zen Mind, Beginner's Mind*).

The idea of joining and belonging again is very attractive to child philosophers. They appear untroubled that their understanding of the waterfall isn't as clear as their intellectual grasp of other philosophical ideas. "I get it but I can't explain it," they tell me, and as a teacher I know too well the challenge of finding the words to convey the waterfall's secret. Kids' responses to their hike with Suzuki vary. Some feel "lost," while others are "found." They feel connected and that "everything might be okay." Many children find it very curious to think that "life and death are not opposites or enemies." Eight-year-old Matthew, a sad child whose dad had died recently, asked me after class where his dad *is* in the waterfall. My answer on Suzuki's behalf was that you can't point to your father as an individual person, here or there, separate from the waterfall. But, just think, your dad was originally part of the water and he is part of it once again. Before he could finish his next question, he turned it into a statement. He guessed that Suzuki would say that he too will be part of the waterfall one day. "Even though you have difficulty falling upright from the top of the waterfall to the bottom of the mountain, you will enjoy your life" (*Zen Mind, Beginner's Mind*).

One little big mind compared the concept of death as *joining* to the ideal to love your neighbor as yourself. He intuited that somehow he would die as a separate person because "I would be so hooked into my neighbor that you couldn't tell us apart." He was not the first child to glean this similarity between Suzuki's waterfall and Jesus' command. "The goal . . . is always to keep our beginner's mind" (*Zen Mind, Beginner's Mind*).

 TEACHING TIPS: THE PHILOSOPHERS

- Death is among the topics that severely test teachers' abilities to put their personal views aside during a discussion. Be vigilant, or you will sneak up on yourself! Make a special effort in your dialogue about death to welcome the children's ideas and feelings so that each child feels free to speak. Also, make sure the kids have the comfort and security of knowing that they do not have to speak.
- Hang a poster in the classroom depicting the waterfall in Yosemite National Park. Display it in full view as you discuss Suzuki's perspective on death. Kids enjoy collecting photographs of waterfalls to decorate the room with festive reminders of Suzuki's theory.
- Write Brahman = Atman and Atman = Brahman on the board and refer to it throughout your look at the *Bhagavad-Gita*. Meaning "Thou art That," that the human soul is divine, this equation is the thread that holds together the Hindu belief in immortality. Kids are drawn to the idea of Atman = Brahman because it indicates that *their* nature is godlike.

DISCUSSION QUESTIONS: THE PHILOSOPHERS

- Do you feel that there is a part of you that never dies?
- Do you think spirit is real? Is there spirit inside you? Inside anything else?

- If you were in Arjuna's place, what would you like to ask Krishna?
- As you look at and listen to the waterfall with Suzuki, how do you feel? Do you want to talk to him?

 EXERCISE: THE PHILOSOPHERS

- Read *The Velveteen Rabbit*. There is no mention of death in this short story of how a rabbit becomes Real. His velveteen existence as a Boy's companion was all right in its way, but he was becoming "old and worn out." After the rabbit is discarded, the Fairy stops his tears and whisks him away to Rabbitland to play forever and ever with the other rabbits. He can now leap on incredible hind legs and has elegant whiskers "so long that they brushed the grass." Read this tale again to the kids after asking them to think about . . . why the rabbit was at home at last in Rabbitland. Ask them to consider what the Fairy *did* to the velveteen rabbit to make him "changed altogether." As they pay close attention on the second reading, they can look for ways that the Boy helped the rabbit to begin to feel Real. Let them look for wisdom in the Skin Horse. In their philosophy journals, have the children write a detailed description of Rabbitland, including the specific things that make it so great.

NATURE'S WAY

Death is folded within every nook in the universe. The cycles of nature and the loss in our own lives remind us that death is here to stay. We are "aware of the weakness in mortal nature, its bondage to birth, age, suffering, dying . . ." (*Bhagavad-Gita*). The fear, worry, and grief associated with death feel unacceptable, yet we can accept that dying is *apparently* one of the things that humans do along with everything else. Can we grow more comfortable with death if we befriend it just a little?

Grief and acceptance are not mutually exclusive, but it does take a lot of room to accommodate them both. However, "your mind and body have great power to accept things as they are, whether they are agreeable or disagreeable" (Suzuki, *Zen Mind, Beginner's Mind*). Think of the way that animals allow death to approach them, the enviable elegance with which animals move along with the process of dying as part of their lives. Yet . . . elephants mourn the loss of a member of their tribe for days, and geese protect those whose flight falters. "Part of myself is the God within every creature . . ." (*Bhagavad-Gita*). When one of the animals in your family dies, the sadness in the eyes of the other animals matches your own. Acceptance and grief shift in a delicate balance.

Suzuki prompts the children to think of ways that they feel that death is a natural part of their lives. Kids know: "I feel it every birthday when I get older." "Sunset reminds me of dying in a soft way, and winter does too." "I was in the hospital and the pain was really terrible and it felt like it *had* to stop." "If I am really, really disappointed deep down, it feels like something in me dies." "When anything you love with your true heart dies, you feel like you're dying too." Kids know.

The natural world offers a contemplative child inextricable links between life and death. "I don't think anything is ever really *dead*. A *dead* tree is full of life in its own way. Rocks aren't *dead*. Air is *alive*. I have no idea why I think this, but I just seem to know it by being out in the world." Young Lizzie looked around the room to see if someone else had come to this profound realization or if the words really came from her very own mouth. Finding herself the center of her classmates' admiring attention, she threw her hands in the air and watched her fingers make shapes, leaving her insight unclaimed, hovering . . . "That which is non-existent can never come into being, and that which is can never cease to be. Those who have known the inmost Reality know also the nature of *is* and *is not*" (*Bhagavad-Gita*). Lizzie, age seven, rides along in Krishna's chariot.

 TEACHING TIP: NATURE'S WAY

- If you broaden the scope of your investigation to include more than just the human realm, this may make it easier to talk about such an emotional subject. Including seals, trees, and squirrels makes death more a part of things. I bring in a photograph of a black angel fish that graced my aquarium for years, whose soaring and gliding through the water on his last night made it a party for all the other fish.

 DISCUSSION QUESTIONS: NATURE'S WAY

- What are some examples of ways that death is a natural part of life? Can you imagine living in your body forever? Can you imagine blowing out the candles on your cake when you turn 150?
- What are some signs in the natural world of the back-and-forth relationship between life and death? Would spring be possible if everything died in the winter?

 EXERCISES: NATURE'S WAY

- Read aloud Christina Rossetti's poem "Caterpillar." Display side-by-side pictures of a caterpillar and a butterfly. "Spin and die, / To live again a butterfly." Tell the children that you would love to know how in the world this happens as you point from caterpillar to butterfly. Listen closely as they explain it to you. Take them outside for a walk and have them look for life that's sprung from what *appeared* to be dead. Ask them not to copy someone else's idea but to keep looking. Encourage original thinking.

- Sing along with John Denver's "Around and Around." His lyrics take you with him as the sun goes down on all the years that have passed him by. Have the children explore what he might mean when he says that he wants to be *there* when he dies. He sings that the world will continue to go around and around *after* he dies. Chat with the children about this notion—that life goes on despite death. He hopes that thoughts of him will bring a smile after he's gone. Invite the young composers to write songs about someone who has died but who still makes them smile.

AT PEACE

Through our discussions of the Hindu and Buddhist perspectives on death, I see the little big minds becoming more accepting of death's inevitability. Both Krishna and Suzuki turn their attention from death to a focus on living fully as the best way to negate death's power. I encourage the children to talk at great length about how they can make their understanding of death part of their ongoing understanding of life. Peace comes with their realization that they can deal better with death by taking charge of the way that they live. This awareness does not solve death's mystery for kids, and it isn't a cure for their heartache. As you help them draw on the lessons gleaned from Krishna and the waterfall, their ability to respond to death with a measure of peace may increase dramatically. What may or may not happen after death becomes of less concern to them. Arjuna *must* get on with his life, and the waterfall *will* continue to flow. "Without accepting the fact that everything changes, we cannot find perfect composure" (Suzuki, *Zen Mind, Beginner's Mind*).

Child philosophers come to their own resolutions concerning death. While philosophizing helps some kids a lot, others continue to struggle. I encourage the children to use what benefits *them* from our dialogues on the Hindu and Buddhist viewpoints, while reminding them that new understanding need not negate any beliefs that they hold dear. Kids find words for their level of comfort with death in a variety of ways. One budding scientist found satisfaction in her belief that "nothing can ever destroy energy." It seemed quite basic to another young philosopher that "what exists, exists." One child explained that if life and death are mixed up together like a waterfall, "maybe the two are *never, ever* separate." Children enjoy chatting together about the way they feel connected to those they love who have died. It's not important to them exactly how the connection survives, but they often decide that after dying "maybe there's *more* life but just different." One grieving child remarked that he still really missed his mom but was not so nervous about it after our conversations. "The big mind . . . is something which is always with you, always on your side" (Suzuki, *Zen Mind, Beginner's Mind*).

Kids tell me that they can give me some good tips for being more at peace with death if I ever get confused or sad. Here are some of their recipes for peace: "You can cry." "Look at photographs and put them all over your house." "You should tell stories that are really funny to bring back young memories. Like, if your cat dies, you can talk about when you found her as a wild kitten." Thinking that I need more suggestions because I am quiet, not realizing that I am speechless at their sensitive intelligence, the kids give me some parting ideas. I can cook my loved one's favorite food so my kitchen smells just the same, and when I am finished cooking, I can use their "old special" tools to fix things or to dig in the garden. "Sorrow melts into that clear peace . . ." (*Bhagavad-Gita*).

At the conclusion of one of my training sessions, a child explained her views so that even I could understand. She told me that death is just part of my whole entire life and that if I would just live I might not even have a name for death.

"Peace. Peace. Peace" (*Bhagavad-Gita*).

 ## TEACHING TIP: AT PEACE

- Students love show-and-tell. To open our chat about death, I bring a photograph of my childhood friend Carter. I introduce her to the children. Among other comments, they wonder why she doesn't have any wrinkles and if she always smiles so wide. When I tell them that the photograph was taken two weeks before she died, they are happily amazed. I use Carter as an example of a person who loved life and could accept the disease that would cause her death. It is terrific to begin your discussion of death with a photograph of someone in your life who died. This creates an optimistic atmosphere, because the person's presence is alive in spite of death.

? DISCUSSION QUESTIONS: AT PEACE

- Do you agree with philosophers who believe that we can live much happier lives if we can get over our fear of death?
- When has death caused you horrible heartache? Were you able to admit how much it hurt and talk about the pain?

- How can you live so that death is not a big worry? How can you become full of life?
- Do you know anyone who handled dying peacefully? Even with humor?
- Did your philosophical investigation of death help you in any way? Was it hard? What will you remember?
- Do you know someone who is grieving? Can you do anything to support this person?
- How can you remain close to someone you love who has died? Would it help to take a familiar walk or listen to favorite music?
- How can grown-ups make it easier for you to cope with death?
- How can you help grown-ups find more peace about death?

 EXERCISES: AT PEACE

- Invite the staff from your local hospice to come for a luncheon prepared by the child philosophers. Explain the mission of hospice organizations. The kids will enjoy preparing the meal and organizing recess for their guests. This is a way that the children can do something for those who assist people who are dying and their families. It makes them feel as if they are a little part of hospice work. Encourage the kids, if they like, to bring a photograph or drawing of someone or something close to their hearts that has died. At recess they can tell the story of their pictures to expert listeners who share the experience of dying every day.
- Recite John Donne's "Death Be Not Proud." For children who are having a hard time seeing death in a positive light, this poem can help them feel that death can be overcome. Take

each line, one at a time, and use it as fuel for philosophizing about death. "For those whom thou think'st thou dost over-throw / Die not, poor Death; nor yet canst thou kill me." The poet feels that death has no power over life even though it may appear that it does. Have the children write dialogues between themselves and John Donne in their philosophy journals based on their responses to each line of his poem. Donne ends his masterpiece by telling death that it will die while everything else will live. Ask the children for ways that they can defeat death every day. Let them tell you how they can live and what they can do. Ask them to write a poem entitled "Death, You Are a Real Loser."

- Read as a group Cynthia Rylant's *Missing May,* a lovely book that exposes both the excruciating pain of loss and the extraor-dinary power of love that somehow survives death. You and the children can take turns reading so that you become part of the story together. Because her parents are dead, young Summer moves in with one relative after another without anyone truly taking her into their hearts. Finally, her uncle Ob and aunt May give Summer her first home and unconditional love. Six years later, however, Aunt May dies. Summer more than recovers from her grief, and her path through heartache is a memorable lesson. Look at her relationship with Uncle Ob. How wonder-ful to have a friend named Cletus Underwood. Ask the chil-dren what ideas Summer gives them to use in their own lives. Have them picture Summer as a grown-up now. Encourage their imaginations as they write a letter addressed to them-selves that is signed "Love, Summer." In the letter they can express what they think she would tell them about death, about how to handle it, and how she feels about her aunt May.

- Listen to the duet "September When It Comes" sung by Rosanne Cash with her father, Johnny. Their voices join together in the promise that they will face his death together. Father and daughter admit that soon he will be going to a place where he can rest, and that they will let his September into their lives when it comes. Ask your young philosophers what they have to offer to those they love who are getting older. Have the children write their own lyrics for a duet to sing with someone they know and love who is facing September, "when the shadows lengthen and burn away the past."

The reality of death has found an unwanted place in the lives of many child philosophers. They long for the freedom to express their feelings despite the emotional strain of talking about death. Kids know that somehow they will be better in unspoken ways if they speak about it. Whether adults choose to have conversations with children about death or not, children are keenly aware of its inevitability. All that they love is at death's mercy, as is the fragility of their own tender lives. The realization that everyone deals with the sadness and the dreaded anticipation associated with death comforts children, and this sense of camaraderie encourages them to open up and say what is on their minds and in their hearts. "Everything dies. It's strange, but I think that's a nice thought."

It is beautiful to watch kids give themselves wholeheartedly to a close inspection of death. Tears and laughter exchange places regularly, as they move through dialogue with emotions that run the gamut. I admire their ability to tuck their insights into their own private places to use as needed, and then get on with . . . what else but life. It is a privilege to observe children saving their lives by going after death. The word *lifeguard* comes to mind.

Resources

- *Zen Mind, Beginner's Mind* by Shunryu Suzuki. There are countless reasons that this book has sold millions of copies. He discusses death throughout the book, most memorably in "Nirvana, the Waterfall."
- The *Bhagavad-Gita,* translated by Swami Prabhavananda and his student Christopher Isherwood. A timeless embroidery of poetry and prose, this dramatic translation shows why this work is of such significance for Hindus, and it is accessible to any interested reader. Paths and practices for spiritual improvement are laid out for our troubled warrior.
- "Death Be Not Proud" by John Donne. This poem is in most of his collections, including *The Holy Sonnets.*
- "Caterpillar" by Christina Rossetti. Sometimes called "Brown and Furry," her caterpillar finds its wings in *Christina Rossetti: The Complete Poems.*
- *Missing May* by Cynthia Rylant.
- "September When It Comes," by Rosanne Cash and Johnny Cash. This duet is on her CD *Rules of Travel.* The photographs on the cover and the liner notes are thought-provoking as well.
- Adagio for Strings by Samuel Barber. Two possible CDs are *Adagio for Strings* with Leonard Slatkin and the St. Louis Symphony, and *Barber's Adagio,* which includes eight different performances of the Adagio including his choral version, Agnus Dei.
- "Around and Around" by John Denver. He sings this in his early years on the CD *Poems, Prayers, and Promises.*
- *The Crooked Cucumber: The Life and Zen Teaching of Shunryu Suzuki* by David Chadwick. The first part of this biography takes a detailed look at Suzuki's childhood and entrance to the Eiheiji Monastery at the age of thirteen. Thinking Suzuki hopeless, his exasperated teacher nicknamed the future Zen master "Crooked Cucumber."
- *The Velveteen Rabbit* by Margery Williams.

PREJUDICE

Can you imagine someone saying seriously:
"There must be something about tomatoes
because I can't bear them."

—JEAN-PAUL SARTRE, "Portrait of an Anti-Semite"

THE TOPIC

What is prejudice? The roots of the word give us a startlingly effective definition. When we *pre-judge,* we draw conclusions and form opinions without any pertinent information. I make some decisions about you and you about me before we have had any time to get to know each other. It's dangerously quick and easy to locate the things that divide us: perhaps appearance, job, or accent. Being aware of difference is inevitable. Noticing similarities is somehow much harder. Being prejudiced based on difference, however, is not a given. Differences can be interesting and exciting complements to our likenesses.

The human tendency to judge others without solid reason has baffled philosophers from the beginning. Are we not more alike than we are different in our shared humanity? Where is the comfort in the belief that those *other* people are not like me? Why are our preconceptions most often negative and degrading? Is our view of the world so narrow that we fail to see the consequences of denying the full humanity of each individual? Across cultures philosophers join hands in sadness because they know, often firsthand, that it is easier to turn away from suffering when those in pain are not like us. We are more likely to drift toward violence against those who do not live as we do. Lying in a fabricated hammock of smug superiority, we stop caring.

As many of us can recall from our childhoods, so much heartache awaits the tap-dancing boy and the overweight ballerina. Some child philosophers are more aware of bigotry than others, but almost all know that it is lurking about, whether skulking around their dinner table or looming over their soccer team. With a little philosophizing, children reluctantly become aware of the dormant stereotypes nestled in their own psyches. And while they realize that there is no vaccine to prevent this illness in anyone, including themselves, they've expressed to me how eager they are to try to overcome prejudice.

Two twentieth-century philosophers, Gloria Anzaldúa (ahn-sahl-DOO-uh) and Jean-Paul Sartre (zhanh-pohl SAHR-tr), paint in stark colors the damage done by prejudice. Anzaldúa was a Chicana who grew up in the borderlands between Mexico and Texas. With one foot in two very different worlds, she had her identity in neither. At a very young age, Anzaldúa began to learn about the damage inflicted by prejudice. Children can identify with her childhood pain at being ashamed of her cultural background at school and feeling pressure to give up her identity. Taking as examples the people who made up his world in France in the years surrounding the Second World War, Sartre revealed the fear and insecurity that motivate the bigot. Through a look at Sartre's rigorous analysis of prejudice, the children realize how severely bias injures the bigot as well as others.

We can do better.

 ## TEACHING TIPS: THE TOPIC

- Write *prejudice* in large letters on the board. Write *pre*: meaning "before," and *judge*: meaning "make a decision," below the word to make its origin clear.
- Define *stereotype*. A definition one of my students gave me might do: A stereotype is "a great big label one person sticks on another person before they get to know them."
- Encourage the connections among kids who share similar stories of prejudice. I have found that children with comparable experiences of bigotry's cruelty feed off one another's comments, and their mutual confidence grows because of their common bond. It would be much more difficult to tell your story if you were the only lefty confused when lining up to play kickball, for example.
- It makes the kids comfortable if you talk about occasions when you have suffered because of prejudice as well as times that you have lapsed into the snare of stereotypes.

? DISCUSSION QUESTIONS: THE TOPIC

- What is prejudice? Why does it exist?
- What stereotypes do you have in your mind and heart? When did you realize that you had these stereotypes?
- Are some prejudices worse than others? Are some kinds of prejudices okay?

- Are there negative words that you have used to describe a group of people, words that should be eliminated from your vocabulary?
- Do you need to feel superior to other people? Why or why not?
- Do you feel inferior to any group of people? Should you?

 EXERCISES: THE TOPIC

- Read Harper Lee's *To Kill a Mockingbird*. Her classic showcases prejudice and two children who learn its lessons well. Kids admire Tom Robinson's dignity in the face of fatal bigotry, and the courage of Atticus Finch in his legal and emotional defense of Tom. They cheer as young Scout, someone their age, unwittingly disperses a mob when she addresses Mr. Cunningham by name. Kids often remark that they would love to have a protector as "different" as Boo Radley. You can decide how best to handle the unjust criminal charge brought against Tom Robinson, depending on the age of the children. Ask the child philosophers how they feel when the people in the balcony stand as Atticus leaves the courtroom. In their journals, have them make lists of the things that they admire about their contemporaries, Scout and Jem. On the next page, ask them each to write a short story that has a different ending for Tom Robinson. Finally, invite the children to sit on the front porch with Scout, Jem, and Atticus in Maycomb County. Have the kids share their thoughts on the changes that people need to make in their thinking to make sure that Tom Robinson will continue to be safe.
- Read Huynh Quang Nhuong's *The Land I Lost: Adventures in Vietnam*. Children meet someone their age as Nhuong tells sto-

ries about his childhood in the land that he still loves, which was destroyed by war. He wants these tales to unite rather than divide his readers, highlighting human similarities rather than differences. In "Opera and Karate," the tables are turned on prejudice, literally and figuratively, to the surprise of the diners in a restaurant. Joining opera and karate in itself dispels some preconceptions! Ask the children to pretend that they have spent a day with Nhuong as a kid in Vietnam and that it is almost time for bed. Make sure that they have enough time to write descriptions in their diaries of this day, as well as their plans for a day that Nhuong will spend with them. Encourage the kids to think hard about activities that will give their Vietnamese friend a feel for their lives, as well as things that might be fun and remind him of home.

THE PHILOSOPHERS

The Other holds a secret—the secret of what I am.

—JEAN-PAUL SARTRE, *Being and Nothingness*

Jean-Paul Sartre's name is almost synonymous with the existentialist movement that flourished during and after the Second World War. Sartre was active in political and literary circles in Paris and was a major force in French philosophical thought. Writing at sidewalk cafés, with his beret at a jaunty angle, he was a well-known public figure. His intellectual versatility is evident in his work as essayist, novelist, and playwright, and his play *No Exit* is alive in theaters today. Sartre's scholarly pursuits rest on the borderland between philosophy and literature.

Sartre challenges people to create their own lives, without excuse, despite the anguish of uncertainty and heaviness of accepting personal responsibility for one's actions. He recognizes prejudice as a tool used by those unwilling to face this challenge. By denying the full humanity of individuals perceived to be different and flawed, bigots can safely focus on the faults of others rather than their own. Understanding the root of prejudice as fear is the first step in undoing its hold.

Bigots are fearful of others because they are afraid of their own human weaknesses as well as their own potential. "The anti-Semite is afraid of discovering that the world is badly made: for then things would have to be invented, modified and man would find himself once more master of his fate, filled with agonizing and infinite responsibility" (Sartre, "Portrait of an Anti-Semite"). Insecure about their place in the scheme of things and unsure of their identities, bigots are afraid of examining their own possibilities and contributing to their world. The bigot chooses to find security in the permanent, irrational, passionate hatred of a group of human beings. "He has chosen to be all outside, never to examine his conscience, never to be anything but the very fear he strikes in others: he is running away from the intimate awareness that he has of himself even more than from Reason" ("Portrait of an Anti-Semite"). Securing the bigot in a superior position, prejudice grants refuge from personal growth through the vicious denouncement of a group of strangers. At least, if only in this one case, the bigot is better than *those others.* Everything seems set in its proper place.

Safe in their fake superiority, bigots become frightening in their dogged irrationality and therefore go unchallenged. Prejudice gives them permission to dismiss reason and justify exclusion, and everyone suffers as a result. Sartre's personal experience of the Nazi occupation of France, which ran concurrently with the slaughter of the Jews, taught him too well the unthinkable results of prejudice. He was convinced that the nightmare would not end with the war because while today it is the Jew, "elsewhere it will be the Negro, the yellow race . . ." ("Portrait of an Anti-Semite"). Bigots destroy their own humanity as they rob others of theirs, shrinking the vastness of the world to the smallness of their little minds.

The suffering they inflict on others boomerangs back into the bigot's meager life. The bigot's small world comes to revolve around who the *other* is *not* and what the other cannot do, and it becomes the effort of a lifetime to prop up the shaky sense of superiority they have constructed. Bigots force themselves to hold rage and contempt exhaustedly within their beings, and this stains every connection, precluding self-awareness and genuine relationships. Sartre is adamant that bigots' prejudices form their character and taint every aspect of it. Prejudice cannot be isolated. "It is a passion and at the same time a concept of the world" ("Portrait of an Anti-Semite"). A mind-set that casually dismisses human beings makes it absolutely impossible truly to be a good father, teacher, or employer and also . . . makes you a bigot.

Child philosophers respond very quietly to Sartre's focus on the bigot rather than the victim. Realizing that prejudice damages the prejudiced person makes an enormous impact on many of them. How horrible to realize that an abiding prejudice means that you can't be a trusted friend, a reliable student, or a loyal team member because you can turn on anybody, anytime! They quickly recognize, sometimes for the first time, the stereotypes alive in their own minds. Soft voices acknowledge "making fun" of the custodian at school, mocking the "guest speaker's clothes," and refusing to listen to music because it wasn't *mine*. Children hope that their stereotypes . . . that girls can't throw a ball and boys can't sew on a button . . . are not yet harmful, but if you ask the girl with a mitt or the boy with needle and thread, it doesn't look good. Sartre's approach demands introspection, and I've seen kids look around the classroom at one another, some sheepishly recognizing their assumptions of superiority.

The child philosophers I've worked with have had lots of questions for Sartre: "Why do I prejudge and act mean if I don't like it when it happens to me?" Kids seek the assurance that some prejudices are all right, and that it's not a problem if you're prejudiced and keep it a secret and don't do anything. "Isn't it okay to be prejudiced against prejudiced people?" "Can't I think foreigners are aliens and don't belong here and be nice to them?" "Stereotypes can be true, I mean, aren't celebrities good people?" Their facial expressions are priceless as they work through their questions from Sartre's perspective and come up with *his* answer.

Ignorance splits people, creates prejudices.

GLORIA ANZALDÚA, *Borderlands / La Frontera: The New Mestiza*

Anzaldúa was born in 1942 in Jesus Maria of the Valley, Texas, at the time Sartre was active in the French Resistance against the Nazis. She was a cultural theorist, a historical analyst, and a writer of fiction and poetry who insisted that human survival depends upon the interrelationships among different cultures. Her major work, *Borderlands / La Frontera: The New Mestiza,* explores her suffering as a woman of color caught between ways of life that were not her own.

In her passionate Chicano language that she so loved, Anzaldúa cried out against the physical, mental, and emotional borders that separate and divide us. Her teachings at the University of Texas and San Francisco State, among other institutions, as well as her writing, still inspire activist movements to overcome bigotry. Anzaldúa's life showcases the many-layered tangle that bigotry weaves.

Young Gloria Anzaldúa grows up straddling the physical borderland between the United States and Mexico. The geographic and internal place she calls home is a unique mix of the shared experience of several traditions and languages, and her cultural heritage has provided her with a strong sense of herself. She savors the sight of her grandmother cooking in a kitchen infused with wood smoke and the sound of crackling cheese in a red–hot pan. She loves the sound of her language and the rhythm of Chicano music such as bolero and corrido. But prejudice soon makes her ashamed of who she is and what she loves, devaluing the world in which her identity flourishes. Gloria is taught in childhood that Chicano life, different from every culture that surrounds and engulfs it, is inferior. It doesn't fit. It isn't right.

"Borders are set up to define the places that are safe and unsafe, to distinguish *us* from *them*. A border is a dividing line . . ." (*Borderlands / La Frontera*). The borders that distinguish *Gloria* from *them* are clear from the start. When she tells her teacher how to pronounce her name, she is punished for talking back and made to stand in a corner. Suspecting Gloria of speaking Spanish at recess, her teacher raps her knuckles with a ruler upon returning to the classroom. Even her mother wishes that her child would speak English like an American and lose her Mexican accent.

What does this Chicana girl learn at school? She learns that it is the role of an inferior person to accommodate the superior people. She learns that skin color matters, that accents define who you are, and that her language is bogus and her cultural traditions highly suspect. "In childhood we are told that our language is wrong. Repeated attacks on our native tongue diminish our sense of self" (*Borderlands / La Frontera*). There are no opportunities to learn about Chicano traditions and the intricacies of this lilting language. Ignorance reigns, and prejudice does its damage.

Still, Anzaldúa pursues her education and returns home as a teacher of migrant workers. Though the principal of the high school forbids it, she sneaks in Chicano literature to teach English to her Chicano students. Throughout her graduate career, she argues successfully for the legitimacy of Chicano literature as the focus of her research. While refusing to bow down to bigotry, Anzaldúa's struggle against it colors her life. She shows us that the most dangerous borderlands of all are the ones living within the mind, dividing the heart and disqualifying others from running in the biggest race of all: the *human* race.

Kids admire Anzaldúa. Many identify with her homesickness and the horror of being ashamed of who you are. Children squirm at her own mom's insistence that she lose her accent. They long for the chance to tell her what they love best and who their family members are. For the first time, many students tell classmates about the awesome sound of Cuban music or their smiling Korean grandparents or tasty Somalian food. Anzaldúa is the impetus for them to speak up and tell one another about their favorite memories and special loves with pride and without borders. I also have listened to many questions that the kids have for her: "How can you value your own culture and learn about others without borders in your mind?" and "Gloria, do you think maybe there are some things about a culture that need changing?" "What if everybody in this room started speaking a different language at the same time?" This thought makes them burst out laughing and move on to their next flurry of ideas—or, as Anzaldúa would say, evolve. Though she died in 2004, I love picturing her as a little girl in class with child philosophers.

✓ TEACHING TIP: THE PHILOSOPHERS

• Whenever possible, show the children photographs of the philosophers. Pictures of the borderlands and of Paris take the children into the worlds of Anzaldúa and Sartre.

DISCUSSION QUESTIONS: THE PHILOSOPHERS

- If you have a prejudice and keep it to yourself, is it still a problem?
- Do you have a prejudice that you can defend to Sartre? What is your explanation? What do you imagine his response to you will be?
- Do you agree with Sartre when he says that if you have a strong prejudice that you refuse to change, this way of thinking will affect your whole character? If you dislike all Mexicans, is it possible for this bias to change your friendship with your Korean pal? What will happen if you have a Mexican teacher?
- Why do you think that someone who is prejudiced against a certain group of people often becomes extremely angry if someone asks why?
- What would you like to tell Anzaldúa about your childhood? What would you like to ask about hers?
- What is the purpose of physical borders, between states, for example? What is the reason for the borders that exist in our minds that separate people?

EXERCISES: THE PHILOSOPHERS

- Listen to a recording of Roger Miller's musical *Big River: The Adventures of Huckleberry Finn*. Tell the children the story of Mark Twain's Huck and Jim, and read excerpts to provide an engaging background for the music. As they listen to the musical telling of the tale, have them write in their journals what they see and how they feel. Encourage them to create a piece of art that would make a good gift for Jim and Huck. Have them picture the successful production of this musical that included sign language. The characters using sign language for the deaf audience were actually part of the show, and any *borderland* between the deaf and the hearing audience disappeared. Ask the child ren to imagine that Anzaldúa and Sartre are in the audience at this production. Have them write a dialogue between the two philosophers after the show.

- Listen and dance to the Latino music that Ry Cooder uses to bring the vanished community of "Chávez Ravine" back to life. The fifteen tracks, sung in Spanish and English, recall this barrio in Los Angeles during the 1940s and 1950s. The music portrays the destruction of this community to build a baseball stadium and brings the story of those who loved Chávez Ravine alive again. Ask the children to imagine Anzaldúa snapping her fingers to conjunto, corrido, rhythm and blues, jazz, and Latin pop. She is home again as she hears the Chicano legend Lalo Guerrero, the Pachuco bounce of Don Tosti, and the beat of Ersi Arvizu of The Sisters and El Chicano. Cooder fuses cultures as Hispanic and American music alternate. Help the children research how many people lived in the barrio and the capacity of the barrio's replacement, Dodger Stadium. Ask the child philosophers to imagine that they are kids living in the barrio in 1945, and have them write an article for the newspaper explaining why they want the stadium built elsewhere. As they learn more about life in the barrio, let the children develop their own theories as to why this site for the park was chosen. Finally, ask them to write a poem describing how they would feel if they had lived in the barrio during those years and were now hearing their music again.

A VICIOUS CIRCLE

As adults, we see all around us—in our neighborhoods, in the newspaper—the destruction that prejudice leaves in its wake. It seems there is no such thing as harmless or benign prejudice, so easily does it grow and multiply. As Sartre wrote in *Being and Nothingness,* "The triumph of hate is in its very upsurge transformed into failure. Hate does not enable us to get out of the circle." Ask the child philosophers if they agree with Sartre. Does prejudice lead to a vicious circle of hate?

By the age of eight most kids have tasted prejudice as a giver or receiver or both. As I listen to children talk about prejudice, I am reminded of Anzaldúa's words when she describes this moment: "Something is taken from us: our innocence, our unknowing ways . . ." (*Borderlands / La Frontera*). Children are surprisingly up front with their painful recognitions and hurts as they talk about how prejudice has made its way into their lives. "My friends tell me I can't be upset about anything because my parents are rich." "I'm so skinny that people act like I can't be good at basket-ball." "As soon as some people hear my accent, they think I must not understand English." "I fast during Ramadan, and people say it's because I must hate America." Such honesty from an assembly of middle-schoolers is both heart-wrenching and beautiful.

In any life, how much suffering is born of a feeling of inadequacy, of not measuring up, of not belonging? Part of bigotry's dark legacy is the internalization of a sense of inferiority in its victims. Once again, philosophical conversation can lead to understanding and even to healing. Ask the kids you are working with to share their experiences of prejudice and to describe how it has affected them. To begin this part of our discussion, I encourage my students to share the ways that being prejudiced *against* makes them feel inside. Quietly, some children have admitted that they feel "wrong," "stupid," "embarrassed," "ashamed," "scared," and "lonely." One of the most difficult admissions to hear came from a nine-year-old child who said quietly to the group: "I am not right and can't ever be because of who I am." One child described his pain as "like the dustballs in my room that start small and get really big." Jesse, a sixth-grader, found words for the damage done by comparing it to what happened with his mom's foot. After she injured her foot, she made up for it by changing the way she walked. When her foot stopped hurting, she forgot about it. But her new way of walking slowly sneaked up on her and damaged her back. Jesse concluded that "what's scary is that kids are young and don't think about serious stuff much, and all of a sudden you can feel really bad about yourself and have no idea *why*."

I have learned in my exchanges with certain children that internalized feelings of inferiority have had a dramatic effect on their childhoods. On a number of occasions I have heard kids admit their own anger in response to their experience of discrimination. Some have described their anger as "all bottled up," "making me sick," and "taking me over." Being angry at the world can explode into others' lives, as this frank admission by a fourth-grader reveals: "I was always nice, but when I went to a new school, I couldn't make friends because everybody said since I was fat I was lazy and dumb. It happened all the time, and it made me so furious that I started to stomp on bugs and pick on the little kids." One candid third-grader stated that "I got in a fight at recess because someone told my sister that black girls make good maids." A child recently released from time-out explained to me that "I was rude to the teacher because I'm mad that my best friend can't come over to play just because we live in a trailer." The child philosophers' testimony is proof that prejudice is a hideous source of suffering, and that further suffering can be caused by the anger of those who are injured by it. Once you have spoken with your group about their experiences with prejudice, be sure to conclude your discussion by noting that prejudice breeds prejudice in a vicious circle—and ask them how they think they might be able to help put an end to the cycle.

 TEACHING TIPS: A VICIOUS CIRCLE

- Give them time. Some of the children may tiptoe around this discussion at the beginning because it makes them look in the mirror and close to home. I find that they will work their way to their own trouble spots and hurtful places at their own pace, in their own way.
- Express empathy for every child's suffering and then move on so that the child does not linger unproductively in self-pity.
- Help the children spot stereotypes in their textbooks as well as in their weekend or vacation reading. You can raise their awareness by asking them what they notice in a particular paragraph in their geography book, or the sample questions for discussion at the end of a poem or short story. As a teacher or parent, you'll find it worth the effort to make sure that what they are reading does not reinforce stereotypes.

 DISCUSSION QUESTIONS: A VICIOUS CIRCLE

- What harm comes from prejudice? Use both your personal experience and your imagination.
- Is prejudice contagious like the flu? Why or why not?

- Do you think it is worthwhile to try to get rid of prejudice? Do you think that it will always exist?

 EXERCISE: A VICIOUS CIRCLE

- Read Carl Sandburg's "Choose." In this powerful four-line poem Sandburg presents Sartre's theory that whether or not to be prejudiced is a choice we make. Sandburg vividly presents to children's imaginations a fist raised in anger waiting to strike, and contrasts the fist with an extended hand willing to clasp another. He suggests that we meet another person in one of these two ways. Talk with the kids about the reasons someone chooses a raised fist or an extended hand. Ask the children to write a poem in response to Sandburg titled "When We Meet."

HEALING THE WOUNDS

You will find in your discussions of prejudice that it is not easy to look at the damage done. Some of the conversations about it are among the most painful you will have with your child philosophers. But I find that as our talks continue, little big minds grow increasingly confident that awareness can begin the process of healing. I remind them from time to time throughout our discussion that clear thinking shines a brighter light on everything we talk about, especially on the lack of clear thinking that leads to prejudice. "Awareness of our situation must come before inner changes, which in turn come before changes in society. Nothing happens in the 'real' world unless it first happens in the images in our heads" (*Borderlands / La Frontera*).

Children are eager to look for solutions and get past the damage exposed in our dialogues. I tell them that our first exercise has two steps. First, I entice them by telling them that we are going to brag about ourselves a bit. They can't believe it! To their surprise, however, they discover that the "bragging" will be about our many individual shortcomings. I begin by announcing proudly that it is almost impossible for me to subtract fractions accurately. As we try to outdo one another by naming our weaknesses, most child philosophers quickly recognize the silliness of *anyone* adopting a feeling of superiority. I then tell them it's time for our second step, which is their opportunity to name a personal strength. Their long list of positive attributes helps many to see that a feeling of inferiority is just as unnecessary as the reverse. Child philosophers can feel the weight of prejudice lifting as we move with optimism toward getting past it.

Sartre's portrayal of the bigot encourages children to want more for their lives than false superiority. Analyzing the bigot's fears brings most kids to the realization that "even though it's easy to make excuses for being prejudiced, once you understand what prejudice is and does, it's obvious that you can't." Anzaldúa urges them to make the effort to change for the better. "I change myself, I change the world" (*Borderlands / La Frontera*). Child philosophers have offered countless ways that they can improve their thinking so that they avoid being hurt themselves by prejudice and avoid inflicting pain on others. "I can stop trying to change *other* people." "I should try harder to get to know people." "I need to remember to feel good about myself. I think that would take care of this problem." "Well, I'll tell myself that either everybody's weird or no one is." These third-graders offer real solutions so simply.

Children can describe vividly the unnecessary borderlands we create: mutt/purebred, old/young, sick/healthy, my church/any other, human/everything else. Is difference a good reason for building borders? I talk with child philosophers about whether or not it is possible *not* to notice difference. I ask them, for example, if it could escape their attention that some people are much older than they are. Is it possible not to recognize any difference between being seven and seventy-seven? Can you still be friends? Can you learn from each other? Can you share a hobby? At the heart of our dialogue is the question, not of whether difference *exists,* but rather if difference *matters.* The child philosophers and I have decided together that what's important is *how it matters.* If we tear down the borders between us, our differences can enhance our appreciation for the many expressions of life. Kids have told me that you can notice what's different, and being different can be great. For example, "Because you're tall and I'm short you can carry me in the three-legged race." "Since I'm good at math and you're good in English, we can study together." "Well, you can drive and I make you laugh, so let's go out for ice cream."

 ## TEACHING TIPS: HEALING THE WOUNDS

- Enjoy foods from different cultures with the children, and invite the kids to join a native chef in preparing the meal, if possible. With music from this culture accompanying cooking and eating, prejudice doesn't stand a chance. (No upturned noses are allowed!)
- Invite your child philosophers or adults who speak Spanish, Russian, or Chinese to read aloud in their language. Rather than being perceived as different or wrong, another language can be appreciated for its unique rhythm and structure when fluently recited by a native speaker. You can follow their reading by reciting the same passage in English and allowing the two languages to complement each other. International organizations at colleges or senior centers are great places to find willing speakers.

- Playing music of all kinds regularly is a subtle and powerful antidote for prejudice. Introduce the children to the Spanish Harlem Orchestra at the start of the day, and as they pack their bags, let Johnny Clegg and his South African band move their feet and hearts.

 ## DISCUSSION QUESTIONS: HEALING THE WOUNDS

- Why is it helpful to keep your limitations in mind when examining prejudice? What are some things that you don't know and can't do?
- How can you see beyond your current way of looking at the world so that you can understand other lifestyles, cherished traditions, and values?

 ## EXERCISES: HEALING THE WOUNDS

- Read aloud from *Dream Keeper and Other Poems* by Langston Hughes. Explore racial reality in the United States in 1932 with the child philosophers. This poetry speaks to children, as Hughes intended, as if it were for and about them. Kids feel a part of these rhythmic poems that sing the blues of pain and struggle along with the beat of hope for a better day. After reading "Youth," have them write a poem of a "tomorrow bright before us." After time for reflection on "I, Too," ask the children what they may have missed that is beautiful in their lives. In "Aunt Sue's Stories," a "dark-faced child, listening, / knows that Aunt Sue's stories are real stories." Ask the children to imagine that A u n t Sue is rocking them in her lap, and have them write poems in response to her. Invite the kids to meet you at the carnival and wonder with you how merry the "Merry-Go-Round" can be if "white and colored / can't sit side by side." Join the kids in writing a group poem of a different and better ride at the carnival. Go around the room and let each child recite a line of "Daybreak in Alabama." After a second group reading, let everyone become the composer of a song about daybreak when everybody can touch "each other natural as dew."

- Create a unique experience of sameness/difference for the child philosophers. For example, I invited Somali children from city schools to join students at a school in the Virginia countryside for games and lunch. I encouraged the Somali children to bring their favorite foods from home, which included flat bread, a chicken and rice dish with a variety of vegetables, and tasty fried corn. The Virginia students volunteered to provide water, juices, fruit, and ice cream. The Somali child philosophers taught their hosts about their lives in a Kenyan refugee camp and were made to feel most welcome. A final game of soccer and volleyball dissolved any borders between their cultures.

- Give each child two weeks to learn five words in another language from a native speaker. Ask them to find out what each word means and how to pronounce it correctly. Let them pretend that they are journalists conducting interviews. Using their philosophy journals as their reporter's pads, have them take notes on what they learn about this culture. For example, have them find how three different traditions are observed, how birthdays are celebrated, and how the elderly are cared for. Encourage the kids to look around them for possible interviewees. They can be classmates, neighbors, or teachers.

Philosophizing with children convinced me of the urgent need to grapple with the issue of prejudice while they are young. Kids want the room to question bigotry and talk about it in detail because they see and hear it all too early. Adult credibility requires vigilance in grown-up lives . . . guarding against passing on stereotypes and judgments through teaching materials, parental expectations for their children, overheard conversations, and keenly observed behavior patterns. As children talk more about prejudice, I see them learning to hold difference and likeness together comfortably, and slowly kids are able to transfer this ability to more and more situations. With their heightened awareness of prejudice, kids are more likely to watch over themselves whether or not they enjoy the demands of their new insights. "'Knowing' is painful because after 'it' happens I can't stay in the same place and be comfortable. I am no longer the same person I was before" (Anzaldúa, *Borderlands / La Frontera*).

Kids make sure that I know that it is far from pleasant to examine the biases they have as well as the painful occasions when bigotry has come their way. Still, with their reliable resilience, they bring welcome humor and humility to this hard topic. One child philosopher told me laughingly that people should "wait until I give them a reason not to like me. No one would ever have to prejudge me because there are so many problems with my personality!" A struggling second-grader, silent during several dialogues about prejudice, sat up straight to announce his solution to the problem: "All we need to do is to remember that everybody is handicapped in their own way."

Resources

* *To Kill a Mockingbird* by Harper Lee.
* *The Land I Lost: Adventures in Vietnam* by Huynh Quang Nhuong.
* *Water Buffalo Days* by Huynh Quang Nhuong. An invitation for a buffalo ride gives kids further glimpses into Vietnamese childhood.

- *Dream Keeper and Other Poems* by Langston Hughes. This edition contains seven additional poems and black-and-white illustrations by Brian Pinkney. "Merry-Go-Round" and "Daybreak in Alabama" are two striking additions.
- *Chicago Poems* by Carl Sandburg. "Choose," in this collection, is among the many poems ideal for a discussion of prejudice.
- *Big River: The Adventures of Huckleberry Finn* by Roger Miller. You can enjoy the CD of the original 1985 Broadway Cast Recording.
- *Chávez Ravine* by Ry Cooder.
- *Borderlands / La Frontera: The New Mestiza* by Gloria Anzaldúa. Anzaldúa mixes poetry with prose and Spanish with English in a way that encourages readers to appreciate all of it. The preface is a powerful introduction to the reality of this Chicana woman.
- *Prietita Has a Friend / Prietita tiene un amigo* by Gloria Anzaldúa. This is the first of Anzaldúa's three bilingual books for children.
- *Friends from the Other Side / Amigos del otro lado* by Gloria Anzaldúa. This second book introduces us to Joaquin and is a powerful depiction of his experience with prejudice as an immigrant child.
- *Prietita and the Ghost Woman / Prietita y la llorona* by Gloria Anzaldúa. You can find a healer and captivating artwork in this book, as well as an occasion to look at Chicano folktales.
- *Hatred, Bigotry and Prejudice,* edited by Robert M. Baird and Stuart E. Rosenbaum. Jean-Paul Sartre's essay "Portrait of an Anti-Semite" is included in the section entitled "What Is Hate?" This anthology looks at the definitions, causes, and possible solutions for prejudice. "Portrait of an Anti-Semite" is also in *Existentialism from Dostoevsky to Sartre,* edited by Walter Kaufmann. Sartre's "Portrait" is a stinging indictment of anti-Semitism in particular and prejudice in all its many forms.
- *Existentialism* by Jean-Paul Sartre.
- *Being and Nothingness* by Jean-Paul Sartre.
- *Across 110th Street* by the Spanish Harlem Orchestra, featuring Ruben Blades. "Un Gran Día en El Barrio" moves the children's feet

to the salsa, samba, tango beat of this CD and is a nice complement
to Ry Cooder's music.

• *Cruel, Crazy, Beautiful World* by Johnny Clegg. Clegg's convictions led
him to fight apartheid in South Africa through his lyrics and multi-
racial band, Savuka. He follows his social protest in "One (Hu)man
One Vote" on the title track with his hope for a better life for his
children.

GOD

To thirst after a comprehension of things as
they really are was my habit and custom from
a very early age. It was instinctive with me,
a part of my God-given nature, a matter
of temperament and not of my choice
or contriving. Consequently as I drew near
the age of adolescence the bonds of mere
authority ceased to hold me and inherited
beliefs lost their grip upon me, for I saw
that Christian youths always grew up to
be Christians, Jewish youths to be Jews
and Muslim youths to be Muslims.

—*The Faith and Practice of Al-Ghazali*

THE TOPIC

Philosophy thrives on asking fundamental yet elusive questions.
Our minds want desperately to understand the big picture. What
doesn't change or die? What is the source of life that seems to be
calling everything home? Is anything perfect and complete? Is
there an explanation for existence in its totality? What is that

something more that dangles beyond the reach of our minds? Is there a god? Is there more than one god?

Through the ages, philosophers have thrilled at the contemplation of the question of god. They also have examined the reality that personal beliefs about this particular topic can lead to argument and sometimes to violence. What happens? Why do humans invest in one belief and exclude all others from consideration? Why do we reject and label as wrong any viewpoint other than our own? The child philosophers I have spoken with about the concept of god find this obstinacy incredible.

Children often fear even saying the word. They sense that their inquiries about god may not be welcome. Perhaps a grown-up will become angry at them for asking the wrong question. Maybe it is inappropriate to ask any questions whatsoever. Their young minds can guess why talk of prejudice and death may be taboo, but the forbidden nature of talking about god is confusing. Who could be embarrassed about this topic, as they might be with a look at prejudice? Why would anyone be afraid to talk about it, as sometimes happens with talk of death?

There may be kids from various religious backgrounds in your classrooms, and many families share strong belief in a particular religious faith. I make it clear at the outset that respect for individual religious values is understood. In introducing this topic to children, a topic that most often they bring up before I do, I make it clear that as philosophers we will analyze the *idea* of god as one idea among the many concepts that we discuss. Children's eagerness to discuss what this concept brings to their minds usually leads to very rich philosophical dialogue. I explain to them that when philosophers investigate the meaning of this idea, they stretch to push past the limitations of the human mind and to go after their highest thought. I remind them that there is a great variety of religious beliefs in the world, and that our efforts will not be to prove or disprove people's faith in their God. Instead, we will explore the hugeness of an idea that appears to captivate almost every human being. We have a world, not nothing, they muse. Why? How? This curiosity moves their minds toward the question of god.

In my experience, when students of philosophy see the word *god*, their personal beliefs and prior associations with a particular god come immediately to mind. These preconceptions shadow open conversation and make free dialogue very difficult. I use a lower-case *g* to remind the child philosophers that the *idea* of god is open for investigation and discussion. That small *g* is a help in putting aside preconceived ideas and beliefs and thereby allowing enjoyment of the dialogue regardless of religious background. Acceptance of a variety of ideas then happens naturally, just as with the topics of friendship, justice, or time. Tolerance is a subtle and magnificent by-product of this free philosophical exchange. The wonder of god increases. Far from showing a lack of respect, that small *g* is a bow of reverence to the grand mystery of god.

I ask the following question every time I introduce the concept of god to children, and I repeat it several times. "When you hear the word *god,* what comes into *your* mind?" Hands go up and down and up and down, but I wait for the kids to settle and focus on that exact question only. Many have told me they think of the earth. Others have said, "Trouble, because it's a word no one is supposed to say." Some declare at the outset that their minds are too little to figure god out and I tell them that's all right. "God is a He/She," said one child, while his classmate offered that "god is *It*." I encourage a wide variety of responses from the little big minds, and I keep reminding them to ask good questions and try to imagine the countless ways of thinking about the idea of god.

Saint Thomas Aquinas (uh-KWINE-us) and Abu Hamid Muhammad al-Ghazali (al-guh-ZAH-lee) will take us on their paths to understand that "something more." Aquinas, a Dominican monk, explores nature with his senses. Who made this world? He finds clue after clue that point to the existence of the Christian God. Al-Ghazali, as well, tries hard to use his senses and his mind to know God. He learns nothing. As a Sufi Muslim, he longs for direct contact with God. He wants to experience the fusion of his human being with God's Being.

Aquinas is on special assignment from the pope in the thirteenth century. Al-Ghazali is a solitary seeker in the eleventh century. Children so want an infusion of special understanding when it comes to the meaning of god. Together, Aquinas and al-Ghazali stimulate young philosophers' imaginations.

 TEACHING TIPS: THE TOPIC

- Remember that children want to talk about the concept of god. It may not be easy to listen attentively and encourage their dialogue without directing it, especially if you have your own specific religious beliefs, but your openness is the key.
- Consider your classroom as a think tank for children's exploration of the magnitude of this idea. Philosophy encourages passionate dialogue about the concept of god, with dispassionate objectivity. Separation of church and state ensures that particular religious beliefs will not be imposed on others. In the public school system, this legislation prevents any coercion or enforcement of one religious view on students.
- Be sure to open your discussion with the one question that serves me so well: "When you hear the word *god*, what comes into your mind?"

DISCUSSION QUESTIONS: THE TOPIC

- Is there anyone who doesn't wonder about god? Who? Where? What *do* they wonder about?
- What is the source of human curiosity about god?
- Who is the one person with whom you would most like to talk about god?
- How much do you think you can know about the nature of god?

 EXERCISES: THE TOPIC

- Listen to the sounds of the New Orleans gospel singer Mahalia Jackson. "How sweet the sound," indeed! Listening to "Amazing Grace," see if the children know how human vocal cords create Mahalia's sound. Ask them what they think grace is. Hearing Mahalia sing "I'm Going to Tell God," ask the young beat-keepers what they have to say to God. Give them time to describe their own forever home as they listen to "In My Home Over There." Children love to sing along with her rendition of "He's Got the Whole World in His Hands." No need for philosophizing, just get in line and dance with them to "When the Saints Go Marching In." Martin Luther King Jr.'s love for her music touched all those at his funeral as she sang his favorite, "Precious Lord." Have fun with Mahalia and the children.
- Listen as those saints go marching in once again, this time accompanied by Louis Armstrong's froggy voice and his trumpet. Celebrate the New Orleans jazz tradition with the children. Maybe they are up for a mild version of jambalaya or

gumbo. Ask the children if they can explain how Louis teaches that trumpet to talk. Where do they think talent comes from? Check with them to see if maybe it's enough to know that the world exists, not why, and to revel in all its wonder. "What a Wonderful World." Listen to Louis! Give the children plenty of time to write the lyrics to their original rendition of a song entitled "What a Wonderful World." They have the freedom to choose who they would like to sing it and what instrument they would like for accompaniment.

THE PHILOSOPHERS

Now because we do not know the essence of God, the proposition is not self-evident to us, but needs to be demonstrated by things that are more known to us, though less known in their nature—namely, by His effects.

—THOMAS AQUINAS, *Summa Theologica*

As a theologian, Thomas Aquinas specialized in the philosophical analysis of the nature of God and God's relation to the world. One of the greatest thinkers of his time, he interpreted and refined Christian doctrine in the thirteenth century. Born in the Italian town of Aquino, Aquinas trained to become a Dominican monk at the University of Paris. It was there that he earned his doctorate in theology, studying with the legendary scholar Albertus Magnus.

The works of the ancient Greek philosopher Aristotle were rediscovered in the late Middle Ages, and these findings were a hot topic in intellectual circles. The Catholic Church did not want to lose any believers in the excitement over Aristotle's views, which include belief in neither the personal God of Christianity nor human immortality. It was Aquinas's huge job to reconcile Aristotelian theories from ancient Greece with the explication of Christian dogma. Referring to Aristotle as "The Philosopher," Aquinas uses Aristotle's emphasis on the importance of empirical evidence to offer the creation of the world as proof for the existence of God as its cause. The Thomist tradition is a dominant force in Catholicism today, and the five proofs are debated still.

It is clear from his writings that the physical world makes sense to Aquinas. There are no inexplicable phenomena, nothing arbitrary, and certainly no flukes. In this quite Aristotelian view of the universe, great emphasis is placed on organizing a structured understanding of the world based on empirical data. There is a reason for everything, an explanation and cause determined for each event. Guided by his reliance on observable cause and effect, Aquinas examines the existence of the universe to point to the presence of God. "The existence of God, in so far as it is not self-evident to us, can be demonstrated from those of His effects which are known to us" (*Summa Theologica*).

Aquinas knows that his investigation will not convert a nonbeliever and recognizes that a gap remains between the clues for God's existence found in the world and incontrovertible proof. His focus is to support Christian faith by offering a sound rational link between the created universe and its Creator. The five proofs are similar and weave together to strengthen Aquinas's case. Pick a spot outdoors, if not physically then at least a place in nature to rest mentally. It is this world that Aquinas offers as proof for God's existence in the following five arguments: motion, causation, necessity/possibility, gradation, and governance.

The world is full of movement. The wind moves the leaves on the trees and blows through human hair and dog fur. Children, trains, and rivers run. Aquinas asks that you trace one motion back to what caused it to move, then look at what caused that one to move, and trace motion all the way back to the first motion that gave the world its start. It is nonsensical to suggest that there can be an infinite regress of motion. Similar to a footrace and a concert, the world must have a starting point. God is the "Unmoved Mover," responsible for the beginning motion that continues in the world today. "Therefore, whatever is moved must be moved by another. . . . But this can not go on to infinity, because then there would be no first mover. . . . Therefore it is necessary to arrive at a first mover, moved by no other; and this everyone understands to be God" (*Summa Theologica*).

Aquinas's second proof based on causation is much like his analysis of motion. The natural world holds together through a tight chain of cause-and-effect relationships. Rain causes vegetables to grow and cold is the cause of a bear's hibernation. Trace this chain back to see what caused this and what caused that, and push it all the way back until the chain stops at the effect that is the universe. It would be odd to think that cause and effect applies throughout the world without being applicable to the world itself. God is the First Cause, the Cause that is not itself caused by anything outside Himself. The world is the effect of God. "There is no case known (neither is it, indeed, possible) in which a thing is found to be the efficient cause of itself. . . . Therefore it is necessary to admit a first efficient cause, to which everyone gives the name of God"(*Summa Theologica*).

The necessity/possibility proof received the most attention in Aquinas's time and continues to enthrall professional and child philosophers today. Hold on! As you look at the world, Aquinas asks that you think of all events as having either necessary (*must be*) or possible (*may be*) status. What is necessary for the world to exist? This woodpecker, that mountain range, and even your mother exist as possibilities that were actualized but were not essential for the world to exist. Those are *may be* examples. As the search for things that are necessary for the existence of the world intensifies, not even one necessary being can be found. "Therefore, not all beings are merely possible, but there must exist something the existence of which is necessary" (*Summa Theologica*). Indeed, what about the world itself? Was it absolutely necessary for the world to exist? Aquinas concludes that the world itself is not a necessity. There could be nothing. A Necessary Being must exist that actualizes the possibility of the world as we know it. If everything were a possibility at the same time, contingent on something else for its existence, there would be nothing. "Therefore, if everything can not-be, then at one time there was nothing in existence. Now if this were true, even now there would be nothing in existence, because that which does not exist begins to exist only through something already existing" (*Summa Theologica*). Whew.

Next, Aquinas points out that there are different gradations of being in the natural world. A plant has actualized more potential than a rock, an anteater has more realized being than an amoeba, and a human is the most actualized instance of being in the universe. The human ability to reason crowns this ascending hierarchy of *isness*. It is clear, however, that humans squander potential and experience limitations and imperfections. There must be a fully actualized, complete Being that is the measure of the qualities of all beings. "Therefore there must also be something which is to all beings the cause of their being, goodness, and every other perfection; and this we call God" (*Summa Theologica*).

Finally, while it is not surprising that reasonable beings can plan their lives, the order exhibited as the planets orbit the sun and as a pig's heart pumps blood through its body is quite curious. The march of ants and the workday of bees have clear designs. Surely humans cannot prod an acorn to turn into an oak tree. "We see that things that lack knowledge, such as natural bodies, act for an end . . . designedly. . . . Therefore some intelligent being exists by whom all natural things are directed to their end" (*Summa Theologica*). God is responsible for the flawless governance of the world. The observable order is His order.

Children engage with Aquinas almost immediately. Many tell me that his proofs remind them of their own thoughts and lead them to new ideas as well as some questions for *him*. As Aquinas's representative, I can count on being asked who made God every time I begin a discussion of this topic. It's a wonderful question, and when I tell them that Aquinas suggests that God is the cause of Himself and no one *made* God, they giggle, pull baseball hats down to cover their faces, and tell me that I just said something really weird. The governance proof reminds some kids that they think of God as beauty. It's the third proof that thrills them. *Nothing?* Their minds tumble out of their bodies. One child philosopher especially loved this proof because she said that it makes *nothing* seem so full of power.

The little big minds I have met would have given this Dominican monk a lot to think about with their questions. They want to know why he thinks that God is outside the world. Any child who really loves an animal wants to know why he places humans at the top of nature's hierarchy. Some question why there *must* be a beginning. I cannot imagine Aquinas's reply to the query of whether or not his proofs will work for anybody's concept of god.

> After that I examined my motive in my work of teaching,
> and realized that it was not a pure desire for the things of God,
> but that the impulse moving me was the desire for an influential
> position and public recognition. I saw for certain that I was
> on the brink of a crumbling bank of sand and in imminent
> danger of hell-fire unless I set about to mend my ways.
>
> —*The Faith and Practice of Al-Ghazali*

Abu Hamid Muhammad al-Ghazali was born in 1058 in Persia, an area currently identified as eastern Iran. He was the central figure in the development of Muslim thought in the Middle Ages. He taught Islamic theology at the University of Baghdad. Despite his success as a scholar and a teacher, al-Ghazali suffered a spiritual crisis that led him to retire from the university and live an austere and solitary life. Regardless of his success in the academic community, al-Ghazali's need to discover certainty whenever possible, but most especially in the case of God, never left him. This thirst for certainty was the foundation and motivation of his spiritual path. He turned to the mysticism of the Sufi tradition in Islam, and with his restlessness resolved through devotion to this approach to spirituality, he eventually returned to teaching.

He knew that his intellectual effort to understand the nature of God dead-ended at the limits of human reason. Knowledge based on the senses, similar to Aquinas's five proofs, also fell short for al-Ghazali. His search was for truth beyond doubt. The mystical experience of union of the human with the divine, of al-Ghazali with Allah, granted him this infallible truth. In this immediate contact he experienced certainty about God's nature. Al-Ghazali's journey was a long one.

Al-Ghazali begins with an incisive inquiry into the foundation of his knowledge. He reexamines how he acquired knowledge, and with certainty as his guide, his plan is to eliminate any source of knowledge that contains even a shred of doubt. He admits that he has accepted the testimony of his senses with very little scrutiny and therefore challenges their reliability. The sun looks so small to human eyes, but this is clearly an illusion. Shadows, as well, play tricks on human perception. And it is in dreams that our senses mislead us entirely! With sensory evidence discarded as a source of certain knowledge, al-Ghazali next probes the first principles that serve as the basis of pure mathematics and science. He wonders if there is any possible reason to doubt that ten is more than three. No, well, maybe . . . what about the source of those first principles? he muses. Perhaps if human intellectual powers were finer, these formerly self-evident principles would be seen to be erroneous. Even though al-Ghazali's faith in Allah's benevolence ultimately restores the validity of the first principles, math and science do not constitute the kind of knowledge that his whole being longs for. He wants to know God. "It was plain to me that sure and certain knowledge is that knowledge in which the object is disclosed in such a fashion that no doubt remains along with it, that no possibility of error or illusion accompanies it, and that the mind cannot even entertain such a supposition. Certain knowledge must also be infallible . . ." (*The Faith and Practice of Al-Ghazali*).

Al-Ghazali retreated from public life, leaving the university to live an ascetic life in order to purify himself of his attachments to the material world. He found direction in the Sufi tradition, which has at its core the promise of the ecstatic union of the human being with Allah. For his being to merge with the Divine, al-Ghazali embarks on the path of becoming a proper receptacle for God. Through spending a considerable amount of time in the desert, he works first on bodily purification. This earnest and relentlessly rigorous discipline leads to the purification of his heart of any considerations other than spiritual repose. Al-Ghazali must empty his mind and heart of any material concerns to make possible the clarity of the intuitive experience of the Divine. "I knew that the complete mystic 'way' includes both intellectual belief and practical activity; the latter consists in getting rid of the obstacles in the self and in stripping off its base characteristics and vicious morals, so that the heart may attain to freedom from what is not God and to constant recollection of Him" (*The Faith and Practice of Al-Ghazali*).

Al-Ghazali achieves certain knowledge of the highest truth. It is with humility before Allah and reverence for the beauty of the experience that he refuses to discuss it. It would diminish the reality of "complete absorption in God. . . ." When the human heart contains only God, "it is hard to describe in language; if a man attempts to express [it], his words inevitably contain what is clearly erroneous" (*The Faith and Practice of Al-Ghazali*). That is All.

Kids think it's pretty neat that al-Ghazali quit his job to figure things out. They say that they feel this way about school sometimes. A few do wonder, however, what happened to his kids when he went off to the desert, and it is a relief to learn that he provided for them and did return to the university. Their understanding of intuition is appropriately direct. Kids tell me that intuition means "in your face," that "there is no static on the biggest screen of all," and that "you know the truth without thinking anymore." They exude confidence in their grasp of the mystical as well. A mystical experience is "a perfect connection," it is "absolutely total," it "wraps everything in one," and "by the way, it actually happens."

The child philosophers do not shy away from their effort to describe al-Ghazali's indescribable experience. They say that in the mystical union "he experienced peace," that "God is in him," and that al-Ghazali was "able to make sense of *It.*" *It?* I ask them. *It,* they answer.

 TEACHING TIPS: THE PHILOSOPHERS

- The word *intuition* and the phrase *mystical experience* may require definitions. You can define *intuition* as direct understanding

with nothing standing between you and what you understand. There is no doubt and you know the truth immediately. For al-Ghazali, a mystical experience is the union of a
human being with God. There is no separation, and the two
become one.

- Be sure to show the children photographs of both the University of Paris and the University of Baghdad. It's interesting for
them to see where Aquinas and al-Ghazali went to work. I've
learned never to pass anything around during conversation.
Concentration on the dialogue evaporates.

- It helps the children to visualize Aquinas's motion and causation proofs if you draw a chain of arrows horizontally on the
board and trace them all the way back to the beginning of
the world. The final arrow points to God. A chain of vertical
arrows with humans at the top of the ladder clarifies the proof
based on gradations.

 ## DISCUSSION QUESTIONS: THE PHILOSOPHERS

- Do you agree with Aquinas that humans are the highest forms
of being in the natural world? Have human beings realized
their potential more than anything else?
- Do you think that knowing Allah is the same experience as
knowing the Christian God of Aquinas? Can two Gods be
different, and if so, how?
- What is Aquinas's best proof in your opinion? How about his
weakest?
- Would you like to have certainty about God like al-Ghazali?
- Do al-Ghazali and Aquinas have anything in common?

EXERCISE: THE PHILOSOPHERS

- Read the poetry of Hafiz, the Sufi master, and laugh out loud with the children. His poems are brief and trigger an immediate response. Like the child philosophers, Hafiz is playful and profound. An excellent collection of 250 poems from this fourteenth-century prankster is *The Gift*. "Two Giant Fat People" delights the children every time. God and the child poet are two giant fat people laughing and bumping into each other in a tiny boat. Ask them if this is how close al-Ghazali gets to Allah. What would it be like to bump into God? In "Startled by God," the young philosopher gets close to God once again. Hafiz learns so much from God that he is no longer a Muslim or a Christian or a Jew or anything else in "I Have Learned So Much." The experience of love frees him completely, and this poem fills the children with ideas and questions. Have the kids write their own poems, inspired by Hafiz, that begin "I have learned so much from God."

STRETCHING THE MIND

When you introduce the idea of god for philosophical discussion to kids, you will find that it stretches their minds in ways that no other topic does. "This science treats chiefly of those things that by their sublimity transcend human reason, while other sciences consider only those things that are within reason's grasp" (Aquinas, *Summa Theologica*). God is unknowable in any ordinary sense of the word, and in their analysis of the concept, little big minds become much bigger as their standard mental turf expands significantly. It is this very mental stimulation that kids most love about their dialogue concerning god. You will see, I think, that the more they talk and exchange ideas with you and with one another, the less their interest lies in proving a point or agreeing or disagreeing with an idea. What's fun is watching one idea build on another, and the buildings children feel they are constructing grow taller and taller as they reach for an understanding of . . . It feels to me as if their big minds are stretching to catch a glimmer of perfection.

I go outside with the child philosophers as our discussion of god warms up and everyone gets involved. I ask them to scatter about and to stretch and extend their bodies to feel even taller and more flexible. We bend and twist and laugh. After about five minutes, I ask them to describe the change they feel in their bodies. Some of these changes have included: "I can reach farther," "I'm not as stiff," "I feel stronger," and "Wow, not only can I touch my toes, but I feel like my fingers can touch a really low cloud, one day." Then we sit and talk. I explain to the limber big minds that philosophical talk about god stretches the mind just as we stretched our bodies: really far, in all directions. Usually, before I continue further in defense of our physical exercise, the kids clarify my rationale for me. For example: "It's good to feel your mind uncramp just like your legs." One demonstrative first-grader pulled the elastic on his waistband out as far as he could and proclaimed, "Look at my mind now!"

When I encourage philosophical dialogue about god as mind-stretching exercise and join the children in this mental challenge, I almost always see two things happen. First, the grandeur that the thought of god holds for a child is magnified. The possibility that something may explain *everything* as its reason and cause is wondrous. Also, through contemplation of the meaning of god, children become believers in the power of their *own* minds. How amazing even a kid's mind must be if it can creep toward an understanding of Aquinas's fully actualized Being and al-Ghazali's certain Truth! "Whoever thinks that the understanding of things Divine rests upon strict proofs has in his thought narrowed down the wideness of God's mercy" (*The Faith and Practice of Al-Ghazali*). I can see children's surprise in themselves, over and over, stretching, reaching, extending.

How far can little big minds stretch? How ready are their minds for the challenge of reaching beyond the visible horizon? Here's Jesse's answer, from his eleven-year-old mind and heart.

Mozart's music was playing as a backdrop for our long-anticipated discussion of god. I overheard Jesse talking in a low voice to a classmate during our "quiet time," and I heard enough of the conversation to turn Mozart off and Jesse up. I asked Jesse to repeat what he had just said to Roxanne, and he replied, "I think that babies and very young children understand every-thing perfectly, that while they are still young they understand it all very simply without trying." I desperately wanted Jesse to keep talking, but I also wanted to stay out of his way, so I encour-aged him to continue by asking an occasional question here and there.

"Was this true for you, Jesse?"

"Yes! Mozart's music is beautiful, but I'm not surprised he could make music when he was so young. We all have unlimited potential in our minds when we're born. Who knows what each of us can do? Who says anyone in this room couldn't be Mozart? I can feel the pure way I understood life slipping away from me. I can remember *that* I understood but not *what* I understood. Babies' bodies haven't caught up with their minds, but if they could keep their baby knowledge safe until they were older, they could do incredible things. There's no telling."

"How smart are babies, Jesse?"

Jesse's spontaneous enlightenment moved him to stand, knocking over his thermos and his chair. "Most people don't listen enough to children. I know it seems like babies are just babbling nonsense. But they're not just making sounds. Babies speak the language of god."

 TEACHING TIPS: STRETCHING THE MIND

- Ask the children to watch you carefully as you erase absolutely everything on the board. Explain to them that this is similar to what they will be doing with their minds. Their minds need to be blank slates to have tons of room for lots of new ideas about god.
- I often play a recording of Mozart's Symphony No. 40 in G Minor in the background as children settle in for quiet time preceding our discussion of the concept of god. Mozart's creativity inspires child philosophers to stretch their minds.

 DISCUSSION QUESTIONS: STRETCHING THE MIND

- How can people learn to stop arguing about their religious beliefs? Can you please give grown-ups some suggestions?
- Why do you think some adults shy away from talking about the idea of god?
- What is prayer? How many ways can you pray?
- Pretend that your mind is a box, and open the box and look for your ideas about god. Where and when did you get these ideas? Do you think they were there when you were a baby?

- Was it hard for you to erase the ideas about god that were already in your mind in order to make room for new ideas? Why?
- Can you define *perfection*? Do you think it exists?

 EXERCISES: STRETCHING THE MIND

- Look from violets to god with Mary Oliver in "Spring." What a wonder, the violet! They're happy making blossoms and just resting, saying thank you over and over. Their leaves are heart-shaped "for the greater glory of _____." Ask the children why they think Oliver left that space empty. Find out if they want to fill in the blank. Have them write poems expressing some of their ideas about god through a close look at one thing in nature. Oliver pictures the violets spending their lives "just saying: Thank you." Tell the children you wonder if they have any idea why the violets might be thankful.
- Listen to a "Prayer for Peace/Harachaman" matched with a "Prayer for the Ancient Trees." You can follow this with a chant from the Dalai Lama coupled with the "Prayer of Saint Francis." These selections are from the CD *Prayer: A Multicultural Journey of Spirit.* As you listen to these voices and eclectic musical instruments, ask the children to describe the sounds of prayer. Ask them to listen closely to see if the voices share similar emotions in different pieces.
- Feel the vibrations of various voices on the meditative CD *Sacred World Chants.* This presents a quiet opportunity to ask the children several questions: Where does the urge to chant originate? Does it come from our bodies or our minds or something else? Are the Jewish and African mantras similar? How do the children feel listening to the chants and the

soaring flutes? What *is* it about sound? Why do we hum and whistle?

MYSTERY

As with any philosophical topic, the more elusive and mysterious a topic becomes, the more adventurous the child explorers become. Because so much of what children learn in their early years seems factual to them and goes unquestioned, most children are stimulated when learning expands to include the unknowable as a legitimate topic.

Aquinas knows that faith is needed for belief in the revelations of Holy Scripture, and "while it describes a fact, it reveals a mystery" (*Summa Theologica*). Al-Ghazali does not *solve* the mystery of God. He becomes part of it. Many kids notice two things that Aquinas and al-Ghazali have in common. Both believe completely in their God, yet neither can *prove* that God exists. Fully taking in the realization that people can believe with certainty in what they cannot prove enthralls children. It is their definition of faith. A fourth-grader concluded that "faith is sure belief in the realness of mystery."

Ah, those child philosophers. The mystery of god is a philosophical amusement park for them. Their minds roam. When I ask them what they want to discuss further about Aquinas, quite often they return to his third proof based on necessity because this allows them to wiggle into a discussion of the concept of nothing. Thinking of Aquinas's question of the possibility of the universe coming from nothing, a sixth-grader exclaimed: "Nothing didn't stay nothing and that's one wild thought." They squeal with laughter and rock back on their heels "because the world didn't have to be here, but here it is and here we are!" I have seen them nudge one another as a child asks me what nothing means. "You should be able to tell us what it is because nothing is *something*." The plot thickens as to the status of that wondrous "nothing" when it seems possible that it may actually be "something." "Does that mean *something* can be *nothing*?" The kids just laugh and I just wonder. Aquinas makes a miracle out of nothing for children!

An endearing characteristic of dialogue with kids of all ages about god is that with every statement comes yet another question. "God's everywhere, so why can't I see Him?" "God is the earth, but does that mean god is an armadillo?" A soft-spoken kinder g a rtner ventures: "I think of god when I listen to my turtle breathe, and I wonder if I am kind of crazy." "God is what you say when there is nothing left to say, and wait, what in the world am I saying?" Still, the concept of god "stays way out there." One child who defined god as change "because everything changes" was at once satisfied and perplexed by his insight. Thinking that "god is all at one *time* but also outside *time*" was not a definitive conclusion for a furrow-browed student. "God is truth I don't get," one ready-for-recess nine-year-old philosopher remarked, satisfied with this stance.

Kids can see many benefits in accepting this mystery. With the saddest of faces, eight-year-old Karen lamented that she was "ridiculed" when she said that she didn't believe "the sea split or that humans came from those two boys, Cain and Abel." She sat up somewhat straighter with her realization that "if god goes back to being a mystery, I can think about god on my own." After class, Karen confided in me how much she enjoyed wondering about god all along.

 TEACHING TIPS: MYSTERY

- Can you describe *nothing*? Is it *something*? Should *nothing* have a name?

- Compare philosophers to jugglers. Jugglers keep lots of balls in the air at the same time, and philosophers keep lots of ideas, sometimes very different ideas, going at once.
- Laughter. Plenty of laughter.

 ## DISCUSSION QUESTIONS: MYSTERY

- If you grow up to be a philosophy teacher, will you introduce the topic of god to children at your current age? Why or why not?
- What is it that we are trying to understand and to express when we use the word *god*? Are there any other words that mean the same thing?
- How did you benefit from your philosophical investigation of the idea of god? Do you think it's important to discuss this concept? Was anything especially difficult?

 ## EXERCISE: MYSTERY

- Explore the universe in Virginia Hamilton's *In the Beginning*. As they think about why the world exists, the children can learn some of the world's countless creation myths. Barry Moser's lovely watercolors pique the imagination as they transport a child to the tales told by Australian Aborigines, the Eskimos, and the Kono clan of Guinea. You will find some of the usual suspects, such as Pandora and Prometheus. Imagine "The Woman Who Fell from the Sky" making contact with the "Turtle That Dives to the Bottom of the Sea"! Ask the children if they think there was a time when there was only ocean. Or only . . .? As an ongoing project, have the children write their very *own* creation stories. Encourage their imaginations and cheer on their creativity. Make a special occasion of the day that the children read their tales. Child philosophers also enjoy making original drawings to illustrate their stories.

Children know that there are religious wars and that a great deal of personal anger is spent in defending religious convictions. This internal and external violence seems to them the antithesis of philosophy. So often questions are not welcomed about god, and kids sense adults' unspoken assumption that they will accept what they are told. The child philosophers cannot figure out how *the* ultimate mystery, of all philosophical topics, closes people's minds and produces the need to insist that one's *own* ideas about god are true beyond doubt. One very young child, recognizing that people believe in many different gods, concluded that she liked this because "it makes god seem . . . so, well . . . like god." The question "When you hear the word *god,* what comes into your mind?" prompted third-grader Mikey to search long for his words. "It's everything. Fullness. A bit of infinity in everything."

Children have been disappointed, hurt, and confused because of the drama and conflict that came from their previous efforts to explore the concept of god. There's real irony here. Kids have so much fun wondering about *it* that when I am with them, their openness to talk about it *all* makes peace seem inevitable. When I return to the *grown-up* world, what stays with me from the children's lessons is that if peace is not inevitable, it is at least possible. I am grateful for their gift every time.

Resources

- *The Faith and Practice of Al-Ghazali,* translated by William Montgomery Watt. This fine compilation contains al-Ghazali's autobiography, as well as a thorough description of how to live daily as a Sufi Muslim in the hope of growing closer to Allah.

- *Deliverance from Error* by al-Ghazali. This is his personal and spiritual autobiography.
- *The Marvels of the Heart: Al-Ghazali's Science of the Spirit* by al-Ghazali. Al-Ghazali examines the relation between the soul and the body and investigates the possibility and nature of a nonmaterial reality.
- *Summa Theologica* by Thomas Aquinas. This enormous achievement consists of 631 fundamental questions about Christian ethics and salvation. Locate Part I, "God," Question II, in Three Articles. The five proofs are in the third article. These proofs can be found in many anthologies, including Steven Cahn's *Classics of Western Philosophy.*
- *Aquinas's Shorter Summa: Saint Thomas's Own Concise Version of His Summa Theologica* by Thomas Aquinas. Shorter!
- *In the Beginning* by Virginia Hamilton.
- *The Gift* by Hafiz. Lovingly translated by Daniel Ladinsky, this collection includes several of the children's favorites, "Two Giant Fat People," "Startled by God," and "I Have Learned So Much."
- "Spring" by Mary Oliver. This poem is one of her treats in *Blue Iris.*
- *At Blackwater Pond* by Mary Oliver. On this CD, Oliver reads forty-two favorite poems from a number of her works. The musical accompaniment, *The Lark Ascending,* is composed by Ralph Vaughan Williams and performed by the English Northern Philharmonia.
- Symphony No. 40 in G Minor (K.550) by Wolfgang Amadeus Mozart. An excellent recording on CD of this symphony, which includes Symphony No. 41, as well, is performed by the Vienna Philharmonic Orchestra and conducted by Leonard Bernstein.
- *Prayer: A Multicultural Journey of Spirit* by Dean Evenson. On this CD you will find "Prayer for Peace/Harachaman" along with "Prayer for the Ancient Trees," and a chant from the Dalai Lama complements the "Prayer of Saint Francis" (Soundings of Planet label).
- *Sacred World Chants* by Dean Evenson.

- *Mahalia Jackson—World's Greatest Gospel Singer and Fall-Jones Ensemble.* You can't go wrong with this CD.
- *The Essential Mahalia Jackson* by Mahalia Jackson. This includes "He's Got the Whole World in His Hands," "When the Saints Go Marching In," and "Precious Lord." Among other bonuses are "My God Is Real," "Dig a Little Deeper," and "Nobody Knows the Trouble I've Seen."
- *Amazing Grace* by Mahalia Jackson. This CD includes "Amazing Grace," "I'm Going to Tell God," and "My Home Over There."
- *Ken Burns Jazz Collection: Louis Armstrong.* This is a great CD that showcases Louis and his trumpet, and you can turn up "What a Wonderful World."

HUMANITY

> If you will to have the requisite energy,
> you can win what is the chief thing in life,
> win yourself, acquire your own self.
>
> —Søren Kierkegaard, *Either/Or*

THE TOPIC

The question of what makes us human has absorbed philosophers for centuries. What are we? Who are we? Do we retain the same identity as time passes? Or are there times when we simply stop being "ourselves"? And what *is* human nature—is there a Platonic essence that we all share?

The great philosophical traditions, East and West, respond to the above questions with an interesting variety of answers. Plato and Descartes supply a Western, rationalist piece of the puzzle. Our minds constitute our identity because it is the ability to think that defines human nature. Locke and Hume remind the rationalists that our senses feed simple ideas to the mind, and without sensory input the mind would remain a "blank slate." Existentialists toss all the pieces of the puzzle into the air. The clues to the existential riddle of who we are never provide the solution to the mystery. Yet they do manage to boil it down to something of a formula: Each of us is our own indefinable mix of emotion, reason, and the fluctuation of our whims and desires. The Hindu answer points to Atman, the spiritual essence within each human being, which is the heart of who we are. Because impermanence reigns in the physical world, the Buddhist response is that the notion of any kind of enduring individuality can only be an illusion.

To open discussion on this topic, I ask child philosophers to write their names on a piece of paper, or say them aloud, and to tell me who or what *that* is. I give them fifteen minutes to think and write as much or as little as comes to mind. Faces scrunch up and heads bob. Kids are truly perplexed at the apparent impossibility of defining the very thing that is closest to them. This must be another philosopher's trick. How can identifying myself *as* myself be so hard? How strange and hilarious! "It's like I'm putting jeans on somebody I don't know." "Why am I so far from being able to explain the person who is saying these words right now?" One child enthusiastically admitted that human *being* does sound important, as if something is actually *happening* . . . After more deliberation, however, she settled on this observation: "I could have been a frog."

When children tire of trying to understand who *they* are, they fall back on asking me who *I* am in the hopes that this will shed light on their nature. I answer by asking who, exactly, wants to know. As we laugh, I remind the kids that we will ask *lots* of questions and uncover even more as we check out the suddenly surprising mystery of human nature. Not only is it a challenge to understand who we are as individuals, but it is even more difficult to look for one thread that ties us *all* together.

Though separated by two centuries, a Danish and an American philosopher would share my students' fascination with the sounds of their own names and the question "Who am I?" Søren

Kierkegaard (SO-run KEER-kuh-gahr) might have snapped bluntly that each of us decides who we *are* by the way that we live *our* lives. Alive and well in Amherst, Massachusetts, Elizabeth Spelman would remind us what we are *not*. We should not be confined by categories such as wealthy, Jewish, white, or female, restrictive labels that we regrettably learn in our early years. Spelman and Kierkegaard insist that each of us has a story to tell that is ours alone. Something exciting unfolds for children as they consider human nature with these two philosophers. *Being* becomes a wonder.

 TEACHING TIP: THE TOPIC

- This topic is humorous to the children. They may become a bit rambunctious when something that should be simple confuses them mightily. Be patient.

 DISCUSSION QUESTIONS: THE TOPIC

- Do you have a definition of human nature that satisfies you? Is there an essence of humanness that everyone shares, like spirit or feelings?
- Do you think of each person you meet as an individual? How about people you know well, like a parent or a teacher?
- What is valuable about being an individual? What is valuable about realizing what all humans have in common?
- What kinds of potential do you have? What can a human being become?

EXERCISES: THE TOPIC

- Recite "Roadside Peddlers" with a bouncy rhythm as you take the children on a boat trip to the Caribbean Islands. They will never forget Monica Gunning's *Not a Copper Penny in Me House* and *Under the Breadfruit Tree*. This elementary school teacher remembers her childhood in Jamaica as a life full of loving relationships and a strong connection to the earth, as well as hurricanes and financial poverty. The poems have a calypso rhythm, and the illustrations in both collections convey the richness of belonging that comes from a strong sense of community. Encourage the children to write a poem that describes a rich human life with no mention of money.

- Read Truman Capote's portrait of the beauty of his friendship with Miss Sook Faulk in *A Christmas Memory*. Through Capote's autobiographical look at his early years in rural Alabama, the child philosophers will enjoy Miss Sook's enduring childhood into her sixties. In their philosophy journals let the children explore what they think draws these two human beings together in their difficult world. Discuss with the children what this relationship teaches them about human nature. As you finish reading this story to the kids, let them imagine and then draw the picture of the two kites that fly at the story's end.

- Describe this true story to the children: A deaf man struggles with the loss of family and friends, and endures depression. Despite these personal problems, Symphony No. 9 in D Minor comes together. In the fourth movement, this revolutionary genius struggles with the inability of musical instruments to express the full range of human emotion. His radical solution is to use voices in an orchestral symphony. Beethoven realizes that a chorus of human voices expresses emotion as nothing else can. Ask the kids if they agree with this composer who could no longer hear the chords and chorus himself. Ask the little big minds how what appears to be a limiting characteristic, such as deafness, can be overcome and not hamper a person's ability to excel in being human. Can any *one* characteristic define a person satisfactorily?

THE PHILOSOPHERS

For to think that for an instant one can keep one's personality
a blank, or that strictly speaking one can break off and bring
to a halt the course of the personal life, is a delusion.

—SØREN KIERKEGAARD, *Either/Or*

Søren Kierkegaard lived in the conservative and largely self-satisfied society of nineteenth-century Copenhagen, a society he felt relied too heavily on science, systems, and absolute standards. To him, greeting the abundance and complexity that life offers to each human being by settling for the security that complacent routine brings is unforgivable. Underlying all his writing is his relentless effort to plumb the inexplicable depths of the human condition. Kierkegaard's philosophizing centers on his consuming quest to understand what it means to be human.

The popularity of his works grew dramatically in the existential fanfare after the Second World War. Similar to other existentialist works, Kierkegaard's writing bears the imprint of his personal life. He uses pseudonyms extensively and through these fictitious characters keeps his audience guessing and, in the end, lets them figure things out for themselves. No easy reading, his style can be repetitious, contradictory, provocative, humorous, and melancholy all at once.

Kierkegaard invites his readers to dive headfirst into the pool of existence with passionate involvement and utter awareness. The discovery of what it means to *be* a human *being* will not come from a hesitant, selective, halfhearted engagement with life. His invitation to every reader is to experience *all* of it and make of it what *you* will. Kierkegaard's interest does not lie in discovering a shared human essence because for him, a loner himself, the complexity of human nature makes this a futile search.

"The thing is to find a truth which is true *for me*, to find *the idea for which I can live and die*" (*Journals of Kierkegaard*). Objective truth that is external to your life means little in the search to understand human nature. People are the authors of their own sense of the truth and are the subject of their lives. Subjective truth comes from full immersion in life and does not suffice as truth for another. Being human is a complicated, lifelong affair, and profound realizations about this intimate matter defy simplification. In introducing Kierkegaard to children, I remind them of the inquisitive nature of philosophizing and show them that Kierkegaard is asking that each of us become an investigator into our own life. Rather than look *at* a concept such as justice or compassion, each child *is* the concept. As their focus turns inward, kids respond with great excitement to their status as an idea deserving thorough consideration. The only way to investigate human reality is through individual perspective. "The individual is the category through which . . . the human race as a whole, must pass" (Kierkegaard, *"That Individual": Two "Notes" Concerning My Work as an Author*).

Kierkegaard issues a bleak warning against the insidious threat posed by the crowd to the project of becoming a human being. He is adamant: Personal identity does not exist in a crowd. Individuals seek truth by steering the course of their own lives, but direction is lost in the midst of a mob. A crowd crucified Christ, all those involved excused by their anonymity. *Individuals* did not commit this act, thereby making it possible. "A crowd in its very concept is the untruth, by reason of the fact that it renders the individual completely impenitent and irresponsible, or at least weakens his sense of responsibility by reducing it to a fraction" (*"That Individual": Two "Notes" Concerning My Work as an Author*). Kierkegaard insists that the mob mentality swallows each individual mind and heart and destroys the possibility of discovering subjective truth.

Children easily understand Kierkegaard's theme of the dangerous crowd. I ask them to describe times when they have been caught up in a crowd. They vividly recall being part of a "million people at the mall," being "pushed in line" for a popular ride at the amusement park, and "having my ears stopped up by all the noise at the football game." Frightened all over again by their memories, kids share their feelings of being dragged along by the crowd's momentum rather than their own, and the desperation that comes from feeling lost and no longer in control. You may want to identify with this feeling of helplessness and give examples from your own childhood as well as your recent experiences of being captive to the human horde.

Leaving the crowd behind as Kierkegaard suggests, he presents people with the challenge to create their own lives through the demanding process of decision making. "When I stood at the crossways . . . my soul was matured in the hour of decision" (*Either/Or*). Our decisions, as well as our failure to make choices, form our character. The best decisions, in Kierkegaard's opinion, are the ones that are arrived at through complete involvement in whatever life brings. These living choices truly belong to the individual who makes them. Kierkegaard insists frantically that the moment to act presents itself with urgency as an opportunity to take ownership of your life. Waffling with trepidation may render your internal debate moot. Alternatives disappear as moments tick by . . . Ask the children if they agree with Kierkegaard that it is satisfying to make a decision at the right time. Perhaps you can offer them a time in your life when you procrastinated in making a decision that you now wish that you had made then and there. This helps them understand that they can lose the opportunity to make a choice, and that this omission will affect their character.

Kierkegaard frequently reminds his readers that it is not *his* word but rather *theirs* that is final in assessing *their* lives. To deflect the surge in his notoriety, he went so far as to write a letter under another name to the editor of a Copenhagen newspaper criticizing that upstart philosopher Kierkegaard! I explain to the intrigued children that Kierkegaard was trying to ward off too much attention to his ideas and give birth to questions for every individual. The notion of using a name other than one's own delights young imaginations. Johannes Climacus, Vigilius Haufniensis, Constantin Constantius . . . child philosophers are tickled by Kierkegaard's use of such aliases. And their first thought? How nice it would be to use pseudonyms on their tests! Together we toy with the appeal of being someone else, if only for a day. Without encouragement they proudly pronounce their own pseudonyms. That no one knows more than anyone else about what it means to be human captivates children. It intrigues them that Kierkegaard believes that each of them will find the definition of human being by *being* human.

> Describing who we are and how we are like and unlike others
> is not always the straightforward process it appears to be.
>
> —ELIZABETH SPELMAN, *Inessential Woman*

A professor of philosophy at Smith College since 1981, Elizabeth Spelman probes the societal categories—homeless and handicapped, for example—that often artificially reduce human beings to their membership in a given group. Spelman relies on the sharp tool of philosophical analysis to make these arbitrary classifications transparent and thereby honors the uniqueness of each person.

As I open our discussion of Spelman's philosophy, I tell the children that sorting things into groups appears to come naturally to humans. "It may seem to us as if who we are, who others are, and what we do and don't have in common are matters of simple observation. Perhaps because we learn the categories so early and are continually asked to reflect our knowledge of them, they seem unproblematic. Ease of application of the categories can be confused with justified certainty about how 'natural' they are" (*Inessential Woman*). For example, I ask them to think of the way we categorize books (adventure, education), how they find music in certain sections in stores (jazz, rock), and how a banana won't be found in the pet food aisle. We subconsciously come to *expect* certain things in certain places. After strolling through many different aisles, the kids and I move to the issue of categorizing human beings. I ask them if they see a difference between sorting food into groups and people into groups. Does sorting have the potential to hurt humans in a way that cucumbers and squash will never know? Now they can see the problem Spelman presents. Spelman uses vivid diagrams of doors that artificially identify human beings forced to walk through them: banker, black, deaf, lower-class, Israeli . . . Framed in the classification of your assigned door, *you* as an individual cease to exist. If you are Polish, you are *only* Polish, and if you are middle-class, you are *only* middle-class. Essentialism is the doctrine that there are fundamental qualities inherent in all members of such groupings. The characteristics associated with that group unfortunately come to speak for each individual within that category. This enormous oversight leads to the assumption that all women's stories are the same, as is the essential story of all Palestinians or all Americans.

In her major work *Inessential Woman,* Spelman examines the damage done to personhood by lumping human beings into categories. She also offers ways in which we can emphasize individuality instead. She proposes that if we voice the stories of our lives as well as *listen* to others' stories, we can move toward an appreciation of the rich variety that flavors humanity. In listening to one another's stories, we learn about a person's interests, loves, connections, and hopes. We can then see and reject the easy descriptors we might have lazily grabbed before. Spelman looks closely at the reasons why such labels as Catholic, Hispanic, or male no longer suffice.

I draw and label some of Spelman's doors on the board for the kids. I show them how, when one door slams closed behind you and the passageway becomes narrower, one door feeds into another and possibilities for an individual's growth are gradually eliminated. Individuality recedes and your smothered identity progressively shrinks. Humanness is reduced to the following: married, Filipino, Christian, teacher. But what about this individual's vast array of actions, feelings, and ideas? These categories do not sufficiently explain what it means to be human, either for ourselves or for others. Categories deprive human beings of the vision of the lovely mess and mix of individual experience. Essentialism is a snare that shuts down every emerging personality caught by this mind-trap.

Ironically, part of the power of the doors is that we can feel isolated and inferior if there is no category to which we belong. There is no way that someone who is a scholar and an athlete can use one door, and there is no frame suitable for the child of a Jewish father and a Muslim mother. "Is there any reason why I should not try to get on the far side of any door I want to? Are the doors there to pinpoint one's 'true identity,' if there is such a thing? Do people have identities independent of what proceeding through the doors would indicate?" (Spelman, *Inessential Woman*).

Kids just stare at the labeled doors I've drawn on the board. They tell me that they despise what the doors imply, yet they realize that they make distinctions based on group membership too. They agree that if they were willing to listen hard to another's story, as well as their *own*, it would give them the ability to knock down the doors with Spelman. Often children proclaim that they could construct better doors, "ones based on the sound of your laugh, if you love to read, and if you are kind." You will enjoy hearing about "better doors" that your little big minds would like to build.

Also, kids are curious about our keeping the doors around when we know they cause problems and don't really work. And the children can tell you exactly why they don't work—you are left out if you are a citizen of India and the United States, if you have no religion, i f you are adopted and don't know anything about your first parents, and if your mom is black and your dad is white. You can imagine which students are reluctant to pass through a door that is marked "special needs."

Think of examples from your life, the news, or a book that you can offer the children as ways to defeat the doors. I give them this incredible example, one that children always understand. While I was directing the tennis camp, one of my pupils, Philip, left for a day on a scholarship to attend a clinic conducted by Arthur Ashe. Prior to his big day, all the attendees watched documentaries not only on Ashe's tennis prowess but also on the discrimination he suffered as a black youth growing up in Virginia. They saw in detail his activism to end segregation in this country and around the world. Days after Philip's return, I overheard his conversation with some tennis campers at dinner. "There's only one real difference between Marietta and Arthur. He says to hold one ball in your hand when you serve, and she says to hold two." It's not that twelve-year-old Philip didn't notice that Ashe was a male with black skin and more tennis ability than I could even imagine. Nor did he forget Ashe's struggles against the long odds of discrimination. But nothing seemed to matter beyond his day of tennis with Arthur Ashe and improving as a player himself. In Philip's heart and mind, he, Arthur, and I were fellow athletes. He did not separate us by using meaningless categories.

TEACHING TIPS: THE PHILOSOPHERS

- Write the word *individual* in the middle of the board. Surrounding the word at different distances, write the word *crowd*. Draw lots of arrows that point from the crowd toward the individual to show how threatening the numbers in a crowd are for the lone individual.
- Cut out pictures from magazines or use actual photographs to make a poster of lots of different doors. Lock each door with a category inspired by Spelman's philosophy. Black, female, white, male . . . the list is unfortunately endless.

DISCUSSION QUESTIONS: THE PHILOSOPHERS

- If you were sitting on a park bench with Kierkegaard, what would you like to ask him or tell him?
- Pretend that you are standing in front of a batch of doors with Spelman at your side. What would you talk about?
- Do you agree with Spelman that every single person has a story to tell? What's yours? Be honest.

- Are there any times in your life that an adult unfairly tries to make you into someone you are not? When? Why would a grown-up be unwilling to listen to your unique story?
- If someone walks through doors marked upper-class, Muslim, African-American, and female, what do you know about that person as an individual?
- Do you use categories to define others or yourself?

EXERCISES: THE PHILOSOPHERS

- Read Shel Silverstein's "Recipe for a Hippopotamus Sandwich." Children feel that his poems and drawings exist just for their enjoyment. The hippo recipe joins "Hector the Collector" in defying categorization. "Just Me, Just Me" celebrates individuality, and "Woulda-Coulda-Shoulda" recalls Kierkegaard's emphasis on making decisions at the right moment. "People Zoo" and "Hungry Kid Island" peek at human nature. Children have fun thinking about their lives with "Hurk," through "Play Ball," and in considering the "Pie Problem." Have the children write poems about what they find "where the sidewalk ends." Ask each of them to compose another original poem that ends with the line "Just me, just me." Their trilogy is complete with a poem titled "Me."
- Watch a documentary with the children on the life of Arthur Ashe. Kids find motivation in his story. As a young boy, Arthur was not allowed to play on the public courts in Richmond, Virginia, yet he grew up to be a world champion tennis player. Ashe's character cannot be contained within the category of athlete, however; he was a scholar and a human rights activist as well. His statue stands amid generals from the Civil War on Monument Avenue in Richmond. Children gather around

Ashe, who dangles a tennis racquet in one hand and holds books raised high in the other. You can choose selections from his autobiographical *Days of Grace* to share with the child philosophers. The dignity with which he faced his terminal illness is human nature in all its beauty.

CLIQUES

Kierkegaard's emphasis on the dangers of the crowd and Spelman's worry about the exclusive nature of her doors are perfect stepping-stones to a rich discussion of the crowd and categories in the lives of children. When I spend time with children outside our philosophy sessions, at recess, lunch, or on a field trip, for example, the gravitation of individual kids into exclusive cliques happens almost inevitably. The shunned expression of withdrawal on the faces of children suddenly left out wrings the heart. What happened to the happy group of child philosophers who were mixing so well together in heartfelt conversation? Now separated into preestablished groups of assumed solidarity, how did rejection replace acceptance?

When you discuss with kids the hurt inflicted by the formation of cliques, what makes it an interesting challenge is that in your classroom you have both the members of the cliques and the lonely outsiders together. Just opening the conversation empowers the outsider and gives pause to the insider. This unfolding of dialogue is a powerful experience for them *and* for me. I begin by asking some general questions that may or may not move a group to look at the specific problems they share. Why do people feel the need to band together in a gang? Why do people act one way in a group and another way when they're alone? Why does membership in a clique imply permission to treat other human beings cruelly? Kierkegaard's reminder that crowds behave in ways that individuals never would weaves itself throughout our discussion of these questions. What happens to the humanity of all involved: those not invited to sit at the lunch table and those eating lunch with a feeling of security in numbers? As dialogue on cliques continues, your child philosophers will develop questions of their own, as you will, based on the personalities and particular circumstances in your classroom.

Younger and older philosophers alike benefit from chatting about the cruelty of exclusion: Is this behavior learned, instinctive, or a combination of the two? The philosophies of Spelman and Kierkegaard lead children most often to an exploration of the clearly *human* capacity for the rejection of others that kids recognize with dismay in themselves. I see their squirming discomfort when they realize how cruel they can be in clusters, and I find their willingness to look critically at this phenomenon most commendable. A fifth-grader admitted that he didn't invite a classmate over to play computer games with the rest of his friends because the classmate's family could not afford a computer, *and he told his classmate that this was why.* Child philosophers are aware as well that there are classmates, siblings, or neighborhood kids who naturally include others in their lives, and they admire these peers. Convincing them of the harm done by cruelty is unnecessary because in every group there are children who endure or inflict cruelty every day.

To create an inviting atmosphere for a difficult conversation, it helps to talk to the child philosophers about your own memories as a grown-up of childhood hurt experienced long ago. I assure them that adults can remember the very moments and exact days that they were excluded by a group or mocked by cruel passing remarks. The hurt that looms large in a child's world can be recalled vividly in the world of grown-ups as well. It really helps the kids for you to identify with them by talking about your childhood hurt at the hands of the crowd. They respond warmly when

I tell them how an entire school bus full of children made fun of my brother and me every day for giving each other a kiss as we got off the bus to go our separate ways.

Cliques are Spelman's doors in action, and they hurt *all* children dreadfully. Even the insiders admit to feeling lost without their security based on numbers. They confess to losing a piece of themselves as part of a gang. Each time I talk to kids about Kierkegaard and Spelman, they express admiration for the idea of being yourself, but they tell me that the experience of being isolated from a crowd is "brutal." Cliques can make you feel that who you are is inferior and that you need to be like someone else. "The greatest hazard of all, losing the self, can occur very quietly in the world, as if it were nothing at all. No other loss can occur so quietly . . ." (Kierkegaard, *The Sickness unto Death*). Elite groups let you know that you are not *popular,* so you eat lunch alone or perhaps you are "the only kid whose locker is not decorated for their birthday." It's puzzling, a few tell me, to "feel like an outsider for being left out of something that you don't really care about anyway." Spelman and Kierkegaard show the children, some for the first time, that they are special and that they are people who count. Those insights are hard to remember when you hear dork, geek, nerd—in other words, *essentially* a loser. Commercials don't help either, a sixth-grade girl told me, because "there is no way that *I* can possibly look like *that.*" As Spelman puts it, "We have to ask what happens when we do not do what we are expected to."

Many children have begun already the painful, lifelong effort to resist the pressure to conform and go along with the crowd. To end our first conversation on this topic, I ask for some successes they have achieved, perhaps without fully realizing them, of being true to themselves. On one occasion a second-grader displayed her hands for me, revealing only her right hand's fingernails decorated with nail polish. She told me all her friends said she should paint her nails, but she wasn't sure if she liked how it looked. A nine-year-old boy told us, as he rubbed his barren head longingly, that he'd been talked into his "first but only" buzz cut by the soccer team. One individual reported that when he told a group at recess that he didn't collect Pokémon cards, the card-players told him to get a life. The first-grader replied that he "already had one." An honest eleven-year-old philosopher admitted that she really liked having a babysitter, even though all her friends bragged that they didn't need one anymore.

Most child philosophers are unwilling to end their investigation into human nature on this note of cruelty emanating from exclusive membership in a clique. Aren't humans more than this?

 ## TEACHING TIP: CLIQUES

- It helps to give examples from your childhood of a time when you felt left out by a group. Often I tell the kids about a basket-ball game when I was in the ninth grade and no one on my team but me wanted to continue to play. When they ask why, and I tell them that we lost the game 103 to 13, they treat me with an endearing tenderness that is almost comical.

 ## DISCUSSION QUESTIONS: CLIQUES

- Are you fearful or uncomfortable in a crowd? When have you felt pressure to do what a group was doing? Saying?
- Are crowds always a threat to individuality? Have there been times when you have been part of a group and have also been yourself?

- When have you suffered because of your treatment by a clique? When have you felt left out? What qualities can you develop to help you rise above the crowd?
- Why do kids in a clique pretend to be superior? How do cliques operate, and what makes membership seem desirable?
- Do grown-ups form cliques? Can you give an example?

 EXERCISE: CLIQUES

- Divide the children into pairs to have a quiet lunch. Their lunch partners should be classmates they do not know very well, if at all. Their first assignment is to enjoy each other and their lunch. Regardless of what else they talk about, make sure that they learn: their partners' favorite holiday and the reason for their choice, the meal that they most look forward to, their special hobby, what they think about when they are going to sleep, a time of year that they especially enjoy and why, where they were born . . . When they are finished, the kids can share with one another what surprised them about their partners' interests. What were some things that they didn't expect, some brand-new ideas to consider?

WHO AM I?

"Is it possible for me to know who I am?" the child philosophers want to know. As soon as the topic is introduced, questions appear as if by magic. Through our class discussions the children soon discover that the meaning of *I* defies a clean, sharp definition and involves a number of factors. But they *love* the investigation. It is obvious to them that a dictionary will not help. A definition of what it means to be human that applies to everyone seems to them a contradiction in terms. Kids can't get their musings out fast enough, though one told me that it makes her "mind feel all shriveled up" to think about human nature. She said that words don't work very well and that she would prefer just to laugh at herself. Then she will make up somebody like Kierkegaard did and describe *that* person perfectly. A kindergartner pondered if he was "still *me* when I am dreaming or asleep." Many kids would like very much to know how they are both different and the same as they were when they were babies. A thoughtful fifth-grader asked me if "I will still be *me* after *I* die, as my body or something invisible, and by the way could you tell me if *I* am my body or something else *now*?"

I ask the children to think of the five points of a star as I draw a big one on the board. I tell them that as philosophers, we will consider five main points *just to get started* on our journey of self-discovery. The first star point for children to consider in thinking of who they are is simply: How do *I* think of myself? The second: Who am I as others see me—my mom, the principal, the bus driver, my friends, my dog? The third point: Do my talents and my lack of certain abilities *both* define me? Should they, and how? Fourth star point: Am I who I am through my relationships, like being part of my family, a member of my third-grade class, or a player in the chess club? And the fifth point to consider: Since it's true that all people are part of the human race, are there things that we all share that make us human? You can settle in for a long afternoon with your talkative private detectives.

I like to leave child philosophers with the ongoing question of whether there is any *one* characteristic that they think sums up who they are. I want them to keep thinking about what defines them because they live in a changing world, and settling for a permanent definition limits their possibilities. "If we observe children," despite any fears of the unknown in themselves, we find them "seeking after adventure, a thirst for the prodigious, the mysterious" (Kierkegaard, *The Concept of Dread*). The child philosophers creep close to Kierkegaard's awareness that total self-knowledge seems out of reach. A number of kids say that just when you think you get it, "the definition of *you* changes because *you* do." It is "easier to know who you *were* than who you *are*." Kierkegaard would appreciate the paradox that child philosophers want to become *just me* but are aware that they can't handle the project of becoming an individual by themselves. They want help and support with this serious undertaking.

 TEACHING TIP: WHO AM I?

- Enjoy making lemonade with the children in two different ways to make individuality a tasty proposition. Lemonade is a much-loved beverage that can be made either from a package or from scratch, perfect analogies for a one-size-fits-all definition of humanity versus a unique creation of the individual. Give them the choice of following the directions for a powdered mix or concocting their own beverage using lemons, water, and sugar.

 DISCUSSION QUESTIONS: WHO AM I?

- Do you ever wonder about yourself? Do you know who you are?
- Are you the same person that you were as a baby? When you were four? Are you still you when you're asleep?
- Does your name tell you who you are? Can you explain how? What if someone else has the same name?
- What activities help you learn things about yourself as well as about other people?

EXERCISE: WHO AM I?

- Clap along with Ray Charles as he does it all for six decades: gospel, R&B, country and western, soul, jazz, and rock and roll. Engage the children in a lively discussion about how this great performer adapted his music to different genres, yet somehow his music remained distinctively his alone. When he sings "Georgia on My Mind," listen with the children to a human voice in love with a tune. Toward the very end of his life, Charles invited some of his friends to come to his studio and make music with him, and his voice joins the voices of his buddies in duets. Ask the kids why they think Charles wanted to sing songs at this time with his friends rather than alone. As he sings "You Don't Know Me" with Diana Krall, have the children think about the people in their lives who really know them. As they imagine "Sweet Potato Pie" with Ray and James Taylor, ask the young poets to compose a song titled "Walking on Cloud Nine." Let them guess what music means to this blind man with a hard life, and then write their thoughts in their journals. Invite them to write a song about what it means to be human to perform with Charles as a duet.

Talking about what it means to be human with the children serves as a crashing reminder to me that I was (am?) one of them. After leaving the classroom, I sometimes pause to connect the years of my life. Watching them marvel at the reality of their own somewhat mysterious being renews my appreciation for *being*. Kids' yearning to be allowed to be who they are is palpable. Their testimony to the damage done to the individual through the crowd mentality of the clique is unforgettable. Child philosophers understand that only as respected individuals can they really belong in their families, in their schools, and in their communities. But they also *really* want to belong. Unqualified acceptance of who they are coupled with the joy of being part of a group is their hope, and they want this to be the grown-ups' hope for them as well. Kids' efforts to understand what it means to be human almost always lead to their desire to improve who they are.

On one memorable occasion a child philosopher caught up with me just as I was exiting her school. Though Ashley was a bit breathless from her sprint down the hall, her words were quite clear. "Maybe the best definition of human being that we can get is that we are all unique. What humans share is being special and that's what our essence is." This realization came from an eight-year-old child already categorized as learning disabled. She can't keep up?

Resources

- *Days of Grace* by Arthur Ashe. This is his compelling autobiography.
- *Citizen of the World.* This excellent documentary on the life of Arthur Ashe is available on video and DVD.
- *Falling Up* by Shel Silverstein. Here you can find "Woulda-Coulda-Shoulda," "People Zoo," and "Hungry Kid Island."
- *Where the Sidewalk Ends* by Shel Silverstein. This includes "Hector the Collector," "Just Me, Just Me," and "Recipe for a Hippopotamus Sandwich."
- *A Light in the Attic* by Shel Silverstein. "Hurk," "Play Ball," and "Pie Problem" await the children in this collection.
- *Not a Copper Penny in Me House* by Monica Gunning. "Roadside Peddlers" is among these poems that invite the children to Jamaica.
- *Under the Breadfruit Tree* by Monica Gunning. This includes "One Hand Washes the Other."
- *A Christmas Memory* by Truman Capote.

- *Genius Loves Company* by Ray Charles and friends. Ray sings duets including "You Don't Know Me" with Diana Krall and "Sweet Potato Pie" with James Taylor on this CD.
- *Standards,* by Ray Charles. "Georgia on My Mind" is among the classics in this sampling of his repertoire.
- *Ode to Freedom,* conducted by Leonard Bernstein. This CD includes Beethoven's "Ode to Joy" from the Symphony No. 9 in D Minor.
- *Young People's Concerts* by Leonard Bernstein with the New York Philharmonic. This nine-disc DVD set consists of twenty-five concerts that were broadcast on CBS between 1958 and 1972. From Mahler and Strauss to the Beatles and the Kinks, Bernstein brings home to kids the experience and understanding of the magic of music and music's tremendous importance to human beings.
- *The Humor of Kierkegaard,* edited and introduced by Thomas C. Oden. Have fun with this collection, which demonstrates Kierkegaard's often overlooked sense of humor and the fundamental role it plays in much of his philosophy.
- *Existentialism from Dostoevsky to Sartre,* edited by Walter Kaufmann. Selections from several of Kierkegaard's works pertinent to an examination of human nature are in this anthology.
- *The Essential Kierkegaard,* edited by Howard V. Hong and Edna H. Hong. This has it all. Good luck!
- *Inessential Woman* by Elizabeth V. Spelman.
- *In Repair: The Impulse to Restore in a Fragile World* by Elizabeth V. Spelman. Spelman looks at the human instinct and motivation to fix things, whether an old bicycle or a broken relationship.

NATURE

The Tao can't be perceived. Smaller than an
electron, it contains uncountable galaxies.

—LAO TZU, *Tao Te Ching*

THE TOPIC

We make "natural" mistakes. "Natural" athletes take to their
sport with ease. Heads nodding in understanding is a "natural" response. A "natural" smile catches our eye. What does it mean to
be natural? What is nature? The Platonic search for meaning begins again, naturally.

Nature casts a spell on our imaginations. It speaks to our hearts
without words. Nature is a magnet pulling us in, yet its mysteries
tumble over and beyond our comprehension. Music and science,
art and poetry, and of course philosophy find inspiration here. Yet
how do we humans fit within the whole of nature?

Philosophers often ground their theories in this elusive natural
world. In Plato's *Phaedo,* Socrates offers proof for the soul's immortality based on the reciprocal processes he observes in nature. Life
springs from the rotting tree trunk, and summer growth appears

from winter's dormancy. He consoles his followers, as his death nears, that human life and death swing back and forth as well. In the eighteenth century, Bishop Berkeley described the natural world as the ideas that God shares with human minds through the pipeline of our senses. For this Irishman, a sunset was a flicker of God's infinite consciousness. Followers of the Jain religion, with its prehistoric roots in India, believe in a world that is completely alive. There is soul in everything—in rocks, in air, in fire. In his writings focused on environmental concerns, Ed McGaa, also known as Eagle Man, celebrates the Oglala Sioux belief that one spirit flows through everything, through the river as well as the human being.

Child philosophers enjoy entangling themselves in an effort to define *nature* and *natural*. When asked to define these terms, a fourth-grader recited fifteen definitions of *nature* from an unabridged dictionary only to announce that she didn't understand any of them. When asked how she herself would define it, she answered, "Where we *are*,"—pausing and then repeating, "Where we *are*." A fifth-grader ventured that it is anything not made by humans, only to stop himself with his acknowledgment that humans are also part of nature. He said that it felt reasonable to think that everything is natural but us. Then again, he asked, "What's the difference between beavers building dams and people building bridges?" Maybe human creations are natural after all . . .

Kids definitely find it interesting that we ourselves can be natural and still change and "maybe improve the world." I often tell my students that nature is part of us and we are a part of it. Perhaps this closeness is what makes nature so hard to define, I suggest, but as philosophers we must try to move toward a definition of nature. I give them this starting point: Nature is the world as it is. Something that is *natural* is what it is and only that.

Children feel nature's pull. Whether they are used to being in nature or not, the pond invites their toes for dipping, and tree branches cry out to be swung upon. I also hear child philosophers express a restless concern about human interaction with nature. A common, somewhat anxious request I hear from them is "Let's talk about technology versus tradition." Children sense that something valuable is lost in the excitement over human discoveries and inventions. They wonder if we can go back to a simpler life, and they question how we should go forward. What are we forgetting as we progress? What have we done, what are we doing, and what should we do?

There are two philosophers, Lao Tzu (lau-DZU) and Baruch Spinoza (beh-ROOK spih-NOH-zuh), whose shared reverence for the natural world makes them natural picks for our discussions. Lao Tzu's intuition and Spinoza's reason merge together in their vision of nature as one complete whole that contains infinite variety within it: the tulip and the tsunami, the cobra and the coyote. Humans are a piece of this variety. We belong to the world; we belong in the world.

In ancient China, Lao Tzu brought the clarity of his earth-bound experience to his writings on nature's flowing balance and harmony. In seventeenth-century Amsterdam, the lens grinder/philosopher Baruch Spinoza presented his intense intellectual analysis of the intricate design of nature's whole. Though coming from very different perspectives, the two meet in awe as they witness nature's countless unfoldings. Lao Tzu and Spinoza agree that peace and happiness can come only from recovering our place as part of this glorious whole.

? DISCUSSION QUESTIONS: THE TOPIC

- Do you feel that you are a part of the natural world? In what situations do you feel most a part of the world? When do you feel least connected to the natural world?

- How can human beings remember that they are a part of nature and relearn how to work with it rather than try to control it?
- Could humans become an endangered species? When?

 EXERCISES: THE TOPIC

- Encourage the children to become involved with environmental issues at the local level. Explain the problem clearly and carefully, whether it's the health of streams and rivers, lack of participation in an intelligent recycling program, or irresponsible development and use of land. You can take the young child activists to a meeting of City Council or the Board of Supervisors, or perhaps a larger gathering of citizens coming together to discuss sustainable growth in your region. Maybe your children would like to form their own environmental organization. With your help, they can become active in working for positive social change. How local is global warming?
- Introduce the children to unforgettable Karana in Scott O'Dell's *Island of the Blue Dolphins*. Karana is a twelve-year-old American Indian girl who survives and thrives for eighteen years on an island off the coast of California. Between 1835 and 1853, Karana finds food from the ocean and warmth in an otter's cape. She meets sea elephants and becomes best friends with a wild dog that she names Rontu. Remind the children that this is a true story. Ask them to imagine living for just one weekend alone on this island. What would they do? Have the kids write in their philosophy journals the questions that they would like to ask Karana, as well as a list of the lessons she teaches them about nature.

THE PHILOSOPHERS

The Tao is nowhere to be found. Yet it nourishes and completes all things.

—LAO TZU, *Tao Te Ching*

Lao Tzu, "the old master," was born in 604 B.C.E.. We know very little about this unassuming man who lived what appears to be a relatively uneventful life. This may explain all the legends that continue to surround him. Was he really conceived by a shooting star and/or born an old man with white hair, as future generations speculated? A more believable account is that he was a record keeper who toward the end of his life wanted to leave town and enjoy retirement in solitude. As he was heading west, legend has it on a water buffalo, the gatekeeper asked him to leave an account of his beliefs. Lao Tzu's three-day effort is the *Tao Te Ching* (dow-de-zhing), or *The Way and Its Power.*

One of the most frequently translated works of all time, this classic celebrates the rhythm of the universe, which flows within and around everything. In order for humans to find again the natural rhythm of our lives, we must resume our natural place as a piece of the universe. Our mistaken sense of separation has led only to misery. The *Tao Te Ching* appeals to human intuition with its invitation to experience life simply, with joy.

Think of any and every preposition. The Tao is within, behind, beneath, around, under and over and through everything. It is the ever-present reality that permeates and saturates everything, the intangible glue that unifies the world. "Its net covers the whole universe. . . . It doesn't let a thing slip through" (*Tao Te Ching*). The Tao, life's eternal principle, lies beyond the reach of sensory experience and intellectual understanding. The mystical experience of the transcendent Tao is unutterable. "It is like the eternal void filled with infinite possibilities. . . . It is older than God" (*Tao Te Ching*).

Manifesting itself as the energetic way of the universe, the Tao "flows through all things, inside and outside" (*Tao Te Ching*). The cosmic rhythm of nature beats within everything, and this beat is constant. Nature's flow is inevitable and cannot be altered. "All things issue from it; all things return to it" (*Tao Te Ching*). The gentle force of the Tao sustains the universe in balance and harmony. Seeming opposites are complementary partners: light and dark, wet and dry, high and low, and in and out. Being and nonbeing, which is to say matter and space, enhance and make possible each other's existence. Old and young, life and death, and stiff and flexible are parts of each other.

Humans are part of nature's unity. The energy of the Tao that resounds within and without us supports every life effortlessly if we are open to it. "It is always present within you. You can use it any way you want" (*Tao Te Ching*). Our lives can breathe with simple clarity as we move with the current of life rather than struggle against the flow. The notion that the human will can succeed in imposing itself on cosmic energy is a foolish one. The perception that humanity, and humanity alone, is above and outside the whole of reality is flawed. Human energy can be synchronized with the energy of the universe, and this alignment sustains and powers our lives. "When you use it, it is inexhaustible" (*Tao Te Ching*). While we cannot force ourselves successfully upon the world, the world's energy can buoy our open spaces. The internal reverberation of the Tao directs us effortlessly in improving and growing in everyday living. Every human being is an organic whole that is contained in the integrated whole of Nature.

Children gravitate to Lao Tzu's teaching with ease. Life is one big circle and everything is inside it. . . . How simple! Upon hearing about the Tao, many have likened it to the way that music makes them dance to its rhythm, while others compare the sound of the Tao to a quiet chant. One impressed boy, holding an imaginary weight above his head, expressed his delight that the world was actually supporting *his* life in this way. And what do the children make of the *Tao Te Ching* itself? Well, a ponytailed kindergartner said that "living the natural way is the opposite of fingernails screeching on a chalkboard. It's more like how an eraser sounds—gentle." Another said being "picked up and swung by the Tao" would allow him to "fill his space in the world like a fish gliding through water." When you think about it, they've told me, everything works better if you relax—sleeping, shooting a basketball, and learning to play the bagpipe, for example. And if you don't follow the Tao? This leads to the frustration of "trying to force a piece of a puzzle into the wrong spot, when you know it's the wrong spot," one very wise little big mind told the group. Surely you can't "take something that grows in the desert and plant it in Alaska and tell it to grow, can you?"

But the children want Lao Tzu to know that it is not always easy to slow down and be in touch with the natural energy of life. It is not easy to "take it easy" when you're told constantly to hurry up! There's "so much noise but only one beat." Kids think Lao Tzu needs to understand that he makes it seem so simple, and that he should remember that maybe it is but maybe it isn't.

> All things are begotten by a certain eternal necessity
> of Nature and in absolute perfection.
>
> —BARUCH SPINOZA, *Ethics*

Baruch Spinoza, despite his short and retiring life, was a major figure in the booming philosophical period of the seventeenth century. Spinoza's family, Portuguese Jews, fled the Spanish Inquisition, and this experience inspired his lifelong pursuit of tolerance and academic freedom. He wrote in Latin so that his academic work would not serve any nation's political agenda. He refused a prestigious position in philosophy at the University of Heidelberg to preserve his professional integrity.

Spinoza is the philosophical model for deductive reasoning. His philosophy resembles mathematics in its movement from generally accepted principles, through a tight chain of logic, to the arrival at particular facts that are known beyond a doubt. In his major work, *Ethics,* Spinoza's search for certainty in philosophy leads him to the quest for a rational understanding of God. The progression of his reasoning took him to a clear vision of the unity of nature's design to which this gentle man responded with admiration, awe, and love.

Spinoza wrote that there is only one substance with infinite powers of transformation. This substance is nature, and it is God. Spinoza's goal was to use the power of reasoning to make the universe transparent to the human mind. With sustained, penetrating concentration, he attempted to lift the veil that covers reality in order to understand the whole of nature through and through. His starting point was the use of definitions and axioms, self-evident statements that do not require proof. One of Spinoza's starting-point definitions is the following: "By substance I understand that which is in itself and is conceived through itself" (*Ethics*). Here Spinoza explains that an individual substance defines itself by its own independent nature. Water is water and fire is fire. And an axiom: "The knowledge of an effect depends upon and involves the knowledge of the cause" (*Ethics*). Here Spinoza suggests that understanding any event depends upon a good grasp of its cause. His growing web of rational knowledge evolved as his deductions based on his axioms and definitions mutually supported one another.

The heart of Spinoza's view of nature comes from his analysis of the concept of substance. This question of *substance* has been of philosophical interest since at least the sixth century B.C.E. For example, pre-Socratic philosophers wondered what the *stuff* of reality was and searched for this unchanging, underlying source of life. They made the following important distinction, as Spinoza did, concerning the nature of substance: The essence of a substance makes a thing what it is, and without this essential quality the substance would be something else. In this way, a substance is identified by its permanent essence. On the other hand, secondary qualities of a substance can vary and change, and a substance can lose or acquire these attributes without changing its essential nature. Spinoza's conclusion is a dramatic one. He identifies one substance with the universe as a whole. The whole universe is God. All the qualities of this substance can be deduced from its essential nature. Nature = Substance = God. Let's look at the process of Spinoza's deductive reasoning that brought him to this conclusion.

Spinoza doubts that the universe is composed of many substances that are separated from one another by their own essential nature. It is more logical to think of the universe as one substance with an infinity of possible manifestations. *Nature* and *God* are interchangeable names for this one substance. Lao Tzu would have added Tao without hesitation. "The following propositions . . . show that in Nature only one substance exists, and that it is absolutely infinite" (Spinoza, *Ethics*).

But why does logic reach the conclusion that there is only one substance? Here is Spinoza's line of reasoning. First, there can't be two or more individual substances with the same essence because you would not be able to identify them. If the essence of zebra were the essence of rose, zebras and roses would be the same. Next, Spinoza ponders the possibility of many different substances with many different attributes. Take any two substances—for example a worm and a tomato. How could you explain any interaction between these two self-contained substances? Can the worm really *change* the tomato by taking a bite? "Two substances having different attributes have nothing in common with one another" (*Ethics*). Because of Spinoza's definition of the nature of substance, one substance cannot be affected or altered by another. A circle can't change the nature of a triangle because they are what they are. Finally, the apparent *change* in the tomato, originally assumed to be caused by the worm, is actually one substance only *appearing* to change. Both the worm and the tomato are forms of one being encompassed by Nature/God.

There is infinite variety within the complete unity of *Nature*. There is no *real* distinction between the attributes of *Substance*. Nature is self-determining as a whole and unfolds according to its own nature. Human failure to understand the completeness of the natural world comes from the emotional and prejudicial placement of the human being at the crown of a hierarchical structure. "Those who are ignorant of the true causes of things confound everything" (Spinoza, *Ethics*). The world does not exist for human ends. The world *Is.* "We see, therefore, that all those methods by which the common people are in a habit of explaining Nature are only different sorts of imaginations, and do not reveal the nature of anything in itself, but only the constitution of the imagination . . ." (*Ethics*).

Many grown-up and therefore sophisticated philosophers doubt that children can understand Spinoza. After discussing his theories and thought process, I use the following metaphor with the child philosophers *just in case there is any confusion*. I ask them to imagine that they are at the beach watching waves roll onto shore one after the other, over and over, forever. It is the same water, but there is variety in each wave. Small hands go up immediately. Children recognize that the one substance can be anything. One eight-year-old child described nature as having "every single possible costume for playing dress-up, so that it could be rain or ant or stone." Another explanation of the myriad manifestations of one substance was an "erupting volcano." A "chick hatching from an egg" was one girl's

especially perceptive comparison to the unfolding of one substance. Her classmate pointed to his freckles, eyelashes, and eye-
brows and reminded us that it was "just one face." An animated
fourth-grader stood up to describe the way that "the sky can go
from blue to purple to green to red as a fire truck to black—and
it's all the same sky!" Yes, the children understand that the universe
recycles itself, fresh and new every moment. A ten-year-old natu-
ralist asked me if her example was a good one. She said that her
neighbor's dog died a year ago and the neighbor had been very sad.
But the other day the neighbor invited her over to look from a distance into a tree. In building their nest, birds had gone to the dog's
favorite spot in the backyard and found his tan and white fur. It was
now the "cushy lining for their nest." Her neighbor was so happy!
The one *substance* unfolds as dog fur and as bird's blanket. "Matter
is everywhere the same . . . parts are not distinguished in it, that is
to say, they are distinguished with regard to mode, but not with
regard to reality" (Spinoza, *Ethics*).

 TEACHING TIPS: THE PHILOSOPHERS

- Listening to *Dawgnation* by the David Grisman Quintet is a fun
  way for the children to feel the beat and the rhythm of music.
  As their toe tapping and finger snapping become more uni-
  form, compare the beat of "Desert Dog" to the beat of the
  Tao. Ask them if nature has a rhythm too.
- Complementing conversation with food native to the culture of
  the philosopher increases philosophy's appeal considerably. Serve
  chow mein and a fortune cookie and Lao Tzu lives forever.
- An explanation of deductive reasoning that children can grasp
  well: step-by-step thinking that reaches a sure conclusion because the steps hold together as tightly as the links in a chain.

- In teaching Spinoza's theory that Substance = Nature = God, keep the word *ONE* written prominently on the board. The heart of his philosophy is that there is only *one* substance, and nature is *one* whole. Seeing the word *one* will remind the children of how all the wondrous variety they see is contained within the whole.

- When you share verses from the *Tao Te Ching*, after you have explained Lao Tzu's general outlook, lead the students with as few words as possible and resist the urge to foist an interpretation on them. Their intuition guides them to a direct understanding of Lao Tzu's *Way* in their own time, and I find that grown-up explanations tend to muddy his simplicity. Define any difficult words if necessary, such as *manipulated,* and reread verses a couple of times if you like.

 DISCUSSION QUESTIONS: THE PHILOSOPHERS

- What do you imagine Spinoza's *one* substance to be?
- How would you describe the Tao to someone who had not studied Lao Tzu?

 EXERCISES: THE PHILOSOPHERS

- Basho's poetry instills delight in the magnificence of nature that complements the philosophies of Lao Tzu and Spinoza. Basho records his travels throughout Japan in haiku form (the *On Love and Barley* collection is my first choice) and captivates philosophers of all ages with his intimate snapshots of the natural world. Frogs and cicadas, snow and cherry blossoms spring to life!

Children take naturally to haiku, and they enjoy the compan-
ionship of this Zen Buddhist monk. Pass his book around the
room several times and have each child read a short poem
aloud. Ask them what images they see immediately of the
monkey and the raincoat, for example. In their journals, have
the children use haiku to describe two trips of their own, one
real and one imaginary. I use the form that limits the writer to
three lines of seventeen syllables, five syllables in the first line,
followed by seven, and concluded with five syllables.

- Travel with the children from Japan to Alaska in Nancy White
Carlstrom's collection of poetry titled *The Midnight Dance of the
Snowshoe Hare.* Her poems, displaying the brilliance of the
northern lights and the midnight sun, are brief and direct in the
spirit of haiku. Children like to pretend that they are Basho as
he travels through Alaska and enjoy recording their trip in
haiku. Ask them what Lao Tzu would think about the balanced
transformation from the snow and darkness of winter to the
light and abundant growth of spring and summer. Sensitive
images of the Alaskan landscape invite the children to visit a
place most of them have only imagined. This is also an opportunity to learn about the way of life in different parts of Alaska
as well as current environmental issues of great importance.
Have them write in their journals how they think Spinoza
would explain that one substance can be ice, aspen, and Eskimo.

RESEMBLANCE

Kids delight in using the theory of unity to find more and more
likenesses in their universe. Child philosophers deduce that likeness between and among things is inevitable because unity is
bound to create resemblance. Their exuberance as they discover
increasing amounts of resemblance is contagious, and similarities
between things previously thought to be different are the most

exciting findings of all. I ask kids to think of Lao Tzu's enclosed circle that includes everything as Spinoza's one unfolding substance. "Each separate being in the universe returns to the common source" (*Tao Te Ching*). I encourage them to remember that if nature has only one essential quality, then there *must* be similarities throughout the universe. How does the world repeat itself in a variety of ways? Kids love this adventure of searching for patterns and designs in unexpected, secret places.

Here's one approach I've used to jump-start the children's awareness of resemblance. I show them a photograph of two images side by side without telling them what the shapes are. They marvel at the similarities even before they can guess the identities of the two forms. Most kids guess that the photographs are of two trees at different times of the year. Their breath catches, just as mine did the first time, when I tell them that one is a tree and the other a human lung spread out to its full capacity. They begin to recognize similarities immediately: Branches are like veins, blood flows like sap, when leaves blow they look as if they're breathing. The contented little big minds sit quietly, looking for more resemblances between the two almost identical shapes of Spinoza's one substance.

When I ask them for their own snapshots of the world that are pictures of similarity, they are so pleased with their examples. All the petals on a flower could be the same petal. (The particular flower that this ten-year-old girl was describing was a dahlia whose petals are a perfect example of repeated similarity.) One nimble boy demonstrated some impromptu yoga poses and asked me if I had ever seen a dog or a cat stretch the same way. Madeline recalled her discovery in the garden that very morning that tulips smell like pancakes, while Jessica responded that mountains look like bunches of broccoli. Struggling to find the words to express her insight, a future health practitioner said that she noticed that her muscles seemed to feel exactly like her emotions. "I do not know why matter should be unworthy of the divine nature . . ." (Spinoza, *Ethics*). Simon oh so accurately admitted that sometimes his hair looked like the quills of a porcupine.

The philosophies of Lao Tzu and Spinoza become clearer as discoveries of resemblance multiply. Many kids are suddenly reminded of how much they look like their parents or siblings, and even people they pass on the street. They want to know if I think rivers look like snakes, if the backbone of a fish looks like theirs, and if fins and wings do the same job. One boy in a group demonstrated convincingly that frogs hiccup. Others asked if I ever noticed how much the sky looks like the ocean. And eyes, oranges, balls, the sun, and ladybugs are all circles!

One of the most exciting resemblances I've ever discovered is that between the philosophies of Lao Tzu and Spinoza. Lao Tzu's intuitive experience of nature's design was matched by Spinoza's intellectual linear progression. When I ask the children what they make of these philosophers coming to the same conclusion by such seemingly different paths, several have been quick to explain it to me. "Great ideas are *like* each other." "The greatest wisdom seems childish" (*Tao Te Ching*). Jocelyn further explained to make sure that I understood: "The ideas behind writing music and building a house are a lot alike." How I wish my mind resembled hers!

 TEACHING TIP: RESEMBLANCE

- Some children have few opportunities to enjoy the outdoors. In conversations with your kids about nature, spend as much time outside with them as possible. By discussing nature *in* nature, it is easier for children to see its many unfoldings.

? DISCUSSION QUESTIONS: RESEMBLANCE

- What shapes and patterns do you see repeated in a variety of ways in nature? What does a sunflower resemble? Why are they called ears of corn?
- How much resemblance exists between a tree and a human being? Describe the kinds of likenesses you see. Sap and blood? How similar is your backbone to that of a fish?
- Do you believe that human happiness lies in our understanding and experiencing that we are a part of some kind of whole?

AWE

Discovering a world of likeness leads naturally to awe. Thinking of themselves as a reflection of the Tao, just like the butterfly and the rainbow and the air, is irresistible to kids. "Every being in the universe is an expression of the Tao" (*Tao Te Ching*). One of the most endearing features of doing philosophy with children is that awe comes easily to them. Kids agree that everything participates in the patterned design of the natural world, from the tiny to the grand, from the human to the meteor.

Children easily share Spinoza's awe that the smallest part of nature's design mirrors the whole. "All things are begotten by a certain eternal necessity of Nature and in absolute perfection" (*Ethics*). I ask the kids what *awe* means to them and how it feels when it runs through their whole being. After they try to fit awe into words, I ask them how this feeling of awe relates to being in nature. An awestruck child philosopher said that if you are in awe of something, "you can't stop staring and you can't get over it, but it gets over you." That one substance "*can* become anything and *does* become everything" stokes their minds. One six-year-old scientist wanted desperately to tell Spinoza that his one substance sounded like primordial ooze, and that "to go from ooze all the way to today is plain magic." "Hence it follows with the greatest clearness, firstly, that God is one, that is to say, in Nature there is but one substance, and it is absolutely infinite . . ." (Spinoza, *Ethics*). "Now, that is *awe*some!" one child shouted from the back of the room when our conversation went from awe to ooze to magic.

The magic continues. "It is mind-blowing to think that I grew inside my ma." "Our roof leaked during the big storm, but the bird's nest stayed perfect in the bush." It seemed impossible, but "in the desert I saw flowers growing out of rocks." Children's astonishment extends from the tiniest pieces of the universe to their sense of the vastness of a whole that they cannot comprehend. Grains of sand, drops of water, minnows, and seeds are so *small*. Redwoods, whales, elephants, mountain peaks lost in the mist, other planets! This world is so *huge*! What about space? Thunderstorms, winds, floods, and rockslides are full of power. Snow, dew, and pollen fall gently. Shooting stars whiz by, and you never actually see a chameleon change its colors. "If you open yourself to the Tao, you are at one with the Tao and you can embody it completely" (*Tao Te Ching*). For little big minds and any grown-up in their company, nature is a miracle and they are part of it.

 TEACHING TIP: AWE

- When children think about nature, many of them express concern about the environment. You may want to devote one session to this topic and a different session on another day to kids' broader exploration of nature's beauty and power. This way they can discuss at length how to care for the environment without distracting them from the philosophies of Lao Tzu and Spinoza.

DISCUSSION QUESTIONS: AWE

- What amazes you most about nature?
- Does nature's power ever make you afraid? When?
- What are some examples of how tender and delicate the natural world is? Have you ever seen a baby bird? What happens when you blow on a fuzzy dandelion?
- How did the carrots we're going to snack on right now arrive in this room? Trace the journey of the carrots.
- What can a computer do well? What can't it do at all? Can nature do some of the things that a computer can't?

 EXERCISES: AWE

- Listen to Alan Hovhaness's soaring orchestral piece *And God Created Great Whales.* Watch the children's faces! Hovhaness composes music to feed the human spirit with his love of nature, using a medley of recordings of whale songs to mesh with the instruments in this uplifting work. While listening to the whale songs, let the kids sketch the world that appears in their imaginations. Allow sufficient time for them to draw a series of sketches. In the following days, study the lives and varieties of whales and their habitats. Then, in a few weeks, repeat this assignment. As the music becomes more familiar to the kids, the whales come alive in their imaginations.
- Accept another invitation from the whales as their songs invite the children into the ocean once again in the two-part "To the Last Whale . . . Critical Mass and Wind on the Water." This haunting tune is a love song for the whales and a wake-up call to human beings. Crosby and Nash question how people can use

harpoons and watch a whale wash up on the shore—all for the production of eye makeup. Excite the child philosophers with an assignment to imagine, as they listen to this song, what the world would look like through the eye of the whale. Have them describe that world in detail. Crosby and Nash salute the whales that swim the ocean following feelings of their own. Ask the children to describe a day that they spend as part of the sea getting to know a whale. How do whales swim?

※

While adults may find Lao Tzu inscrutable ("Some say that my teaching is nonsense") and Spinoza too demanding, children come softly to the realization that everything can work well *together*. One kindergartener expressed his admiration for the crows who eat from the family compost pile and make room for more. Kids know for a fact that their efforts to impose their own will are often unsuccessful, and they are keenly aware of how awful it feels when they are pressed into submission by another force. They gleefully describe the *natural* desire to wiggle free from anything that seeks to curb their spontaneity. Perhaps because children grow up surrounded by competition and the push to win and to be better, most would, if they could, relax and feel a part of the world. I see through my conversations with them how much we suffer when we are divorced from nature's rhythmic beat.

Are children *natural* philosophers? Picture the mustard-covered face of seven-year-old Simon, his clothes redesigned by finger paints, as he raises his hand nonchalantly at the end of our discussion of Lao Tzu and Spinoza. "It's the space that does it. I think in the very beginning there was empty space, but it wasn't chaos. Then tiny things came out of it, like a speck of dust, a speck of mineral, and one drop of water like the point of a pin." Struggling to keep up with him, I asked Simon what made the tiny things come out of empty space if space were really empty. He answered me matter-of-factly, "Question in its purest form. Even now, we still question our world, don't we? Question powers everything."

Resources

- "Act Naturally" by the Beatles.
- *Dawgnation* by the David Grisman Quintet. This ode to the canine community, available on CD, includes "Cha Cha Chihuahua," "Why Did the Mouse Marry the Elephant," and "Desert Dog."
- *Tao Te Ching* by Lao Tzu. I recommend Stephen Mitchell's translation. Delicate and graceful, it shuns heavy language and reads with lighthearted grace. Another translation, by Gia-Fu Feng and Jane English, includes the stark beauty of black-and-white photography as well as Chinese calligraphy.
- *The Tao of Pooh* by Benjamin Hoff. Pooh, Eeyore, Piglet, and friends are perfect teachers of Taoist philosophy.
- *Ethics* by Baruch Spinoza. His look at nature is in Part One, "Of God." Each section is a paradigm of deduction. Propositions XIV and XV warrant a close look, and the Appendix sums up Spinoza's conclusions.
- *Island of the Blue Dolphins* by Scott O'Dell.
- *And God Created Great Whales* by Alan Hovhaness. An excellent CD of this work is performed by the Philharmonia Orchestra, conducted by David Amos.
- *Mysterious Mountain, Letters in the Sand,* and *Mount St. Helens* by Alan Hovhaness. Children also enjoy letting their imaginations roam while listening to these symphonies.
- "To the Last Whale . . . Critical Mass and Wind on the Water" by David Crosby and Graham Nash. This is available on their CDs entitled *Wind on the Water* and *The Best of Crosby & Nash: The ABC Years.*
- *On Love and Barley* by Basho.
- *The Midnight Dance of the Snowshoe Hare* by Nancy White Carlstrom.

COMPASSION

From the time we were little children we
have all of us, at moments at least, cherished
overwhelming desires to be of use in the great
world, to play a conscious part in its progress.

—JANE ADDAMS, *Peace and Bread in Time of War*

THE TOPIC

Children collect money for victims of a recent tragedy because
adults tell them it is good to be compassionate. They're told that
the world is a global community, but what sense of immediate
community do they have in their own lives? Can it be true that
everyone is your brother and sister when a quick glance at the
playground reveals a punch being thrown and insults being whispered behind cupped hands? Philosophical dialogue is the perfect
way for kids to take a careful, analytical approach in order to gain
an understanding of this lofty ideal of compassion.

In keeping with my definition of philosophy as the art of clear
thinking, I define compassion for children as the art of pure feeling. Much more direct than feeling something *about* someone or
something, compassion means sharing another's feeling with as

little resistance and selfishness as humanly possible. Child philosophers nod at my definition, but then quickly seek to improve it.
Some definitions from seven-year-olds: "Compassion involves
stepping over myself and into the person, and it's like the line
between us disappears." A classmate continued the line analogy
by comparing compassion to an "endless line that keeps wrapping
and wrapping itself around two hearts." Many kids define it as
"feeling the way someone else feels in your *own* heart." It is like
"crying inside another's tears." For one of my students, the sound
of compassion is "*boing,* like two people listening to music and
the vibration is the same in both bodies."

Kids understand why they need to take a long philosophical
look at compassion. They freely admit that anybody can *act* compassionately while not *being* compassionate. "It's like being at a
dress-up party but the clothes aren't really yours." Compassion
can be "just another word on your vocabulary test."

Two Nobel Peace Prize winners make their philosophical
theories come alive through their tireless, lifelong dedication
to serve others and work for the common good. The Dalai
Lama (DAH-lie LAH-mah) and Jane Addams share the belief
that the human tendency toward generosity is innate. A life without compassion goes against human nature because compassionate living is in everyone's best interest. It's smart to allow
empathy to move you to work for a better world. It is your world,
after all.

? DISCUSSION QUESTIONS: THE TOPIC

• What are some examples of compassionate acts? What actions
  may seem at first to be compassionate but turn out to have
  selfish motives behind them?

- Do you see many examples of kindness and compassion in your daily life? Is there more compassion in the world than you realized?
- When does being compassionate come easily to you, and when is it harder for you to be compassionate?

 EXERCISE: THE TOPIC

- Listen to the former Beatle on *The Best of George Harrison*. He offers many opportunities to discuss compassion. You can explain the misery endured by millions prior to listening to "Bangladesh." Harrison insists that everyone "lend a hand." He sings that he can't neglect his responsibility to help save lives. He asks the listener to try to understand the people of Bangladesh rather than turn away from them. As they hear Harrison's guitar "gently weep," ask the children to write a thoughtful description in their journals of how they can keep from turning their backs on suffering, what they have turned away from already, and why. Harrison chooses the phrase "take hold of my hand" to repeat over and over, almost like a chant in "Give Me Love (Give Me Peace on Earth)." Have the children write a poem titled "Take Hold of My Hand." In "Think for Yourself" and "What Is Life?" Harrison sings of his hope for a brighter future. Have pairs of children write a duet including the changes they can make to help create a better world.

THE PHILOSOPHERS

Compassion . . . brings us an inner strength. Once it is developed,
it naturally opens an inner door, through which we can
communicate with fellow human beings, and even other
sentient beings, with ease, and heart to heart.

—THE DALAI LAMA, *The Four Noble Truths*

Tenzin Gyatso, the fourteenth Dalai Lama, was born in the province
of Amdo in Tibet in 1935. Monks proclaimed him the reincar-
nation of the Buddha of Compassion when he was two, and he
trained and studied from an early age to be the spiritual and political leader of the Tibetan people. The Chinese invaded his beloved
homeland in 1950, beginning an occupation that escalated into
devastating revolution turned against the people and culture of Tibet. Since 1960, the Dalai Lama has lived in exile in Dharamsala,
India, "home" of the displaced Tibetan government and approximately ten thousandTibetans.

Winner of the Nobel Peace Prize in 1989, steadfast in his insistence on nonviolence despite the slaughter of a million Tibetans
and the destruction of most of their monasteries and cultural treasures, the Dalai Lama lives the meaning of his name: Ocean of
Wisdom. Many of the child philosophers I've worked with over
the years have been affected by his compassionate spirit, some of
them having had the chance to meet him and become pen pals.
The kids often feel that I personally know Plato or Lao Tzu because I take on their voices in presenting their philosophies, but I
was actually in the audience to see and hear the Dalai Lama share
his philosophy at a 1998 conference of Nobel Peace laureates.
Unbeknownst to me, one of my college students assisting me in
teaching philosophy to children brought a group of little big minds

in hopes of glimpsing the Dalai Lama after his speech. While the
kids waited outside the auditorium on a golden fall afternoon, I
anticipated my first time in the presence of Tibet's holy leader.

Over a two-day period in an intimate setting before several
hundred people, each laureate gave a speech that was followed by
dialogue with one another and people in the audience. The purpose of the conference was "bringing together great hearts and
minds" for conversation about human rights, conflict, and recon-
ciliation. The Dalai Lama was the last speaker, and his talk would
bring the conference to a close. The mood in the auditorium
shifted suddenly as he stood to go to the podium, growing more
quiet than silence. The other laureates riveted their attention on
him, and their note-taking and asides came to a halt. Who *is* the
Dalai Lama? Before I saw him in person, I knew him only as the
monk who suffers with his countrymen as they look to him for
guidance, traveling the world to plead the Tibetan cause while
insisting on nonviolence. This is the man I saw:

The sorrow in his face was covered by radiant joy. He showed
three-hundred-sixty-degree sensitivity to others. He was always
the last person to come onto the stage and the last to leave, stopping to talk to any accessible children along the way. Inconspicu-
ously he poured water in others' glasses and was aware when it
was time for a refill, filling his cup last. The Dalai Lama's twirling
in an effort not to turn his back on his translator, who was trying
desperately to be invisible, was natural for him and dizzying fun
to watch. He laughed with a playful sense of mischief, yet he was
clearly a serious man with exhausting responsibility. He emanated
unshakable strength of will while being gentle in his movements
and interactions. This monk in his patched orange robe seemed
uncomplicated and without guile. It occurred to me that he would
be just this way even if he were alone.

The title of his talk was "The Need for Compassion in Society:

The Case of Tibet." While compassion was his central theme as expected, he never mentioned the Chinese, the plight of the Tibetan people, or his own exile. He said that there was no need to discuss world peace and that internal disarmament would be his focus. People need to look within their *own* hearts to find what weapons lie inside. Anger, aggression, and revenge born of the refusal to forgive those who hurt us are motivations for violence. We must disarm our inner selves by controlling our minds, diminishing our anger so that our sameness as human beings shows itself clearly. Weapons do not fire on their own but require a human to pull the trigger. Forget the focus on nuclear disarmament and turn within to examine what motivates you. As members of the audience thought about what drives their actions, the stunned expressions on the faces of the laureates indicated that perhaps some were questioning their motives for the first time. *Why,* exactly, do I work so hard for the banning of land mines? What moves me to fight against apartheid in South Africa? What is the source of my concern for the safety and well-being of children?

In this speech and in his writings, the Dalai Lama shows us that negative emotions block the natural human tendency toward compassion. What has happened to our minds, he asks, that we can no longer understand that everything is related? Think of the whole world as your mother and extend the closeness of that relationship in the womb to all beings. It is faulty reasoning that leads us to believe that isolation is possible. Where can you or I go? It is clear that each of us, every living being, depends on all beings and the earth itself for happiness. Compassion honors this interdependence, and we cannot be happy surrounded by the suffering of our relations. "Emotions without proper reason are what we call negative emotions. The other kind of emotion, which includes compassion and altruism, is emotion with reason because through deep investigation you can prove it is good, necessary and useful.

Furthermore, although by nature it is a type of emotion, it is actually in accord with reason and intelligence" (*The Four Noble Truths*).

Doesn't everyone appreciate kindness? "The mere growth of our body requires another's affection" (*The Four Noble Truths*). As the Dalai Lama came to the conclusion of his talk, part of the marvel was that his simple remarks had cast quite a spell. I was reminded of the Buddhist concept of "big mind" that can see reality simply as it is. With compelling sincerity, he extolled us never to give up hope, and he insisted that losing hope is the only mistake we can make. This exiled Tibetan proclaimed several times that the world is getting better every day. Appearing the slightest bit awkward for the first time, he looked down and said that if there were something useful that we could draw from his comments, that was fine. But if not, that was just fine as well, so "forget about it!" With his translator sidestepping behind him, he closed his talk with the same deep bow of humility with which he began. The eruption of applause, joined by expelled breaths, felt like wind moving the building.

My college student and the child philosophers got their wish! They came upon the Dalai Lama outside the auditorium as he chatted casually with a small group. He invited the kids to join in, and they told him they were studying compassion in philosophy class and starting to do service projects. The kids told me excitedly that he seemed interested in their lives, bending down to their level and asking them questions, so they got his address to write to him.

Almost all child philosophers respond with both enthusiasm and a bit of reservation to the Dalai Lama's policy of kindness. Kids understand how handy altruism is: As you serve others compassionately, you also improve the world in which *you* live. Feeding the hungry and comforting the lonely create a happier world for all. Still, the kids have lots they want to tell the Dalai Lama.

"Dissing the bad stuff in your heart" (internal disarmament!) is not easy. Their list of undesirable weapons is not short: greed, jealousy, guilt, bragging, tricking people, laziness, feeling spoiled . . . They wish they could tell him that it's not always possible to identify with someone else unless you've experienced something similar. One child stated to our group, "I can't imagine being a kid with a war in my country, and both my parents are alive so I don't know what it feels like to have a parent die." I assure them that their honest thinking about the Dalai Lama's philosophy will lead them to closer identification with others.

> Our deepest morality says we must stand by the weak and the wretched
> and bring them into some sort of decency of life and of social order.
>
> —JANE ADDAMS, *A Centennial Reader*

Born in Cedarville, Illinois, in 1860, Jane Addams was very close to her father and deeply affected by his friendship with and admiration for Abraham Lincoln. She graduated from Rockford College only to have her medical studies cut short by health problems associated with curvature of the spine. Her passion for healing others switched direction from medicine to social reform. She was an unyielding pacifist who fought for women's right to vote, and a founding member of the ACLU and NAACP. She was involved in labor law, the juvenile court system, and international peace efforts. Though she was awarded an honorary degree from the University of Chicago and won the Nobel Peace Prize in 1931 (shared with Nicholas Butler), her heart was in social work. Ending hunger and establishing world peace were her immediate and long-range goals.

One of Jane Addams's greatest achievements was Hull-House, the Chicago settlement she founded in 1889 with her friend Ellen Starr, a place that was her own home as head resident until her death in 1935. A home and gathering place for the displaced in this heavily populated urban area, Addams envisioned Hull-House as an example of American democracy in practice. With Hull-House, Addams defined compassion.

As a child, Addams was stirred by an insistent desire to contribute to the world, and she was touched by her father's tears at Lincoln's death and at the human cost of the Civil War. She never lost her hope to improve the world, but as a female college graduate in the late nineteenth century, her options for positive action seemed few. Though an educated woman, she lacked the right to vote and was not sure how to move through society as an agent of change. On a European trip, Addams witnessed with horror and heartache the starving masses in east London. These scenes became the foundation of a lifetime of incredible public service, showing her the path to fulfill her childhood dreams. Of what use is an education if it doesn't address unthinkable suffering? "Many unsavory conditions are allowed to continue which would be regarded with horror if they were considered permanent. Meanwhile, the wretched conditions persist until at least two generations of children have been born and reared in them" (*Twenty Years at Hull-House*). Hands reaching for rotten cabbages to eat with rotting teeth made Addams wonder how industrialization could justify the cold contempt with which the larger society turned away from such human misery. She was convinced that the saturating stench surrounding the lives of the homeless in big cities was too easy to forget, and that people should not turn their backs on the desperation of others who are hungry through no fault of their own.

A settlement house for the homeless in Chicago felt like a necessity rather than an option for Addams. One can imagine this residential complex that lifted people from streets marked by killing hunger and sheer desperation. First, and always, food, food,

food! Hull-House quickly became the social center of the neighborhood, with smells of ethnic cuisine and freshly brewed coffee permeating the hallways. Sounds of laughter came from kids at play and in the day nursery. Music, art, and theater encouraged creativity in children and adults alike. Reading and writing classes were well attended, and Addams insisted that teachers make the reading relevant to the lives of the kids. Adults could attend school at night, and there were many clubs that encouraged a vigorous social life. There was a Shakespeare club, a Kindergarten club, and, of course, a Plato club. Hull-House was an unexpected haven for the formerly hopeless. At the height of its activity, more than a thousand people regularly used the facilities each week, whether to meet all their needs as residents or to connect with their neighbors over cross-cultural coffee.

Child philosophers are struck by the fact that Addams seems as though she knew all along that she wanted to get into the lives of those who suffer. After talking about life at Hull-House, the kids are full of observations and imaginings. Children new to the United States, like Vlade, for example, are quick to notice Addams's compassion for those who had come recently to America. A child philosopher smiled at Vlade and confidently told him that "we are all immigrants sort of, and Jane Addams would not have turned anybody away from Hull-House." Many kids wondered if other people in Chicago were doing anything to help out at this time, and whether they helped "with their *own hands* or just with money." One young girl told me that it was a good thing that Jane suffered a broken heart in London because "it made enough room for tons of people to fit in it." By far, their most lasting impression is that "Jane *lived* at Hull-House," sharing her home with the homeless.

Kids are realistic and often ask if they will become and remain compassionate as time goes by. They would like to think so but are not completely sure. Addams assures them that the answer will be yes, if grown-ups invite them respectfully to play a big part in the world. "We have in America a fast-growing number of cultivated young people who have no recognized outlet for their active faculties. They hear constantly of the great social maladjustment, but no way is provided for them to change it, and their uselessness hangs about them heavily" (*Twenty Years at Hull-House*).

 TEACHING TIPS: THE PHILOSOPHERS

- The Dalai Lama can come alive for your child philosophers through documentaries and photographs. The films *Kundun* and *Seven Years in Tibet* give intimate looks at the Dalai Lama's childhood, his heavy responsibilities, and the people and landscape of Tibet. You can use this beautiful country for lessons in geography and share pictures of Tibet's exquisite art and architecture. Perhaps a member of the Tibetan community can come speak to your group.

- Be sure to define words that may be unfamiliar to kids. A *settlement* is a place to live and share community in a congested urban environment. I like to point out that the root, *settle*, meaning to sit comfortably, works well with Addams's vision for Hull-House. Break down *internal disarmament* for them: *internal* means inside you and *disarm* means get rid of your weapons. A *motive* is the real reason for an action. A *pacifist* opposes violence of any kind. *Immigrants* are people who leave their country to live in another one and have plans to stay.

- In your look at internal disarmament, you and the children inevitably will discuss personal qualities that are hard to admit at first. Perhaps you will need to remind the children that they are looking within themselves and not at their classmates. If there is any friction among the students, they may use this *self*-examination as an opportunity to go after a classmate's sensitive spot.

- Show the children the illustrations in Addams's *Hull-House.* Kids can relate to the fatigue of "A Spent Old Man," for example, while other drawings give them a feel for the layout and activities at Hull-House.

 ## DISCUSSION QUESTIONS: THE PHILOSOPHERS

- Do you agree with Addams and the Dalai Lama that compassion is a natural tendency? Does it come naturally to you?
- Why does the Dalai Lama love to laugh?
- Do you agree with the Dalai Lama that compassion is smart? How does compassion improve the world?
- How can the Dalai Lama forgive the Chinese? What allows a person to forgive even tremendous suffering?
- Why do you think Jane Addams chose to live in Hull-House?
- Do you want to help others as Addams did as a child? What do you want to do?
- Why do you think Jane Addams won the Nobel Peace Prize? How about the Dalai Lama?

 ## EXERCISES: THE PHILOSOPHERS

- Listen to Ravi Shankar and Yehudi Menuhin, two close friends, use Shankar's sitar to merge Indian classical music with Menuhin's majestic violin. Children enjoy the loving conversation between these two instruments on *West Meets East: The Historic Shankar/Menuhin Collection.* Shankar and Menuhin echo the faith in peace shared by the Dalai Lama and Jane Addams, and they are generous with their musical gifts. Shankar brings Indian music to the West and includes George Harrison among his students. Menuhin opens a school for young musicians who play in prisons and hospitals, following the example of their Russian/Jewish mentor who played for survivors of the concentration camps at the end of the Second World War. Menuhin thinks that music can be a tool for peace. Ask the children to explain why he might say this and if they agree. Shankar believes that sound is sacred. Discuss the possibility that sound, a drum beat for example, connects people of all times and places. Spin the globe and let the children choose the places that they would like to go to hear music. Help them explore the music of that culture. Ask the children to explain to you what they can learn about people through music.

- Read *The Goat Lady* by Jane Bregoli. In 1988, the author and her children met Noelie Houle, a French Canadian woman born in 1899. Noelie seems odd and mysterious to most of the townspeople in Dartmouth, Massachusetts, because she keeps goats in her yard, dresses funny, and lives in a farmhouse with peeling paint. The curiosity of Bregoli's children, who move in next door, develops into a loving friendship with this white-haired woman who donates her goat's milk to needy families and some of her herd to the Heifer International Project to provide milk and cheese around the world. Bregoli creates watercolors of the good-hearted Noelie and her animals to put on display at the town hall, softening the hearts of her neighbors. Without trying, the goat lady teaches the people of the town the importance of kindness. Bregoli tells this story from a child's perspective, and it is terrific to read aloud, showing the illustrations to your child philosophers as you go along. In their philosophy journals, have the kids explore the lessons they learn from this true story, the examples of Noelie's compassion and the kindness of the two children and their mother, and how they think the Dalai Lama would respond to Noelie.

GRATITUDE

Through their study of the philosophies and lives of the Dalai Lama and Jane Addams, children understand the many ways that compassion enriches one's own life as it benefits others. I therefore ask them why any person would *not* be compassionate. For a lot of children, the realization that compassion is lacking in their lives lingers in the background of our conversations. I find it effective to talk with kids about what might block kindness in a potentially giving heart. I encourage them to keep talking with me and one another so that we can figure this out together. Once we look at reasons for this blockage, the way is cleared for the solution: gratitude.

First, what gets in the way of compassion? Katy explained to our group that as far as she could tell, she "didn't care about anything that didn't affect *her.*" Her classmate quickly added that he "didn't care about *anything* a whole lot." The expression of one eight-year-old's heartfelt reluctance was most memorable: "I don't want to feel bad, *too,* if I open up to somebody's hurt. I just don't want to take it inside my body if I don't have to."

After we've considered the difficulty in becoming compassionate, I involve the kids in looking at two different ways of being in the world. I tell them that one way of living comes from the feeling that life owes you plenty, so you direct all your energy toward the payback you feel that you deserve. If you are stuck in this mind-set, your life becomes dedicated to *your* needs and expectations only. You do not owe others anything. I ask them if they sometimes live this way, and many are relieved to say yes. Kids understand that this way of thinking prevents compassionate living: If you identify only with yourself, identification with another is impossible. When I tell them that there is another way of being in the world that can help them—as they put it, "get over myself"— they are both glad to move on from the allure of self-absorption and eager to discover this other way of being in the world.

I ask the children: Would it help us to become compassionate people if we taught ourselves to be thankful for small things as well as larger things, day in and day out? Being grateful is the other way of living in the world. It is the willingness to appreciate what you are given and how much life offers you. I explain to them that part of being grateful is the feeling that it is *you* who owes something to others and the earth. Life is full of opportunities to practice kindness, and a thankful heart is not picky about these chances. "If I had stayed in Lhasa and there had not been a Chinese invasion, I might still be isolated. I'd probably be more conservative than I am. Therefore I am very grateful to the Chinese for giving me this opportunity" (the Dalai Lama, *A Policy of Kindness*).

Next, I join the children in thinking of examples of things in our lives for which we are really thankful, so grateful that we feel moved to pay back our good fortune. I give them this easy example from my own life. I am deeply grateful for philosophy's gifts to me, for the tools that philosophy has given me to improve my life. This thankfulness makes me want to share philosophy so that others can also benefit from it. I tell the grinning children that the fullness in my heart had to get out, and it shot me into their classroom. Not only do they think that this image is hilarious, but they now understand the connection between gratitude and the motivation to give back to the world.

Here are just a few of the marvelous connections kids have made between their reasons for thanksgiving and its link to kindness to others. "I am grateful for *my* health, so I want to visit my friend who is too sick to come to school this year." "I am very thankful for *my* family, so I'm going to invite my friend over who stays at home by himself a lot." "When I see how happy *my* dog has been since we saved him, I think I could start a food collection for the animals that we didn't take home from the shelter." For all the Dalai Lama's emphasis on the importance of motivation, the child philosophers and I agree that gratitude is the best motivation for compassion. Gratitude opens the compassionate heart.

Kids love making lists of the things for which they are grateful, and their faces beam as one realization after another strikes them and they hurry to lengthen their list. One of the greatest stories of gratitude I have heard came from a nine-year-old girl who told us that "Once when I was running in PE, just about to turn the corner around the fence, my shoes were *soaked,* so heavy my feet squished water out when I ran, and I thought, Why am I doing this? Then I thought of my teacher who teaches us well. He takes time out of his days just for us. I kept thinking all wonderful things until I was done, and I couldn't stop. I ran two extra laps so I could keep thinking all those things, getting happier and happier." As it turned out, Danielle with the squishy shoes became a quiet force behind several years of service activities at her school.

☑ TEACHING TIP: GRATITUDE

- Gratitude is a concept that can easily fall prey to superficial treatment. To broaden the child's perspective, refer to specific examples of the gratitude that can emerge in a variety of settings, like the library or the ballpark.

DISCUSSION QUESTIONS: GRATITUDE

- What are you deep-down grateful for in your life?
- How does gratitude help you to be more compassionate?
- Can a hard life take the feeling of gratitude away completely? How about an easy life?

 EXERCISES: GRATITUDE

- Introduce the children to a new friend, Zlata Filipovic, age eleven, through *Zlata's Diary*. You may want to give some background information about the situation in Sarajevo during the time Zlata kept her journal, 1991–1993. She tells the story of the drastic changes in her childhood due to war. Zlata's life at the beginning of the diary could be any child's life, as she writes about school, music, and vacation plans. Suddenly the diary entries tell of relentless bombing, hunger, and being housebound with no electricity. Zlata details the effects of war on her parents and especially on children. Help the children identify with Zlata and all the different emotions she feels. Join them in a discussion of what her diary can teach anyone about gratitude. Ask them to imagine that they are sending her a care package and what they would put in it. They may need frequent reminders of her circumstances—that there is no electricity, that she cannot leave the house, and that she loses a lifelong friend. Eventually Zlata escapes and moves to Paris. Pretend with the children that you will all go on a trip to spend a day with her. Ask the kids to make a list of their questions for Zlata and the things they want to tell her.

- Read a five-line poem from the thirteenth-century Sufi poet Rumi, in which he invites the children to a field and promises to meet them there. I find that kids welcome discovering ideas for themselves that are not spelled out in detail, and you can encourage their childlike creativity to search for insights on compassion in this poem, even though the word is never used. Rumi insists that the world is so beautiful that the words *each other* no longer make any sense to him. I engage the children in a lively discussion of what the word *other* suggests, and how identifying with another through compassion chips away at the sense of separation implied by *other.* Have the wide-eyed philosophers draw pictures of themselves with Rumi in his field. Ask them to tell him in their own poems why, if the world's beauty fills their soul with gratitude, the words *each other* no longer have meaning.

- Listen to contemporary composer Libby Larsen's *Missa Gaia: Mass for the Earth.* With the theme of the circle at the heart of this work, Larsen weaves together Native American poetry, medieval mysticism, the Bible, and current environmental poetry. The voices and the instruments blend together to celebrate the community that is our planet. Ask the children to explain how gratitude for everyone's home, the earth, can help people become more compassionate. Encourage them to use their imaginations and think hard. Have them write a poem for Larsen to include in the Mass about the feeling of compassion that comes from being aware that the whole world is a community. Let them decide on the music that they want to accompany their poems, and encourage them to draw paintings of the scenery they would like to see onstage to complement the performance of their masterpiece.

SERVICE

Compassion and service are inseparable. I define *service* for the children as the gift of time and energy that comes from their ability to identify with another's life. No one is excused from the responsibility to work for the common good on a planet that provides for the entire human family made up only of related brothers and sisters. Like so many grown-ups, most kids just want a way to contribute, and they savor an assignment. "They are longing to construct the world anew . . ." (Addams, *Twenty Years at Hull-House*). The Dalai Lama's twinkling laugh and Addams's ever-growing commitment to social action prove that it can work for them! Kids remember the focus on compassion in action of these two simple, straight-talking philosophers. You can help the kids develop a sense of purpose in their own lives by making them aware of possibilities for service on a regular basis. Among all the topics we discuss, service to others is a direct result of comprehending the nature of compassion. The kids' grasp of interdependence greatly reduces any concern on their part about how *they* will be rewarded in return for their service.

But service does reward the giver. What does service bring to the lives of little big minds? They explain to me that helping others from the simple desire to do just that "makes me full up and feel excellent for the first time." The practical benefits are also obvious to them. "If I help to feed the hungry, there will be less stealing and violence and I'll be safer." "When I work with a local environmental group to protect ecosystems, the air quality will be better and so will my asthma." "If I can just understand that other people have lots of problems, then I will be less angry about my own little bothers, and *believe me* when I say my anger is a problem." Kids' genuine pleasure on occasions when they see the results of their service is a source of joy for them as well as the adults in their lives. "It was really cool to see smoke coming from the chimney of the neighbor whose wood I carried inside." After going on a "major" trash pick-up, their grins wrap around from ear to ear at recess when they hear other kids and teachers talking about how clean the playground is. And how exciting it is to "see the lonesome student that I made friends with feeling strong enough to play with other kids now." Parents and teachers consistently testify to the improvement in many kids' own academic approach as a result of their service efforts. "Of course I can do better in social studies! Didn't I already teach a kindergartner to read?"

The child philosophers who met the Dalai Lama received quick return mail from Dharamsala. Through his secretary, the Dalai Lama asked the young philosophers to make kindness their life's work, and he assured them that the world needed their help right now. I see kids from a wide variety of backgrounds relishing their chance to work to reduce suffering. They understand that the feeling of compassion moves you to give what you can, to work for Family in the largest sense from the fullness of a grateful heart. "If it is natural to feed the hungry and care for the sick, it is certainly natural to give pleasure to the young, comfort the aged, and to minister to the deep-seated craving for social intercourse that all men feel. Whoever does it is rewarded by something which, if not gratitude, is at least spontaneous and vital and lacks that irksome sense of obligation with which a substantial benefit is too often acknowledged" (*Twenty Years at Hull-House*). As an eighth-grader explained the attraction of service for her: "I love doing something my heart tells me to do."

It is a privilege to see children's instinctive joy in service. As we come to the end of a full-bodied look at compassion, I present several options for service projects. Kids jump at the chance to serve, whether individually or through participation in a group activity. How happy they are, whistling and talking to classmates whom they knew less well than others, engaging teachers and parents who get caught up in their energy. Even those for whom gratitude is a stretch because of the difficulty of their lives realize that they can help their teacher clean the board or their bus driver search for forgotten items. "Youth is so vivid an element in life that unless it is cherished, all the rest is spoiled. The most praiseworthy journey grows dull and leaden unless companioned by youth's iridescent dreams" (Addams, *A Centennial Reader*).

 ## TEACHING TIPS: SERVICE

- Sometimes you may need to make sure that the kids are in tune with the circumstances and feelings of those they want to help, rather than getting caught up in a flurry of activity that in part may be imposing their own goals. Cleaning up someone's yard because the young philosophers think it looks awful is not service. Wanting to give clothes to those who proudly wear the traditional garb of their culture would be unintentionally offensive.
- Be sure to encourage the children's desire to be involved in their world by giving them interesting, practical opportunities for service activities. Often kids come up with terrific ideas as soon as they fully understand a philosopher's theories. Service enhances children's perception of their abilities and hones their skills in social interactions.

 ## DISCUSSION QUESTIONS: SERVICE

- How does service benefit the giver?
- Is it possible to be content if others suffer?

EXERCISE: SERVICE

- Determined to help children with cancer, one group of children reached out by placing collection jars on the counters of willing community businesses and starting a drive for donations at their school. The children collected games, videos and DVDs, books, stuffed animals, art supplies, and CDs of all musical genres. They wrote letters to the young cancer patients, but somehow they knew it was not appropriate to include photographs of themselves. When they delivered the boxes of goods to the cancer center accompanied by teachers and parents, a girl with leukemia chose to come out to thank them for the gifts. She talked to the child philosophers about her illness, how she coped, and what her hopes were. This one child gave the kids an invaluable lesson in the meaning of compassion. While she was grateful on behalf of the other patients, she instilled gratitude in the children for the good luck of their current health and appreciation for their ability to make a dent in excruciating suffering.

One group of little big minds' outreach to children at a cancer center is but one of so many projects over my years with them. Child philosophers identify with kids whose lives are on hold and whose education is disrupted for whatever reason—a house fire in their neighborhood, a hurricane on the Gulf Coast, or floods in the Dakotas. An entire school became lovingly involved in collecting items for kids sheltered in temporary housing with their moms. Animals at the SPCA pick up their heads when children burst through the door, and a walking trail appears brand-new after their cleanup. The memorial garden planted and tended at one school will continue to bring pleasure, and who knows the number of unsuspecting nursing home residents who have welcomed a hug from a grand child?

Resources

- *The Goat Lady* by Jane Bregoli.
- *Zlata's Diary* by Zlata Filipovic.
- *The Essential Rumi*, translated by Coleman Barks. "Out beyond ideas of wrongdoing and rightdoing" is in Section 4: "Spring Giddiness: Stand in the Wake of This Chattering and Grow Airy." There is no finer translator of Rumi than Barks, and no better invitation than growing airy!
- *Missa Gaia: Mass for the Earth* by Libby Larsen. This magnificent choral piece can be found in part on a variety of collections, and in its entirety on the CD performed by the Oregon Repertory Singers (Koch Classics).
- *Dreaming Blue* by Libby Larsen. This opera, available on CD and conducted by Brian Groner with the Fox Valley Symphony, is for and about children and, in many ways, by kids. Fourth-graders discussed issues that were important to them with Larsen, and their words make up much of the libretto. Kids' drawings are the blueprint for the scenery, and their concerns with isolation and personal identity come to life in Larsen's characters.
- *West Meets East: The Historic Shankar/Menuhin Collection* by Ravi Shankar and Yehudi Menuhin. Children especially enjoy the improvisational duet in "Tenderness" on this CD.
- *The Best of George Harrison* by George Harrison. Here you'll find "While My Guitar Gently Weeps," "Give Me Love (Give Me Peace on Earth)," "Bangladesh," "Think for Yourself," and "What Is Life?"
- *Shankar Family and Friends* by Ravi Shankar. George Harrison is among the friendly collaborators on this CD.

- *Twenty Years at Hull-House* by Jane Addams. The stark illustrations enhance Addams's intimate portrayal of her Chicago settlement. There are lots of books about Addams for kids of all ages.
- *Peace and Bread in Time of War* by Jane Addams. The link between compassion and pacifism comes alive in Addams's look at the First World War.
- *A Centennial Reader* by Jane Addams. Many of Addams's speeches and powerful essays are arranged by topic in this collection.
- *A Policy of Kindness* by the Dalai Lama. There is a vast array of books by and about the Dalai Lama. This one has a personal feel and is good for working with children. They can look at his childhood and his hobbies as well as his joy in repairing transistor radios. The chapters entitled "Kindness and Compassion" and "Living Sanely" have much to offer kids. Also featured is his Nobel Peace Prize Lecture and his Evening Address to accept the Prize.
- *The Wisdom of Forgiveness: Intimate Conversations and Journeys* by the Dalai Lama with Victor Chan. The Dalai Lama's forgiveness of the Chinese is obvious in these tender conversations with his good friend.
- *The Four Noble Truths* by the Dalai Lama. The Dalai Lama explains the basics of Buddhism through interviews and talks over the course of two days in London. The appendix is a speech on compassion given in the Free Trade Hall of Manchester, England.

FREEDOM

It is not true that the recognition of the
freedom of others limits my own freedom:
to be free is not to have the power to do
anything you like; it is to be able to surpass
the given toward an open future; the existence
of others as a freedom defines my situation
and is even the condition of my own freedom.

—SIMONE DE BEAUVOIR, *The Ethics of Ambiguity*

THE TOPIC

The human story is the story of an unquenchable desire for freedom, a freedom that must be had at any cost. Throughout the
ages philosophers have hinged their definitions of what it means
to be human upon the possession of free will. A free person, neither mentally bound nor physically shackled, thinks and moves
without restraint. Yet so many of us are or have been held back
from experiencing this fundamental human liberty.

Thoughts of freedom come with qualifiers and nagging questions. Surely one is not free to do *anything,* so what are the proper
limits of free action? Are humans born free, or is freedom a possession that you can earn if you meet certain criteria? If the value

of liberty is so obvious and intrinsic to human beings, what—if anything—excuses those who steal liberty from some to serve their own needs? Is there any way to predict why some people handle freedom better than others? So many questions surround such a basic idea. What *is* freedom?

Fascination with freedom runs throughout the history of philosophy. In ancient Greece, Aristotle championed free will. Because we can think and deliberate between existing alternatives, humans are not coerced into their actions and are therefore responsible for their free choices. In opposition to Aristotle, various schools of determinist philosophy have suggested that heredity and environment are the true causes of human behavior and that free will is an illusion. In his philosophical novels *The Brothers Karamazov* and *Notes from Underground,* Fyodor Dostoevsky complicates the free will question by laying bare his suspicion that most people would rather be told what to do, despite their realization that freedom is the most valuable human possession. Political philosophizing runs the gamut from democratic theory that celebrates the vast potential of the free individual to the Communist viewpoint that fears freedom's inevitable decline into anarchy and recommends state control in freedom's place.

How is freedom a part of children's lives? Where is that fine balance between the early experience of their freedom *now* coupled with kids' need for security, protection, and guidance? What are the ideal limits of adult exercise of power over children, limits that respect the essentially free natures of developing human beings?

Making sense of freedom for child philosophers whose lives require clear adult authority is a delicate undertaking. It is tricky because kids are quick to admit that youth temporarily curtails the full exercise of their personal freedom, but they want to feel free in their lives. I have experimented with different ways of introducing the topic of freedom to little big minds and found that the best way to begin is by asking the kids if freedom is important to them, and why. I allow as much time as needed for the children to say how they feel about the topic until every voice has been heard. With so many volunteered ideas for us to consider, the complexity of the issue makes itself clear to everyone. Kids then settle in for a philosophical examination of the concept of freedom, curious to see where the dialogue will take them.

A definition of liberty for a child that rings true to me and to them is that freedom is your chance to experiment with being alive in order, gradually, to invent your own life. In their exuberant response to my definition of freedom, children describe a world that is opening for them to move through without having their hopes dismissed as ridiculous and without "getting stomped on." Several have expressed that they never again want to feel as if they are "in trouble for being alive." Furthermore, they want to be "as alive as *anybody*." And you can count on the young freedom fighters demanding a few liberties *now*. When I ask them what they consider their rightful freedoms as kids, they insist that they are free to ask questions and adamant that the freedom to play is absolutely essential. Also, I'm told frequently that everybody, especially children, can have wild imaginations and also big dreams of accomplishments. Some say, desperately and sadly, that they want to be free from fear and worry so that they can begin to figure things out for themselves. Oh, I mustn't forget that a free kid is also one who is read a story at night and tucked into bed.

John Stuart Mill and Simone de Beauvoir (see-MONE duh boh-VWAHR) ground their philosophies in the question of personal freedom. Mill presents freedom as the key ingredient of human happiness, and de Beauvoir proclaims that the exercise of freedom is the *one* way to become a human being. A world of free adults is an absurd expectation for both philosophers unless unlimited possibilities are unveiled for children.

 TEACHING TIPS: THE TOPIC

- Have fun making the atmosphere for your discussions on freedom especially free. Perhaps the kids can sit wherever they like or even stretch out on the floor. Invite them to wear a favorite hat or a pair of socks that they associate with their own "free spirit." (Kids are into socks.)
- Play James Booker *playing his piano.* His music is *the* perfect overture and finale to a discussion of freedom. Booker frees the piano keys in his unforgettable version of "On the Sunny Side of the Street," and kids' energy soars as the chords build. It's not possible to sit still when he sings that "everybody let freedom ring" as we all pitch in to "Make a Better World."

 DISCUSSION QUESTIONS: THE TOPIC

- What does it mean to be free?
- What does the expression "free as a bird" mean to you?
- Do you think of yourself as a free human being? Do you like the idea?
- Up to this point in your life, when have you felt most free?
- What is slavery? Why would someone want to own another person?

- How do people lose their desire for freedom? Could it happen to you?
- Is your mind free? Do you like to think for yourself? How can grown-ups help you to learn to think for yourself?

 EXERCISE: THE TOPIC

- Read, ponder, and laugh with Pablo Neruda's seemingly made-for-child-philosophers *Book of Questions.* In a style uniquely his own, this Chilean poet opens wide the philosophical wonderland of thrilling questions that defy answers. When I share Neruda with kids, they tell me that their minds actually *feel* free. Assurance that their minds are free regardless of other limitations on their young lives is big encouragement for children to continue in the uninhibited spirit of inquiry. Have a free-for-all with the kids in the release from the structure of linear thinking that pursues definitive answers. Let them romp in the unfettered world of ideas with Neruda in his untitled poems that consist of questions. Wink at smiling rice, picture the shape of yellow, and guess what trees learn from the dirt. Think hard with the kids whether the convict's light is the same as yours, and ask them to write poems about the ways the light is the same or different or both for the prisoner and the free person. "Why doesn't Thursday talk itself / into coming after Friday?" is Neruda's invitation to the kids to play Ping-Pong poetry with him and match his questions with ones of their own, back and forth. Then, with a partner, continue the game as each child writes a two-line question/poem and passes it to a friend when both are ready. Kids love "using short poems for conversation." Continue with Neruda's questions until Thursday comes after Friday.

THE PHILOSOPHERS

The only freedom which deserves the name is that of pursuing
our own good in our own way, so long as we do not attempt to
deprive others of theirs or impede their efforts to obtain it.

—JOHN STUART MILL, *On Liberty*

A child prodigy, John Stuart Mill was educated by his father, James,
and grew up to be one of the premier Western philosophers of
the nineteenth century. He viewed his devoted friendship and
eventual marriage to Harriet Taylor as the chief inspiration for his
philosophical work. He dedicated *On Liberty* to her memory as
testimony to their collaborative efforts.

In Mill's two major works he reveals the inextricable link between happiness and freedom. In *Utilitarianism,* Mill advocates a
moral theory that promotes the greatest happiness for the greatest
number of people affected by a decision, based on short- and long-
term consequences. His justification for this utilitarian standard of
morality is that happiness is the goal of human life. In *On Liberty,* he
details the central role personal freedom plays in the attainment of
happiness. Mill makes a powerful case for individual freedom in his
adamant opposition both to the legislation of morality and to the
interference of social pressure in the private lives of free individuals.

Throughout his work Mill refers to the unattractive human
tendency to impose one's own ideas of good living on others.
Mindless conformity inspires many people to feel comfortable in
the world only if others live and think as they do. Mill urges readers to realize this unruly controlling streak in themselves and to
determine not to foist their preferences on their neighbors. The
central thesis of Mill's political philosophy is that the only legitimate reason for government interference with the freedom of in-

dividuals to live as they see fit is to protect citizens from harm. Be it in the personal or the political arena, Mill declared that a sense of moral rightness as to how people should live their lives is not sufficient justification for interference in another's life. Mill's belief in the basic decency of human nature and his faith in our ability to change our minds and to improve our behavior is the foundation of his philosophy of freedom.

According to Mill, individuals have the right to create their lives to suit their own character, and this freedom comes right after food and water as the most basic of human needs. It is the right of all humans to follow our "tastes and pursuits" and to frame "the plan of our life to suit our own character, of doing as we like, subject to such consequences as may follow, without impediment from our fellow creatures, so long as what we do does not harm them, even though they should think our conduct foolish, perverse, or wrong" (*On Liberty*).

Mill acknowledged that children need guidance and protection. While his ideal of freedom is one that he envisioned for adults, he insists that both grown-ups and children require a climate suitable for freedom's flowering. Regardless of age, the emergence of genius, innovative thinking, and unique accomplishment requires an atmosphere that supports and cultivates nonconformity. In a fertile climate of freedom, originality is encouraged and the eccentric's refusal to live bound by custom is applauded. "No one's idea of excellence in conduct is that people should do absolutely nothing but copy one another" (*On Liberty*). Spontaneity's instinctive discoveries are recognized as interesting and worthwhile, rather than the whimsical meanderings of a disordered life. Originality, eccentricity, spontaneity and genius all have a forward, future-seeking momentum. These things cry out for freedom.

It is possible to give up on freedom and its promise of present and future happiness. Like any garden left uncultivated, human

290 LITTLE BIG MINDS

aspiration can die out without nourishment. One can become accustomed to a restricted life and accept it as inevitable. This mediocre contentment with a limited existence is a sad substitute for the real happiness that can be experienced only as a free person. Mill pleads with every reader to "aim at something better than customary, which is called . . . the spirit of liberty or . . . progress or improvement" (*On Liberty*).

Mill's philosophy of freedom resonates with kids. One of my students, Nico, listened intently during our discussion of Mill's ideas, and then told the class the story of his Cuban grandparents' fight for freedom. They worked hard to get permission from the government to go on a short holiday. Agreeing to return in two days, they left Cuba with weekend bags packed and papers signed. With tremendous pride, Nico reported that his grandparents never went back because a new start in America meant more to them than ever again going back to their home and seeing their old friends. Invariably, child philosophers have no difficulty seeing the tight connection between happiness and freedom. Kids have shared countless thoughts on the joys of freedom with me: Wearing mismatched socks is a delight. "Perfect conversations are the ones that just go where they go." And it's a terrible feeling when your mind feels suffocated because "my mind can fly." Kids enjoy becoming newly aware, through Mill's philosophy, of the many ways in which they are already free: free to sing, to try harder, to change their minds, free to say "hi" first, to love, to enjoy having only a little responsibility now. They do hope, however, that Mill knows that he makes it sound easier than it really is.

> To will oneself moral and to will oneself
> free are one and the same decision.
>
> —SIMONE DE BEAUVOIR, *The Ethics of Ambiguity*

Simone de Beauvoir was Mill's twentieth-century French partner in thought. She chafed at the restrictions first imposed on her in childhood. Her determination not to conform to traditional female roles and to live as an independent person began at an early age.

De Beauvoir was drawn inevitably into the exciting world of French existentialist philosophy, with her focus on the fulfillment of human nature made possible through freedom. In her landmark work *The Second Sex,* she exposes the damage done to women, and men as well, by constraint of the natural freedom of woman. She warns against the lure of apathy and the easy temptation to submit to another's will in *The Ethics of Ambiguity.* In each work, she explores in vivid detail the richness of a life grounded in awareness and acceptance of free will.

Only as free beings can we discover the breathtaking joys of human existence, much like children at play gleefully experiencing an apparently unlimited world. Freedom allows people to define their values and priorities and to determine the very quality of their lives. "The source of all values resides in the freedom of man" (*The Ethics of Ambiguity*). De Beauvoir insists that individuals must consciously and relentlessly *will* the project of their lives, fueling their essence and becoming more real as human beings in this lifelong project. Freedom empowers us to surpass the given circumstances of our lives and to thrust forward vigorously into the open space of a future that is not restricted to just one thing. The future is to be announced by free beings for themselves, and this personal navigation of life is *the* source of abiding self-respect.

According to de Beauvoir, humans, born free, are made for free living. They can choose otherwise, however, and can opt out of a free response to life. De Beauvoir labels this unfortunate forfeiture of freedom "self-deception," the peculiar human ability to keep bad faith with ourselves. We lie to ourselves that society's demands and life's inherent difficulty are in cahoots against *us,* and the oddity is that we force ourselves to believe this lie. In the blur of keeping bad faith with ourselves, we choose to become indifferent to our freedom. What are we doing?! Others are free and responsible, of course, but we decide through laziness and cowardice to trick ourselves out of being the authority figures in our own lives. "If I persist in beating my fist against a stone wall, my freedom exhausts itself in this useless gesture . . ." (*The Ethics of Ambiguity*). In this mire of self-deception, we refuse to see ourselves or the world honestly. We spend precious energy on the production of a web of airtight alibis, freely woven, to excuse ourselves from humanity.

Like Mill, de Beauvoir maintains that ethical living necessitates that we encourage and work for freedom for others. Individual freedom can be realized fully only in a culture of freedom. Your freedom enhances mine, and no one can be free in isolation. Freedom should be contagious. This culture of freedom applies directly to children in de Beauvoir's philosophy. Respect for others' freedom and the willingness to fight for it cannot exclude children.

Children with an innately free nature inherit a world not of their own making. Young human beings deserve the respect accorded to all human beings, and it is the task of adults to win new possibilities for a visible and attainable future for these soon-to-be independent individuals. De Beauvoir encourages adults to reach down and take children's hands and spread their future before them. Adults can either demand that children conform to their given world or can nurture children's sense of personal liberty in the shaping of their own lives. Even if the world is preset before their arrival, children soon realize that their lives are not ready-made. Cheer on creativity and spontaneity as the free communication of childhood, de Beauvoir recommends. A child's free explorations are the building blocks of their self-propelled progression.

To negate children's essential freedom, which is developing in their beings, requires adult self-deception. You must intentionally dupe yourself to believe that stifled personal growth is good for children. De Beauvoir will not back off. You are kidding yourself if you think that a child needs to fit the norm for the sake of status. You keep bad faith with yourself *and* children in denying their burgeoning freedom. Only self-deception allows you to justify such needless imposition of authority. Children's freedom is a condition of adult freedom as well. A free climate consists only of free beings in dialogue. How can a free individual spring from a child whose free expression and yearning for discovery are clipped early on? Children seek and need love and support in so many ways. Guidelines and hand-holding are essential, but no one can think or live *for* a child.

De Beauvoir greatly encourages child philosophers, and they are glad that she remembers the lessons of her youth. Many want to tell the woman from Paris that she's right about their having lots of questions about the world. A thigh-slapping child philosopher wanted to know "who the experts are." She pictured the expert vividly as this person who knows exactly what the right way to live is, and she was curious about the qualifications for such expertise. When I didn't reply immediately, she explained kindly that I wasn't an expert because all I do is ask questions! They ask de Beauvoir why their "play time has to be so organized," and if they need to be serious when they grow up. A number of Mill's band of eccentrics want to know why there is an "honor roll at school only for certain things," and if they will be free not to go to college. Seeing the advantages of being cared for, some kids wonder when their childhood will be over. The many kids who find their refuge in the school day want to know why school stops for the summer months.

TEACHING TIP: THE PHILOSOPHERS

- Neither Mill nor de Beauvoir believes unrestricted freedom benefits anyone. At the outset, kids will sometimes trivialize their chance to discuss freedom. You may hear a demand for a driver's license or the option to discontinue their education. I suggest that you stop such requests right away by reminding them that the opportunity to talk about freedom will open new worlds to them.

 ## DISCUSSION QUESTIONS: THE PHILOSOPHERS

- Where does your freedom stop and another person's begin?
- What can you do to support freedom in other lives?
- What do you consider unnecessary restrictions on your freedom?
- Are you eccentric in any way? Why does Mill appreciate eccentricity?
- Even though you're a kid, how can adults treat you as a free human being, as de Beauvoir wants?

 ## EXERCISE: THE PHILOSOPHERS

- Snap your fingers and tap your feet as you and the children listen to *Buena Vista Social Club*. The child philosophers can compare this sense of freedom found in music to the constraints placed on freedom in Cuban society. Have them explain how such free expression can occur in a world full of limitations, and how they can apply their insights to their own lives right now. Let the children pretend that they are music critics for the local newspaper. Have them listen to "Pueblo Nuevo" several times, and then describe in very clear writing the random thoughts and feelings that the music inspires so that their readers can see, almost, Rubén González's fingers on the piano. There is a fine documentary of the making of this CD, with live recordings as well as conversations with the artists about their lives in Cuba. Also titled *Buena Vista Social Club,* this video gives kids a close look at life in Havana and the magical way the musicians' soulful music liberates them from governmental restrictions on Cuban freedom.

SPONTANEITY

Children buzz at the freedom from inhibition that comes with their spontaneous actions. While there are countless ways to introduce them to the joys of spontaneity, there are very few reliable methods for discouraging it! One approach that I enjoy taking with little spontaneous minds is the following: Without any explanation I ask them to go and stand in a place of their choosing in the classroom. "Strike the pose that best expresses freedom to you at this moment," I suggest. Some are sorry that they chose to crawl under a desk or stand of their own volition in the corner! But the results of the exercise are always a pure delight to behold and an excellent overture to discussing the relationship between freedom and spontaneity. Every pose is unique, neither right nor wrong, a playful exercise in freedom.

Mill invites readers of his work to quit their search for society's anonymous approval. He questions anyone's timid retreat into fearful living, as if under the eye of hostile censorship, when so many possibilities for freedom surround us. "The danger which threatens human nature is not the excess, but the deficiency, of personal impulses and preferences" (*On Liberty*). Let there be spicy variety in our hearts and houses and our minds and manners. May every radio be tuned to a different station. The realm of the possible is quite great in comparison to the short reach of limitations on our liberty. We forget how free we can be, indeed how free we are, in our unhindered and unfiltered actions. Walk backward. Face sideways.

Spontaneity is freedom's expression, a basic, unimpeded instinct that leaps into existence with no push from behind or pull from above. Through their spontaneous activity, children enjoy a direct experience of freedom. Immediate attention to a project is the germ of originality, creativity, and fearlessness. "I love the shape of that cloud and want to follow the disappearing pieces wherever they go." "This blade of grass is telling me a story so I can't sit up right this second." "I'm talking to a squirrel right now, and she's telling me about her nut sale." Having no *planned* direction or goal, spontaneity lacks order and is often unwelcome. "Individual spontaneity is hardly recognizable by the common modes of thinking as having any intrinsic worth, or deserving any regard on its own account" (Mill, *On Liberty*). But "human spontaneity always projects itself toward something" (de Beauvoir, *The Ethics of Ambiguity*). Natural feelings, questions, and impulses propel the adventurer fully into life. Spontaneous action is part of free living for all ages.

Children give countless spur-of-the-moment examples of the beauty of spontaneity. They get "excited like crazy" when deciding what to wear in the morning, and everyone knows the "crayon you *choose* for no reason is the *only* one." Kisses, laughter, and "having a question fly out of your mouth before you really think about it" are real because they just happen. Curious inspection of something for the very first time is like going on a search for a great mystery. "It's cool to pretend you're a clown and make people laugh, almost as much fun as crawling like an alligator." Sometimes it's "even fun to pretend to be a grown-up, but hey, maybe grown-ups could pretend that they're kids too, because then . . ."

"Sensitivity is nothing else but the presence which is attentive to the world and to itself" (*The Ethics of Ambiguity*). Kids *being* spontaneous defines the word spontaneity. Eavesdrop on this impromptu dialogue: "Sometimes I yell as loud as I possibly can for no reason and I can look out the window without blinking forever and c'mon let's see how far we can run and have you ever gone digging for rocks and it's awesome to touch a worm and I can bark like a dog so I'm trying to teach the bark of a tree to woof and see how far you can count and make up your own language so you can start using words like *lotteepoopah* and I want to trade places with my teacher for an hour." Bunch of originals, one teacher, lots of fun.

 TEACHING TIP: SPONTANEITY

- I like to ask kids to establish definitions for the words *spontaneous* and *eccentric*. Samples: *Spontaneous* actions go with your natural feeling right then. An *eccentric* person doesn't do what most people expect.

 DISCUSSION QUESTIONS: SPONTANEITY

- What do you enjoy about being spontaneous?
- What are some amazing things you have discovered by going with your natural feeling at that very moment, right then?

 EXERCISE: SPONTANEITY

- Recite Lewis Carroll's "Jabberwocky" with vigorous animation. "Oh frabjous day! Callooh, Callay! / He chortled in his joy." Dance around with the illustrations as you invite the kids into the joys of a poem with lots of rhyme but no particular reason. Ask them how Carroll felt free enough to write such a poem. Let the giggling head-shakers decide if they think that someone gave him permission to write it. Tell them it's also up to them to figure out why "Jabberwocky" is called a "nonsense" poem. Have them explain to you how a spontaneous poem that flies in a lot of different directions for no clear reason can make sense in its *own* way. Let them dig into their imaginations and write their own poems entitled "Nonsense." Invite them to make a series of crayon drawings to illustrate their poems. Be very sure to write your own!

FUTURE

Freedom opens the future like a hand-held fan. Each widening movement of the fan depends on the folds that came before, and by feeding on itself the fan continues to spread out and expand. Freedom fans the future. Having faith in a free future empowers the individual and creates even more openings and options. Liberated people surge toward their futures by following the spontaneous rhythm of their own lives. Free to change their minds and directions, they transcend limits as they flash by. Valuing freedom's crucial place in their lives, free individuals work to liberate those languishing without it. The future for all becomes increasingly vast as more beings realize the potential in their own lives.

Begin your discussion with your child philosophers about the relationship between freedom and their future by having them ask Mill's key questions, "What would suit my character and disposition?" and "What would allow the best and highest in me to have fair play and enable it to grow and thrive?" (*On Liberty*). Kids love to feel that grown-ups believe in their ability to handle free will and make a good life. Spitting their words out as fast as they can, my students have expressed their faith that they can "somersault into the future," with adult help of course. Talk of their future makes their confidence grow, both in themselves and in that future. Others offer how great they feel "just thinking about what they want" to achieve. It is like standing on solid ground for them to realize that their "*possibilities* are real" because *they* are.

Many have also mentioned the flip side: Having their future already planned *for* them makes them "feel like puppets." Ask your young philosphers if they ever feel they are being prepared for futures they are not sure they want. Kids are honest and smart and quick to point out current and foreseeable difficulties in living freely. A number of children admit in a matter-of-fact manner that they are free to "mess up their lives" and are afraid that they will. Also "it would be easy to be lazy and go around blaming everybody else, especially since I can be really mean already." Because of the harsh circumstances of some young lives, it is almost impossible to imagine a future that will not be determined by other forces. "They can exercise their freedom, but only within this universe which has been set up before them, without them" (de Beauvoir, *The Ethics of Ambiguity*). For these struggling children, their biggest dreams are to be free from chronic hunger because they are poor, to move out of a scary neighborhood, or to have even a little peace at home. And "What if I am not good at *anything*?" Michael went on to say that he hated school and didn't care about being free. At the end of our many months together, he took me aside and explained that he couldn't read even one word or spell his name. Education is the key to a society of free individuals for Mill. If education fails, tyranny triumphs.

"The future remains largely open" (de Beauvoir, *The Second Sex*). Mill and de Beauvoir place the responsibility for the free future of every child squarely in adult hands.

TEACHING TIPS: FUTURE

- Invite someone who has left an enslaved existence behind for the promise of freedom in the United States to speak to your group. You can contact international organizations or social service agencies for possible guests. Be sure to provide a translator, if necessary.
- Take a child to a July Fourth citizenship ceremony. The excitement of a new beginning with an inviting future can be felt in the laughter and tears, the exuberance and quiet delight of these full-fledged citizens from around the world.
- Show the children a photograph of the Statue of Liberty, especially lit from within at night. Share her history.

 ## DISCUSSION QUESTIONS: FUTURE

- What would you like to be free to do with your life?
- In what ways are you glad that you are a child and not yet totally free? In what ways do you want grown-up protection and guidance? When are rules helpful or necessary?
- Do you like the idea that your future waits for you to create it?
- Is there anything scary about freedom?

 ## EXERCISES: FUTURE

- Read *Dear Mrs. Parks: A Dialogue with Today's Youth*. Kids feel close to Rosa Parks and understand her pivotal role in the American civil rights movement through children's letters to her over the years and her clear and simple responses. Give your students a vivid picture of life for black citizens in Montgomery, Alabama, in 1955. Parks had the courage and the energy to keep sitting in *her* place on the bus rather than be moved to the back by the lingering legacy of slavery. Her freedom to be herself was motivation to risk everything, and through her act of hopeful defiance she made a free future for all black citizens a better possibility. Let the children take turns reading a letter from one of their contemporaries in the book, and you play the role of Parks as you read her reply. Discuss with the children how unbelievable her act was in 1955, and ask them to share their ideas about the mind-set that took liberty away on the basis of skin color. Next, in their philosophy journals have the children draft letters that they would like to send to Parks. After much discussion of the issues surrounding Parks's life, let the children give the letters to adults they know from whom they would really like a response. Finally, have them explore in their journals how important freedom is to them.

- Bring a civil rights leader into your classroom. Once the kids learn about the circumstances that made Parks's courage necessary, yet totally unexpected, they become absorbed in listening to the voices and watching the faces of individuals active during the civil rights movement. Perhaps you know such a person, or someone who does, and can invite the individual to speak to your group. You can also contact your local chapter of the NAACP or ACLU for suggestions. A documentary that brings this time alive works well, too. *Rosa Parks and the Civil Rights Movement* holds children's attention with dramatic reenactments and archival photographs of Parks's life before and after her stand against segregation.

- Read selected chapters from Harriet Beecher Stowe's novel *Uncle Tom's Cabin*. There is value in reading a period piece, in this case a work written in 1852 by a woman steeped in the abolitionist effort to end slavery. *Uncle Tom's Cabin,* a long novel that makes good summer reading for older children, has many sections that can stand on their own in portraying life in the South for any child. The loss of freedom is reflected unfortunately well in Stowe's subtitle, "Life Among the Lowly." In the chapter entitled "Liberty," the child philosophers can ponder this question while recalling Mill's philosophy: "What is freedom to a nation, but freedom to individuals in it?" Talk about the concept that a country cannot be free unless *all* people possess liberty. Divide the children into small groups of three or four to work together on a short speech that explains, with examples, why this statement is true. Each member of the team can deliver a part of the speech so that everyone participates. Next, let them use abstract art, without words or the portrayal of humans, to show the exhilarating feeling of liberation from slavery expressed in "Liberty": "Who can speak the blessings of that rest which comes d own on the free man's pillow . . . ? They had nothing more than the birds of the air, or the flowers of the field,—yet they could not sleep for joy."

My time with child philosophers makes me a believer in their futures. I have an intuitive confidence that if they are trusted with their inherent freedom now, then a good future will find them in its time. I see them coming into their own as they teach trees to bark, and I like to think of a world populated by adults who had full-bodied childhoods. Kids' wisdom warrants faith in the unfolding of their personal lives.

"The saving of time and the conquest of leisure have no meaning if we are not moved by the laugh of a child at play" (de Beauvoir, *The Ethics of Ambiguity*). The children move me plenty.

I always leave their presence with the conviction that anything is possible.

Resources

* *The Ethics of Ambiguity* by Simone de Beauvoir.
* *The Second Sex* by Simone de Beauvoir.
* *Memoirs of a Dutiful Daughter* by Simone de Beauvoir. This autobiography of her childhood and adolescence shows glimpses of her simmering attraction to open spaces. Though designed for an adult reader, there are some passages and events that you can share with children.
* *On Liberty* by John Stuart Mill.
* *The Subjection of Women* by John Stuart Mill.
* *Uncle Tom's Cabin* by Harriet Beecher Stowe.
* *Dear Mrs. Parks: A Dialogue with Today's Youth* by Rosa Parks.
* "Jabberwocky" by Lewis Carroll. Kids love Joel Stewart's illustrated version of this poem.
* *The Book of Questions* by Pablo Neruda. A bilingual version makes Neruda's native tongue come alive and can provide an easy way to learn basic words in a new language.
* *A Taste of Honey: Live in New Orleans* by James Booker. "On the Sunny Side of the Street" and "Make a Better World" are included on this 1977 live recording. Booker's versatility, from Leadbelly to Chopin, is an irresistible blend of Mill's originality and genius.
* *Buena Vista Social Club* featuring Rubén González, Eliades Ochoa, Compay Segundo, Ry Cooder, and Ibrahim Ferrer, among others.
* *Buena Vista Social Club,* directed by Wim Wenders. This documentary is available on DVD and VHS.
* *Rosa Parks and the Civil Rights Movement.* This VHS video makes its mark in twenty-four minutes.
* *Voices of Civil Rights,* produced by the History Channel. In numerous episodes the activism of Parks, Evers, and King, among others, is examined on this DVD.

LOVE

In the final analysis, love is not this
sentimental something that we talk about. It's
not merely an emotional something. Love is
creative, understanding goodwill for all men.
It is the refusal to defeat any individual. When
you rise to the level of love, of its great beauty
and power, you seek only to defeat evil
systems. Individuals who happen to be
caught up in that system, you love, but
you seek to defeat the system.

—MARTIN LUTHER KING, JR.
"Loving Your Enemies"

THE TOPIC

Plato takes us to a dinner party in ancient Athens in *The Sympo-sium*. After dinner, a heated debate begins on the timeless topic of love. At first the guests attempt to hammer out distinctions between physical and emotional love, or love for another person and intellectual love of truth. As the night grows long, the dialogue begins to revolve around a possible definition of love, and it is decided that love is a universal need that fulfills human longing for Beauty itself. Round and round the table the conversation goes until only Socrates is still awake, wanting to ask more questions and keep the dialogue alive. In the end, however, questions about love's essential nature go unanswered. The topic remains under investigation to this day. Indeed, what *is* love?

Some variation of the following scenario plays out whenever I introduce the topic of love for the first time to a group of child philosophers. I ask them to tell me about love. A lot of bouncing around and hand-raising ensues. Aha! they think, I've gotcha this time, philosophy, I know the answer to this one. But when I call on an especially excited child, an initial pause lengthens into surprising silence, and other hands lower automatically as these kids recognize what the speaker soon will admit. "Hmm. I thought I knew, but I don't, but I still think I do." Numerous children have pointed out the impossibility of putting love into words. "It's more than *words*." I commiserate and tell them I, too, find it very hard to put love into words. I suggest that we just sit and think about love for a few minutes.

As it turns out, many kids are already somewhat confused about love. They are picking up different signals about what love is or should be, and none of these messages seems satisfactory. Kids have a lingering internal sense that this word symbolizes something fundamental to life, something more than they yet understand but something they certainly feel. Though they may find it difficult to articulate what love *is,* they find it relatively easy to tell me what it's not. These are some of their examples of what love isn't: It's not an "embarrassing romance," it shouldn't involve "jealousy or hurt," and "it isn't really something that you can lose." They wonder if love is one thing or different things depending on . . . and if it matters who or what you love. "Do you love mountains the way you love your cat?"

I begin the process of thinking and conversing about love in a variety of ways. I once asked a group to show me what it *looks* like. An eight-year-old girl mimed tugging on an imaginary rope to illustrate how love pulls you, adding that "it keeps pulling because it doesn't run out." "How does love *feel*?" I asked a group of fourth-graders. I was told that "love is pure softness and makes you feel at home wherever you are," that "it makes you feel like playing duets because you're in love with the music." "Love makes you feel so happy it can make a dog live with their fleas." "Love can also make you feel like crying." With self-consciousness evaporating, now they are ready to ease into an attempt at defining love. How well I remember young Philip raising his hand immediately to define love as proof that you're not very good at tennis. Using his knowledge that love means zero in *that* game, Philip wanted out of *this* game right away! Usually coerced into going first, I define love as a bond of the deepest affection that holds fast. Some of my favorite little big mind definitions for love are the following: "Love is a permanent link between you and whatever you love." "It's a hook that never lets you go." "It is accepting somebody or anything into the bottom of your heart." "Love is always love no matter what."

Martin Luther King, Jr., urged that we follow Jesus' command and practice unconditional love for all beings. Bertrand Russell looked at a very special brand of love, a philosopher's love of wisdom. The words of King and Russell help children think of love as a positive force in their personal lives and in the world.

 TEACHING TIPS: THE TOPIC

- First, invite the children simply to talk about love so that they warm to the topic. Then their energy level will tell you when they are ready to search for a definition.

- At the beginning of the discussion, put an end to any nervousness or awkward embarrassment kids may feel about this subject. Tell the child philosophers that King and Russell will show them that there is more to love than just romantic attachments between two people.

 ## DISCUSSION QUESTIONS: THE TOPIC

- What is love?
- Can you explain how love is gentle yet strong?
- Do you love yourself? Can you love yourself without being self-centered?
- Do you remember when you were first aware that you loved something? When and what?
- Who and what do you love no matter what?

 ## EXERCISES: THE TOPIC

- Read Elizabeth Barrett Browning's Sonnet 43, "How Do I Love Thee?" Let the children count along with Browning the many ways she loves. Keep the poem on the board for the children to reread for several days. Then, extract Browning's description, "I love thee . . . with my childhood's faith." Ask the kids to reflect privately and write in their journals what that phrase means to them. Suggest that they continue to make notes in their journals, and when they decide they're ready, have them write their Sonnet 44 titled "Love That Comes from My Childhood's Faith."

THE PHILOSOPHERS

Long before modern psychology came into being, the world's greatest
psychologist who walked around the hills of Galilee told us to love.

—MARTIN LUTHER KING, JR., "Loving Your Enemies"

Martin Luther King, Jr., was born in Atlanta in 1929. His roots
were firmly planted by his pastor father and grandfather in the
Ebenezer Baptist Church. After a stint as pastor of the Dexter
Avenue Baptist Church in Montgomery, Alabama, he returned, as
co-pastor with his father, to Ebenezer. King earned his doctorate
in systematic theology in 1955 from Boston University. He studied
in depth and became a fierce advocate of the nonviolent political
strategy used by Gandhi in India.

While in Montgomery, King followed Rosa Parks's act of
courage by leading a successful bus boycott that ended in desegre-
gation of that bus system. His activism in Birmingham in 1963 led
President Kennedy to send civil rights legislation to Congress that
became the Civil Rights Act of 1964, which was also the year that
King won the Nobel Peace Prize. In 1967 King focused his energy
on the "Poor People's Campaign" and against the war in Vietnam.
While in Memphis supporting sanitation workers on strike, King
was assassinated on April 4, 1968, the day after this very weary man
consoled his followers that he had been to the mountaintop and
seen that victory would be theirs.

King's philosophy of love, neither sentimental nor impractical, comes directly from Jesus' command to love your enemies. For
King the power of this passage from the fifth chapter of Matthew's
gospel lay not only in its biblical context but also in the sheer
wisdom of the command on which he based his lifelong battle
against oppression and injustice. He felt that through philosophi-

cal analysis we can discover how important it is to love even our enemies.

King presents three central reasons for becoming Jesus' model of loving one's enemy. First, hate intensifies and increases hate, lengthening the disastrous consequences of animosity in a never-ending chain. If humans inject love into the universe then this cycle can be snapped. Hate will wither and die with nothing to feed upon. Second, hate destroys the personality of the hater. The person who hates cannot see clearly, thinks and acts irrationally, and becomes sick. King describes an individual suffering from hatred as one who can't see beauty or goodness or truth. The hater's character is destroyed because hatred rots the heart. Finally, the why of love consists in its constructive, creative, positive presence in the world, leaving more love in its wake as it rolls on. For a sound, well-integrated personality, we must respond to life with love, either choosing to love everyone or facing our own destruction from within. King pleads that *somewhere, somebody* has got to have this kind of loving intelligence or the downward spiral of hate dooms humanity to destruction. His words, voice, and face are clear indicators that this prospect of utter ruin, far from being abstract and distant, is frighteningly real.

King recognized the struggle that exists between better and worse human instincts in every life. As he observed the dangerous escalation of frustration and anger in his country, his efforts were unrelenting to ensure that the response of those fighting for equality would be a loving one. King presented three ways in which to respond to the reality of hateful oppression: resigning to oppression without a fight and thereby cooperating with the evil of injustice; resorting to physical violence against your oppressors and consequently multiplying the chaos that violence breeds; or resisting oppression peacefully while loving your oppressors. "Will we be extremists for hate or will we be extremists for love?" ("Letter from Birmingham Jail"). King recommends the third option of nonviolent resistance, of active and passionate, loving noncooperation with all oppressive mind-sets and systems.

The capacity to love our enemies can be developed through a step-by-step process that begins with self-analysis. We must look within our own hearts and at our personal behavior to ferret out what in us may evoke anger and hatred in others. With the humility that results from self-examination, we can more easily recognize the elements of good that are present even in the enemy, and when hate surfaces, we are better able to discipline ourselves to remember these good points.

A lot of kids are shocked at their first philosophical consideration of loving their enemy. "What!" They laugh. When I ask most groups if they have ever heard this statement, many children acknowledge that they have heard it "but have never been forced to think about it." I suggest that we begin with a philosophical analysis of who an enemy *is*. Kids have defined an enemy as someone who "is set up against me," "not friendly in *any* way," and "wants to hurt me." Some child philosophers express their sense of an enemy as someone who has the force to come *at* them. An enemy is an opponent, "but not in a game." When we move on in our discussion to examine the way having an enemy makes us feel, the wisdom of King's philosophy creeps slowly into many kids' minds. It makes them feel "scared," "angry," "shaky," "like fighting," "sick to my stomach," and "worse about myself."

I explain for them that King distinguished between *loving* your enemies and *liking* them. *Phew!* The kids are ready to hear more. King says that we like our friends and people who are good to us, but sometimes it's extremely difficult to like someone who hurts your feelings or steals your cookies, for example. His suggestion is that while it's natural to dislike being hurt or having your dessert taken from you, the key is not to make an enemy of the human being responsible for the act. No one can be your enemy unless you choose to hate them. At this point in our dialogue, I have found that some kids can offer ways to begin their attempts to love their enemies. Some expressions of individual baby steps: "I don't have to see them that way." "I can learn to hate the way hate makes me feel." "I can try to hold on to love." "I can be smart and surprise that kid by *offering* him a cookie before he can steal it."

Kids love hearing that King reminded his congregation that Jesus "wasn't playing," even though he knew his command was quite demanding. Children associate King with discussions about justice and freedom, and this look at his philosophy gives them many new insights into the meaning of love. A number of kids have explained to me in detail that people feared and hated him because deep down they knew that love works. A fourth-grader warned our group: "Love changes lives, and if you want things to stay the same, look out!"

> The individual, if he is filled with love of mankind, with breadth of vision, with courage and with endurance, can do a great deal.
>
> —BERTRAND RUSSELL, "If We Are to Survive This Dark Time"

Born in 1872, Bertrand Russell was one of the central figures in international politics and philosophy in the twentieth century. His publications showed uncommon diversity of interest: logical analysis, clarification of language, philosophy of math and science, ethics, politics, and social reform. Russell's life and career were marked by controversy that began with his opposition to England's entry into the First World War. He later became a vigorous denouncer of the United States' involvement in Vietnam, and he worked with Albert Einstein toward the control and eventual disarmament of nuclear weapons. At age eighty-nine, Russell was jailed for a week in connection with his work on nuclear disarmament. He died at the age of ninety-eight.

Russell was dedicated to countering the seemingly endless criticisms leveled against philosophy. As he saw it, philosophy had been largely undervalued since the beginning, from aggravation toward the Socratic method in ancient Greece to the preoccupation of his Western contemporaries with the scientific method. He acknowledged that many think philosophy consists of nothing more than abstract questions that defy definite answers and lead nowhere. Russell replied that criticism of philosophy misunderstands the final goals of life and what kind of goods philosophy produces. In fact, philosophy goes *everywhere,* exploring the outermost reaches of the universe and pushing beyond. And philosophical contemplation can increase the human capacity to love.

One of the crucial questions asked by its critics is how philosophy benefits the lives of those who study it. Do lovers of wisdom improve their personal lives and the world around them? To this, Russell booms a resounding *yes.* In his very short essay "The Value of Philosophy," Russell makes a strong case for philosophy's character-enhancing qualities. "Questions enlarge our conception of what is possible, enrich our intellectual imagination and diminish the dogmatic assurance which closes the mind against speculation . . . through the greatness of the universe which philosophy contemplates, the mind is also rendered great . . ." (*The Problems of Philosophy*). For Russell, the goal of asking philosophical questions and engaging in dialogue is not to prove one's viewpoint or, indeed, any particular human perspective at all. Philosophy instead can teach those in pursuit of wisdom to view the world unselfishly and therefore lovingly. A mind expanded by philosophical wonder improves the individual to the point that impartial love is not only possible but inevitable.

Russell sees clearly our natural tendency to view the world with our needs and concerns as the focal point. We see events in our neighborhoods and the larger world as important mainly in their relation to our lives. With this view, we interpret the world in a way that makes us comfortable and we reserve love only for those in our immediate circle. The power to love is severely diminished in such a self-centered life. Russell recommends as an alternative the impartial lens of the not-self through which to contemplate the world.

His theory of the not-self is central to Russell's connection between the love of wisdom and the love of humanity. When we look at life from a *self*ish perspective, we can see only bits and pieces of it: *my* friends, *my* children, *my* bills, *my* property, *my*self. Russell insists that both the world and human potential are so much more than what this limited perception shows us. The not-self is the human mind working to its very fullest potential. It is the big mind that shows us the enormity of the universe. With this big-mindedness, we would be willing to give up the notion of our self as the center of life and see the world as it is. This larger world is infinite and includes everyone in its unimaginable entirety. I ask child philosophers to imagine looking through a high-powered telescope through which they can see the whole universe and everything in it extending into space forever. I explain to them that Russell's hope is that our minds can become more and more like this telescope.

Without the narrow, obstructed lens of our limited self as our reference point, the not-self opens the way for the majesty of the universe to present itself to the philosopher, and a bit of this infinity rubs off on the opened minds of those engaged in philosophy. We become dramatically aware that our capacity to love is as endless as a universe that to our minds now has no bounds. This impartiality in observing the world can transfer itself amazingly into our actions and feelings. "The impartiality which, in contemplation, is the unalloyed desire for truth, is the very same quality of mind which, in action, is justice, and in emotion is that universal love which can be given to all, and not only to those who are judged useful or admirable" (Russell, "On the Value of Philosophy"). As we become more aware of the whole world, we can see our expanded self as an essential part of that whole. This striking awareness directs us to love, a universal love that can be given to all and not restricted to those valued by a self absorbed with private concerns.

Some child philosophers are quick to remind me that they've been learning in philosophy to "be true to yourself, stand up for yourself," and "be your own person." They want to know what happened to being an individual! Did I really mean to write "*not-self*" on the board? What is striking to most of them is that *not,* a symbol of negation, can be good when attached to their selves. I explain that Russell is not suggesting that they lose their self-confidence or self-awareness. By trying this new way of looking at the world, the philosopher's way, they lose only the parts of themselves that hold them back mentally and emotionally from loving. Russell assures them their not-self is a much improved self.

I ask kids to think of things that could hold someone back from loving. Some of their suggestions have included "being afraid of being hurt," "not feeling like I'm worth it," and "thinking that it wouldn't work." By far the most common characteristic blocking love in kids' minds is "being selfish," "wanting to have everything my way." But "I tell you what," a loquacious third-grader told me, "Bertie shows me how to get over myself." His classmates were quick to add their own comments. "It's a very funny thought that if I can get out of my *own* way, then love will be easier." "The bigger the world is, the more room for us."

Russell maintains that if we teach our children as well as ourselves to see from the view of the not-self, universal love can become a reality. "Suddenly, as when the mist dissolves from a mountain top, the landscape would be visible and the way would be clear. It is only necessary to open the doors of our hearts and minds to let the imprisoned demons escape and the beauty of the world take possession" (*New Hopes for a Changing World*, from *The Basic Writings of Bertrand Russell*). Ultimately, with time and effort, the not-self widens our perspective even beyond humanity itself. With a big mind, nothing should be excluded from the world or from love.

 ## TEACHING TIPS: THE PHILOSOPHERS

- Use reading glasses, a camera, or a telescope as a fun analogy for looking through Russell's lens of the not-self. When the lens is in focus, the big world appears. As the world gets bigger, the mind expands too!
- There is no substitute for the sound of King's voice. Let the kids listen to audio clips first, perhaps, so that they can concentrate on his message of love. Then, you can watch with them as King moved the world in 1963 with his "I Have a Dream" speech.

 ## DISCUSSION QUESTIONS: THE PHILOSOPHERS

- If you were explaining King's philosophy of love to someone unfamiliar with it, what is the one point that you would emphasize?

- How would you explain the distinction that King makes between loving and liking?
- Do you agree with King that hate confuses your mind? In what ways?
- Why does King insist that hate and violence never have and never will provide a permanent solution to a problem? Do you agree with him that hate and violence cause even more problems, and if so, can you give some examples?
- Do you agree with Russell that philosophy can improve your life so that you will have a positive effect on the world? How?
- How does the world look when you look at it through the lens of the not-self?

 ## EXERCISE: THE PHILOSOPHERS

- Listen to Richie Havens' voice of loving protest. Ask the children how they think Havens' tone in his protest songs reflects the spirit of King's nonviolence. Let them describe the *sound* of his somehow gentle voice in his music that denounces war, racism, and environmental destruction on the CD entitled *Résumé*. Invite the children to hear his plea, approximately thirty years later on his *Wishing Well* CD, for love in our neighborhoods and in the larger world in the powerful "Handouts in the Rain." Talk with them about the ways that philosophy can help all of us be more mindful, as he suggests in "Alone Together." From his *Grace of the Sun* CD, listen several times consecutively to "Pulling Up the Stone." Ask the child philosophers as they listen to the song to write in their journals about the ways that they can "change tomorrow." Have them describe how the philosophies of King and Russell are directly related to this song. In "Scarlet Flowers," Havens sings that love is the only religion and that we must love the lonely and feed the hungry. Ask the children to decide one way in which they can love the lonely on this very day, and encourage them to do so. Be sure to tell them what *you* are going to do.

FROM BIG MINDS TO BIG HEARTS

After practicing philosophy for a while with any group of children, one of my favorite activities is to talk with them about how philosophy is affecting their lives. To test Russell's belief that philosophy stretches our willingness to love as it stretches our minds, I spend an entire session listening to their reflections on the connection between philosophy and love. I make a list on the board of the philosophical concepts that we have studied together and give them some quiet time to think about any change in their characters based on a particular topic. You can choose one topic for this look at love, or several that have been of special interest to your little big minds.

It is amazing that for the most part kids do not need me to guide them in linking love to other ideas. The following are some of the children's especially memorable revelations. One child, remembering our discussion of the similarities among things in nature, told me that "when I saw that everything is tied to me, I thought about how I could love everything because I'm part of all of it." Recalling our examination of friendship, it was clear to a second-grader that "once I started listening to other people, I found out that there were some reasons to love them." A number of honest kids have said that after looking at prejudice, "I didn't know how I was hurting people and I'm working on it." One common refrain from kids of all ages is that a full investigation of death "taught me to love life." For some smiling philosophers fresh out of a discussion of happiness, it's obvious that "when I'm happy, there's no reason not to love." With incredible philosophical awareness, a fourth-grader said that "by building courage in myself I have more hope. When I'm not afraid of what's going to happen to me, I go ahead and love."

Through these children's answers, Russell clearly passes my test. Lovers of wisdom *can* progress toward a more inclusive ideal of love. "Something radiates from their lives, some light that shows the way to their friends, their neighbours—perhaps to long future ages" (from *The Basic Writings of Bertrand Russell*, quoted in *The New York Times Magazine*, September 3, 1950). Many teachers and parents confirm what I see happening to the children, through their projects based on their exploration of the world of ideas. Though a particular activity may have been tied to an analysis of responsibility or compassion, working for others so increased kids' awareness of interconnection that they could extend the reach of love in their lives. They work for people they don't know—in shelters and hospitals—and love's ripples multiply. I find that it is quite beneficial to pause to take a look back with the little big minds from time to time and discuss with them how both individual and group projects, based on specific concepts, have affected them personally. You can share with your group the ways in which *you* see love growing naturally in them as a result of their service activities. For a lot of kids, philosophy "sneaked up on me." An eighthgrader put it especially well: "Even if sometimes I don't love, I do know that there is no good reason not to."

"If the study of philosophy has any value at all for others than students of philosophy, it must be only indirectly, through its effects upon the lives of those who study it" (Russell, "On the Value of Philosophy"). I've learned from the grown-ups in many child philosophers' lives that the children's study, while it certainly benefited the children, also improved the family dynamic and the level of tolerance in the classroom. Several parents have commented that it is becoming easier for them to discuss sibling relationships with their children, and a number of teachers have reported observing their students catching themselves immediately after moments of insensitivity. As love grows in the hearts of child philosophers who better understand the world of ideas, it spreads into the lives they touch.

 ## TEACHING TIP: FROM BIG MINDS TO BIG HEARTS

- Write the definition of *philosophy,* the *love of wisdom,* and King's belief in the *wisdom of love* on the board so that the children can see the possibility of reversing the phrases.

 ## DISCUSSION QUESTIONS: FROM BIG MINDS TO BIG HEARTS

- How can the study of philosophy increase your ability to love?
- How can love be a strong force in your life?
- Will your heart grow bigger and allow you to love more as you grow older?
- Is there an endless supply of love in your heart, or can it run out?

 ## EXERCISE: FROM BIG MINDS TO BIG HEARTS

- Read *Love That Dog.* I use this gem with great results, particularly with middle-schoolers. Love fills the pages in ways that touch children's hearts. In this short, poetic novel, Sharon Creech introduces us to a boy named Jack who thinks he can't write a poem but who nevertheless becomes a poet through his unconditional love for a dog named Sky. I tell the kids upfront that though Sky has died, Jack writes: "I hope it doesn't make people feel too sad." His love for Sky endures and is the inspiration for his growth as a poet. Jack's teacher, Miss Stretchberry, is his constant source of loving encouragement. Through her questions and creativity, she fills Jack's imagination with growing wonder. Discuss with your kids how Miss Stretchberry's teaching is a good demonstration of Russell's theory that by expanding our minds, our hearts will open to the world as Jack's does to poetry. Invite them to talk about what fills their hearts the way Sky fills Jack's to the brim. For several weeks, have them keep poetry diaries of their thoughts and observations concerning love. Just like Jack, kids are thrilled to have real live poets come to their class and read from their very own books. Like Miss Stretchberry, invite a local poet to come for a visit with the kids and have one of their best days on the job.

LOVE AND PEACE

King saw a world consumed by human conflict, and he never wavered in his resolve: All of us must realize in our minds and hearts that love for all is the *only* way to achieve lasting peace. He acknowledges that many think the command to love one's enemies proves that Jesus is an "impractical idealist," a dreamer of paradise on earth. The reality, however, is that the method and practice of love is a practical necessity if civilization is to survive. For King, love eventually transforms even those who most resist it. "Sooner or later, all the peoples of the world will have to discover a way to live together in peace, and thereby transform this pending cosmic elegy into a creative psalm of brotherhood. If this is to be achieved, man must evolve for all human conflict a method which rejects revenge, aggression, and retaliation. The foundation of such a method is love" (Martin Luther King, Jr., "Nobel Peace Prize Acceptance Speech"). Love is the most powerful weapon. It alone can bring peace.

King turns to a Greek word for love, *agape* (ah-GAH-pay), to describe the selfless, other-centered love that makes peace possible. This deepest of all possible loves is unlimited and all-encompassing, an overflowing love that seeks absolutely nothing in return. Unconditional and unrestricted, agape trickles down, around, into, and through every life it reaches. This ideal of love, requiring sincere commitment and much effort, is the foundation of the command to love your enemies. You will find that when you connect agape to loving your enemies, the children in your group will understand more easily that unconditional love erases even the *concept* of "enemy." Chat with them for a bit about what happens to an enemy in a heart that loves all.

Most child philosophers understand that agape is a kind of love to strive for. Several have told me that they've "never really seen it anywhere." One six-year-old boy said that "you just don't expect people yelling at each other to hug." Still hopeful, I ask them for times in their lives when they may have felt that they loved absolutely everything. I have watched their looks turn from skepticism to the sudden realization that "Wait—I've felt it!" Here are some of their examples of "loving it all": "On the last day of school, I loved every single person at the picnic." "One time when I was sad somebody was really nice to me and I wasn't expecting it. It made me feel total love." "I loved everything when I got my first goldfish to take care of." "A few times when I've been really happy, it felt like I loved the whole world." We talk together about how it can make them feel to love everyone no matter what. Among their answers: "Life's more fun." "Very relaxing." "Very peaceful."

Is it possible for kids or grown-ups to be rooted in unconditional love? Talking with little big minds about having "love for all" as a lifetime *goal* makes King's noble philosophy seem doable to kids. You can have incredible conve rsations with your child philosophers about the results of taking even small steps in the direction of agape. Many children realize rather quickly that love for all rules out violence. "If I love everybody, who would I hurt?" "You don't fight somebody you love, do you?" "I get it! I'm going to learn not to hurt myself either. It's about loving *all*." The central question of a life directed by agape is what constitutes a loving response in any and all situations. King teaches that when we train ourselves in agape, we can see the image of God in *every* face. As the working foundation of a person's life, this love wills a good life for all. Agape should be the North Star that guides inner emotions and directs our lives. If we are constantly attentive to human goodness, a new mind-set conducive to peace can develop.

"Children should from an early age be made aware of . . . the importance of cooperation and the folly of conflict" (*New Hopes for a Changing World,* from *The Basic Writings of Bertrand Russell*). In my experience, child philosophers cannot get enough talk of peace. "Peace and love" no longer seems such a cliché. Plenty of kids exude optimism that an active understanding of agape and the not-self can bring peace, and their descriptions of a peaceful world make for a heartening discussion. "No one would be against anyone." "People could lean on each other and everybody be held up." A group of nine-year-olds animatedly acted out with sound effects and movements how love can create peace: "Love explodes into the air like fireworks, and the sparks sprinkle far and wide!" One of my favorite images came from a third-grader who had searched a long time for her words. Pausing ever so briefly after each word, she described peace as "harmony like a perfect piece of music."

TEACHING TIP: LOVE AND PEACE

- Share with the kids examples of successful nonviolent action. For example, you can look at the heroism of the Madres in Argentina, Gandhi's resistance to the British in India, underground movements against slavery in the United States, and efforts to protect Jews in Germany.

 DISCUSSION QUESTIONS: LOVE AND PEACE

- How do you explain the connection between love and non-violence?
- How would you describe a life without love? How about a world without love?
- Had you thought before that you could use love as a force to solve difficulties?
- Can you think of times in your life when you felt love for everything? Can you describe the feeling?
- Do you think you can teach yourself to see the best in people? How?
- What can love accomplish?
- Do you think grown-ups should talk more about agape? With one another? With you?

 EXERCISES: LOVE AND PEACE

- Recite Henry Timrod's sonnet "Most Men Know Love but as a Part of Life." This is a perfect poem to look at the beauty of having love color every aspect of one's life. "Ah me! why may not love and life be one?" Timrod asks. Have the children write in their journals how love can become their way of looking at and responding to everyone. Do they agree with the poet that most people feel and express love only at certain times? "Love, like a visible God, might be our guide . . . ," Timrod suggests hopefully. Have your kids continue their writing by describing what a day in their lives would be like with love as their constant guide. Give them plenty of time to work on their own sonnets titled "How I Know Love."

• Read and perhaps hand out a copy of the "Prayer for Peace" by Saint Francis of Assisi to your child philosophers. "Lord, make me an instrument of your peace," the prayer begins. Ask the children to reflect first through discussion and then by writing in their journals on ways they can use the knowledge gained through philosophy to become an "instrument of . . . peace." Keeping in mind the unconditional love advocated by King and Russell, explore the second line: "Where there is hatred, let me sow love—." Just as a farmer plants seeds in the fields, ask the kids to imagine themselves planting seeds of love. Invite them to create works of art that show what these promising seeds can produce. Talk with them about all the suggestions in this prayer for ways to move toward peace in their personal lives and in the larger world.

Being a disciple of little big minds has changed my life. They have taught me well, most especially about love. When they engage in heartfelt dialogue about the meaning of love, they convince me that love *can* work the wonders that King and Russell envisioned. In one bustling conversation about love, I overheard the following rapid exchange between two eight-year-olds who were clearly oblivious of their wisdom. Tying his shoe, one child announced, "Love is a living thing that has a mind of its own." Drinking from her thermos and stopping in mid-gulp, his classmate responded, "What else is there?"

Resources

- *The Problems of Philosophy* by Bertrand Russell. The last chapter is "The Value of Philosophy," which illustrates the expansion of the self into the not-self.
- *The Basic Writings of Bertrand Russell,* edited by Robert E. Egner and Lester E. Denonn, with a preface by Bertrand Russell. Here you will find lots of Russell writings from various works and publications, neatly arranged by topic.
- *Love That Dog* by Sharon Creech. Some of Miss Stretchberry's poems used in her teaching are included as a bonus.
- *Walk Two Moons* by Sharon Creech. Creech celebrates love and the many benefits of walking two moons in another's moccasins.
- "How Do I Love Thee?" (Sonnet 43), from *Sonnets from the Portuguese* by Elizabeth Barrett Browning.
- *Grace of the Sun* by Richie Havens. "Pulling up the Stone" and "By the Grace of the Sun" are two beauties on this CD, as well as the thought-provoking "Scarlet Flowers."
- *Résumé: The Best of Richie Havens* by Richie Havens. "Here Comes the Sun" and "God Bless the Child" complement his loving protest tunes "Handsome Johnny," "What About Me," and "The Klan." Kids love "Rocky Raccoon" on its own merits.
- *Wishing Well* by Richie Havens. "Love Is Alive," "Alone Together," and the haunting "Handouts in the Rain" are included on this CD.
- *At the River I Stand* by David Appleby. This one-hour video documentary is the story of King's last days in Memphis as a weary participant in the struggle of the sanitation workers. His fatigue is palpable but so is his love.

- *A Call to Conscience: The Landmark Speeches of Martin Luther King, Jr.* Included in this collection are his "Acceptance Address for the Nobel Peace Prize," as well as "I Have a Dream," and "I've Been to the Mountaintop," among others.
- *Strength to Love* by Martin Luther King, Jr. "Loving Your Enemies" is included in this book.
- *Why We Can't Wait* by Martin Luther King, Jr. "Letter From Birmingham Jail" can be found here.
- *A Knock at Midnight: Inspiration from the Great Sermons of the Reverend Martin Luther King, Jr.*, edited by Clayborne Carson and Peter Holloran. "Loving Your Enemies" is among these sermons.
- *The Symposium* by Plato. You can join Socrates and his friends for dinner.
- "Most Men Know Love but as a Part of Life" by Henry Timrod. This sonnet is in a collection of his works titled *Poems of Henry Timrod*, which includes a memoir and portrait. In addition to a grouping of his sonnets, there is also a section titled "Poems Written in Wartime," and you may find a poem here that is suitable to share with your child philosophers that encourages them to work for peace.
- "Prayer for Peace" by Saint Francis of Assisi. This prayer can be found in *The Best-Loved Poems of Jacqueline Kennedy Onassis*, selected and introduced by Caroline Kennedy.

THANKSGIVING

Little Big Minds made some good friends in the process of becoming a book. How I appreciate the encouragement of the children's classroom teachers, their parents, my college students, and the numerous participants and onlookers who were amazed to see the power of philosophy in a child's hands.

Swirling gusts of enduring gratitude for:

Patty Moosbrugger, my agent, whose big mind grasped the book's potential immediately, big heart supplied unwavering commitment, and homing instincts found just the right publisher. Thank you, Patty, for believing in child philosphers and including me in the group.

Sara Carder, my editor at Tarcher/Penguin, who envisioned the completed book and took me through the process of writing it with wisdom and sensitivity. Sara, your unfailing enthusiasm, candor, and flexibility were welcome gifts. Hearty thanks as well to Kat Kimball, Sara's assistant editor.

The Three Ladies of the Laptop: Jackie Dettor, steady and determined from the book's start to its finish, the embodiment of faithfulness: thank you, Jackie, for taking one step at a time with me. Raquel León Alcántara, my generous and spirited taskmaster: *muchas gracias para siempre,* Chica Española. Aimie McLaughlin, both student and scholar, a born wordsmith with a sparkling future: thanks for giving more than your all, Aimie.

Jeanne Reilly, my high school English teacher, who read this final exam with the old rigor and offered valuable insights. We came full circle.

Everyone at Piedmont Virginia Community College, especially my students, who inspire me with their ability to use philosophical dialogue and new ideas to enrich their lives and their communities. And among my talented colleagues, a deep bow to the book's very close friends: Kay Bethea, Letty Macdonald, Charlotte Self, Benjamin Sloan, and Angelsims Cavanaugh.

Carter Miller Forrester, Don Marineau, Sean Chandler, and Paige Turner, sure soulmates, endearingly unaware that their gifts were wafts of energy taking me across the finish line. Yes.

My family, all of whom are lodged in my heart, with an unflinching look in the eye reserved for my father, Mac, for asking me to "write that book" and remaining its inspiration. My mother, June, for the tender, knowing-her-child way in which she made sure that I did. My cousin, Maria, and her two little big minds, Will and Nelson, believers from the beginning. And my dog, Mel, whose flexibility makes it possible for eight small hands to pet him at once and whose face boosts my credibility in every classroom.

And, of course, unutterable gratitude for the child philosophers, every single one . . . those who fill these pages and the ones yet to come.